P9-DNP-462

Professional Learning Communities at Work™

Best Practices for Enhancing Student Achievement

Richard DuFour

Robert Eaker

Solution Tree | Press

a division of

Solution Tree

Association for Supervision and
Curriculum Development
Alexandria, Virginia

Copyright © 1998 by Solution Tree Press

All rights reserved, including the right of reproduction of this book in whole or in part in any form.

555 North Morton Street
Bloomington, IN 47404
800.733.6786 (toll free) / 812.336.7700
FAX: 812.336.7790

email: info@solution-tree.com
solution-tree.com

Cover design by Grannan Graphic Design, Ltd.

Printed in the United States of America

FSC

Mixed Sources
Product group from well-managed
forests and other controlled sources

Cert no. SW-COC-002283
www.fsc.org
© 1996 Forest Stewardship Council

ISBN 978-1-879639-60-7

Dedication

To the two men who have had the greatest impact upon my life—my father and my son.

—Richard DuFour

To my wife, Star, and my children, Robin and Carrie. And to my mother, Jewel Eaker, and in memory of my father, Raymond.

—Robert Eaker

Acknowledgments

We gratefully acknowledge Nancy Wagner and Tammie Allen for their work in the preparation of this manuscript. Robert Granner made a tremendous contribution to this project with his thoughtful and thorough editing of rough drafts of each chapter.

For the past 15 years, the faculty and staff of Adlai Stevenson High School in Lincolnshire, Illinois, has been engaged in the hard work of building a professional learning community. Much of what we have learned can be attributed to them. We also gratefully acknowledge the Board of Education of the Stevenson District for providing the leadership, support, and encouragement that has sustained this long improvement initiative.

Table of Contents

About the Authors ix

Introduction xi

One   The Disappointment of School Reform 1

Two   A New Model: The Professional Learning
Community 19

Three   The Complexity of the Change Process 47

Four   Building the Foundation of a Professional
Learning Community: Mission and Vision 57

Five   Building the Foundation of a Professional
Learning Community: Values and Goals 87

Six   Sustaining the School Improvement
Process 105

Seven   Embedding Change in the Culture of
a School 131

Eight   Planning for Learning: Curricular Focus
in a Learning Community 151

Nine   The Role of the Principal in a Professional
             Learning Community 181

Ten   Teaching in a Professional Learning
             Community. 205

Eleven   The Role of Parents in a Professional
             Learning Community 235

Twelve   Staff Development in a Professional
             Learning Community 255

Thirteen Passion and Persistence 279

Appendix A Sample Vision Statements 289

Appendix B Curriculum Standards, Models, and
             Concepts 301

Bibliography 319

About the Authors

Richard DuFour, Ed.D., is the superintendent of Adlai Stevenson High School District 125 in Lincolnshire, Illinois. He is the only school administrator in Illinois to receive the state's highest award as both a principal and a superintendent. He was presented the "Distinguished Alumni Award" of Illinois State University, was named as one of the nation's "Top 100" school administrators by *Executive Educator* magazine, and was designated as an "Instructional Leader" by the Illinois Principals Association.

Dr. DuFour has helped to develop a video series on the principalship for the Association of Supervision and Curriculum Development and is a featured columnist for the *Journal of Staff Development*. He has authored four books and more than thirty professional articles and has consulted for professional organizations, state departments of education, and school districts throughout the United States and Canada. During his tenure at Stevenson, the school has been named as one of America's best schools six times and has received commendations from the United States Department of Education and the College Board.

Robert Eaker, Ed.D., is the dean of the College of Education at Middle Tennessee State University and a former fellow with the National Center for Effective Schools Research and Development. Dr. Eaker has written widely on the issues of effective teaching, effective schools, helping teachers use research findings, and high expectations and student achievement. Drs. Eaker and DuFour coauthored *Creating the New American School* (Solution Tree [formerly National Educational Service], 1992). Dr. Eaker has spoken at numerous national meetings, such as the National Association of Secondary School Principals, the Association for Supervision and Curriculum Development, and the National Center for Effective Schools. Dr. Eaker was chosen by Phi Delta Kappa for the "People in Educational Evaluation and Research" interview series that appeared in the October 1986 issue of *Phi Delta Kappan*. He regularly consults with school districts throughout the nation on school improvement issues.

Introduction

The most promising strategy for sustained, substantive school improvement is developing the ability of school personnel to function as professional learning communities.

That is the message of this book in a nutshell! Everything else provides context and details—but careful examination and constant probing of context and detail are critical elements in becoming a professional learning community.

Each word of the phrase "professional learning community" has been chosen purposefully. A "professional" is someone with expertise in a specialized field, an individual who has not only pursued advanced training to enter the field, but who is also expected to remain current in its evolving knowledge base. The knowledge base of education has expanded dramatically in the past quarter century, both in terms of research and in terms of the articulation of recommended standards for the profession. Although many school personnel are unaware of or are inattentive to emerging research and standards, educators in a *professional* learning community make these findings the basis of their collaborative investigation of how they can better achieve their goals.

"Learning" suggests ongoing action and perpetual curiosity. In Chinese, the term "learning" is represented by two characters: the first means "to study," and the second means "to practice constantly." Many schools operate as though their personnel know everything they will ever need to know the day they enter the profession. The school that operates as a professional *learning* community recognizes that its members must engage in the ongoing study and constant practice that characterize an organization committed to continuous improvement.

Much has been written about learning organizations, but we prefer the term "community." An organization has been defined both as an "administrative and functional structure" (*Webster's Dictionary*) and as "a systematic arrangement for a definite purpose" (*Oxford Dictionary*). In each case, the emphasis is on structure and efficiency. In contrast, however, the term "community" suggests a group linked by common interests. As Corrine McLaughlin and Gordon Davidson (1994) write:

> *Community means different things to different people. To some it is a safe haven where survival is assured through mutual cooperation. To others, it is a place of emotional support, with deep sharing and bonding with close friends. Some see community as an intense crucible for personal growth. For others, it is simply a place to pioneer their dreams.* (p. 471)

In a professional learning *community,* all of these characteristics are evident. Educators create an environment that fosters mutual cooperation, emotional support, and personal growth as they work together to achieve what they cannot accomplish alone.

This book offers specific, practical recommendations for those who seek to transform their schools into professional learning communities. The recommendations we offer are based on research, evident in best practice, and consistent with standards of quality adopted by various national organizations. References to and brief summaries of standards for curriculum, teacher preparation and development, school leadership, professional development programs, school-parent partnerships, and assessment practices are provided throughout this book.

We have not, however, limited our study to research, practices, and standards in education. We also examine organizational development, change processes, leadership, and successful practices outside of education. We rely heavily on the work of Linda Darling-Hammond, Michael Fullan, Andy Hargreaves, Milbrey McLaughlin, Fred Newmann, Seymour Sarason, Phil Schlechty, Ted Sizer, Dennis Sparks, and others who have focused on steps that can be taken to improve public schools. But we also have sought out the lessons that can be found for educators in the work of Warren Bennis, James Champy, Steven Covey, Terry Deal, Peter Drucker, John Gardner, Rosabeth Moss Kanter, John Kotter, James Kouzes, Burt Nanus, Tom Peters, Barry Posner, Peter Senge, Robert Waterman, and others.

Some educators may object to any suggestion that schools could benefit from the lessons that have been learned in the private sector. These teachers and administrators are often quick to point out that they have no control over who their "customers" are or will be; that while the private sector can focus on finding its niche in the market or enhancing the quality of its processes, schools must take all students, regardless of their abilities or levels of support from parents and the community. It is certainly true that children are not products and that educators are not assembly line workers. There are many differences between schools and industry, and those differences should not be minimized.

Nevertheless, one characteristic of a learning organization is a willingness to learn from its external environment, and it is this willingness that most educators have not demonstrated. In his study of school cultures, Seymour Sarason (1996) concludes that school personnel are remarkably uninterested in issues outside of their daily routines: "It is as if they are only interested in what they do and are confronted with in their encapsulated classrooms in their encapsulated schools" (pp. 329–330). Educators have been too quick to dismiss as irrelevant the experience and insights gained by those outside of education. Over a decade of research has established that the most successful people in any area look outside their narrow field for fresh perspectives and new ideas (Kanter, 1997). We believe that school practitioners can and should learn from the organizations outside of education that have struggled with some of the same issues that public schools face today. The best of these organizations have struggled to find answers to the following questions:

- How can we clarify and communicate the purpose, vision, and values of our organization?

- How can we initiate, implement, and sustain a change process?

- How can we provide strong leadership at the same time that we empower those closest to the action?

- How can we shape organizational culture and provide structures that support the culture we seek?

- How can we create collaborative processes that result in both individual and organizational learning?

- How can we foster an environment that is results-oriented yet encourages experimentation?

This book attempts to summarize the important lessons successful organizations have learned as they have struggled to answer these questions. Thus, the book merges educational research with research from areas outside of education.

The book also represents a merger of another kind—a merger of theory and practice. Too often, researchers and practitioners have different interests, speak different languages, and live in different worlds. This book attempts to bridge the chasm between theory and practice through the collaboration of its authors—the dean of a college of education whose background is in research and the superintendent of a nationally recognized school district. We have reviewed the research, but we have also worked in school districts in 40 states. We have observed and struggled with the perplexities of school improvement. Our experiences have given us insights into the practices that enable a school to function as a professional learning community and have helped us identify the obstacles a school must overcome in the pursuit of that goal.

Chapter Overviews

"Life," Kierkegaard said, "must be lived forward, but it can be understood only backward." While this book strives to describe a better future for public schools, it begins with a look backward. Chapter 1 provides a brief overview of educational reform efforts during the second half of the twentieth century with an emphasis on the Excellence Movement of the 1980s and the Restructuring Movement of the 1990s. It describes the reactions of despair and defiance that accompanied the failure of these movements to fulfill their promises of significant improvement in public education. It suggests the reasons for the failure and presents the assertion that the best hope for significant school improvement lies in transforming schools into professional learning communities.

Chapter 2 contrasts the factory model that has characterized the traditional school environment with the model of a professional learning community. It presents examples of the consistent research findings that have concluded that creating professional learning communities represents the best hope for sustained school improvement, and it specifies the characteristics of such communities. The chapter concludes with a scenario that describes one professional learning community at work.

Chapter 3 examines the complexity of the change process and the often confusing and contradictory advice that research on the change process seems to offer. It urges a realistic acceptance of the difficulty and complexity of substantive change and identifies common mistakes that are made when any organization attempts significant reform. It examines the assertion that a sense of urgency is a prerequisite for change and considers the possibilities for creating a sense of urgency in public schools.

Chapter 4 begins the examination of the four building blocks of a professional learning community—mission, vision, values, and goals. Each building block asks a question of the people in the school. When educators work together to answer these questions, they establish the foundation of a learning community. The *mission* building block probes the question, "What is our purpose?" to which schools often provide a trite and superficial response. Chapter 4 suggests how the issue can be examined in a way that serves as a catalyst for improvement. This chapter also examines the *vision* building block, which asks the question, "What do we hope to become?" It offers strategies for developing a shared vision, examines common questions related to articulating a vision, provides summaries of research that can be used to inform the process, and suggests criteria for assessing a vision statement.

Chapter 5 examines the third and fourth building blocks of a professional learning community—*values* and *goals*. The *values* block poses the question, "How must we behave in order to make our shared vision a reality?" Value statements articulate the attitudes, behaviors, and commitments that each group is prepared to demonstrate to advance toward the shared vision.

The chapter offers examples of value statements for different groups in the school and suggestions for developing such statements. The remainder of the chapter is devoted to the *goals* building block, which clarifies the nature and timetable of the specific steps that will be taken in the initiative to move the school toward its vision. Goals help move the improvement effort from rhetoric to action and can provide the intermittent successes critical to sustaining the improvement process. The chapter identifies common mistakes that schools make in developing goals and presents criteria for assessing goals.

Chapter 6 emphasizes the importance of sustaining an improvement initiative through communication, and it offers a series of questions that can be used to audit the effectiveness with which educators communicate what is important in their schools. The chapter also makes a strong case for job-embedded collaborative structures as a *sine qua non* of a professional learning community. It suggests different structures that can be used and outlines the prerequisites for effective collaborative teams.

Chapter 7 discusses the importance of embedding a change initiative in the culture of a school—the assumptions, beliefs, values, and habits that constitute the norms for the school and that shape how its people think, feel, and act. It stresses the idea that inattention to culture has been a major flaw in past efforts to reform schools, and it suggests several strategies for shaping culture through the articulation of shared values, creation of structures that facilitate reflective dialogue, communication of symbolic stories, and attention to celebration. The chapter concludes with an examination of the interrelationship between the culture of a school and the policies, procedures, rules, and relationships that constitute its structure.

Chapter 8 discusses how the professional learning community addresses the critical issue of curriculum and argues for giving teachers a greater voice in curricular decisions. The chapter describes a process in which teachers work collaboratively to design a research-based curriculum that reflects the best thinking in each subject area and clarifies the knowledge, skills, and dispositions that each student is to acquire. It calls for a reduction of content so that all parties can focus on essential learning and for assessment procedures that give teachers relevant information that can guide their instructional decisions. The attention to this cycle of clarifying what students need to know and be able to do, monitoring student achievement, analyzing results, and making adjustments to instruction based on the actual versus the desired results is the prime example of the commitment to continuous improvement essential to a professional learning community.

Chapter 9 examines the complex role of the principal in the professional learning community. Principals have been torn by research that seems to offer contradictory advice. Some research findings urge principals to function as strong, forceful, aggressive, and assertive leaders. Other findings suggest that schools rely too heavily on principals and that it is time to transfer power from principals to teachers. Principals of professional learning communities are able to maintain the appropriate balance in addressing not only this dilemma but also all the other competing demands that seem to pull them in opposite directions. Chapter 9 describes the part the principal must play in creating a professional learning community and offers specific guidelines for him or her to follow. It concludes with observations of a nationally recognized principal on the challenge of her role in a professional learning community.

Chapter 10 examines the role of teachers in a professional learning community. It begins with the premise that is impossible to create good schools without good teachers, just as it is impossible to create professional learning communities without teachers who function as professionals. The work of the National

Council of the Accreditation of Teacher Education, the Interstate New Teacher Assessment and Support Consortium, and the National Board of Professional Teaching Standards provide frameworks for the professionalization of teaching. The chapter reviews that body of work and also provides a synthesis of the research on teaching. It describes the unique perspectives and priorities that distinguish teachers in a professional learning community from their more traditional colleagues. It concludes with reflections on teaching in a professional learning community from a former National Teacher of the Year.

Chapter 11 considers the important role that parents play in the education of their children and presents strategies for creating meaningful partnerships between parents and schools. In effective business partnerships, each party is expected to bring specific skills and expertise to the enterprise, to offer a different perspective on issues, to provide support in difficult times, and to contribute toward the achievement of mutual goals. Effective parent-school partnerships are based on similar expectations. This chapter examines the national standards that have been identified for partnerships between parents and schools and suggests ways schools can meet those standards.

Chapter 12 examines staff development practices in a professional learning community. Although many school districts provide a variety of incentives to encourage staff members to improve their individual knowledge and skills, individual learning does not automatically translate into enhanced organizational effectiveness. The professional learning community emphasizes developing the collective capacity of the faculty to achieve school goals. Chapter 12 examines the national standards that have been identified for effective staff development. It argues that opportunities to learn should be integrated in the daily activities of educators, and it offers suggestions for staff development that is anchored in the workplace rather than in workshops.

Chapter 13 stresses the need for patience and persistence when attempting the systemic changes needed to transform traditional schools into professional learning communities. This transformation represents not a task to be accomplished or a project to be supervised, but rather an ongoing commitment to continuous improvement.

Appendix A offers examples of vision statements developed by Stevenson High School in Lincolnshire, Illinois, and the Tintic School District in Eureka, Utah. Appendix B provides a brief summary of several different models that schools might use in their investigation of improvement and curriculum initiatives.

Any individual or organization that is committed to improving public schools should seriously consider how professional learning communities could transform education. Colleges and universities can reference *Professional Learning Communities at Work* in their preparation programs for teachers and principals. Boards of education and administrative teams can use it as they develop strategic plans for districts and schools. Faculties can use it as the basis of their school improvement efforts. We hope that this book will be used as a tool to stimulate the shared mission, vision, and values; the collective inquiry; the collaborative teams; the action orientation; the commitment to continuous improvement; and the focus on results that we believe are critical to the survival and success of public schools.

Chapter 1

The Disappointment of School Reform

A significant body of circumstantial evidence points to a deep, systemic incapacity of U.S. schools, and the practitioners who work within them, to develop, incorporate, and extend new ideas about teaching and learning in anything but a small fraction of schools and classrooms.

—Richard Elmore (1996, p. 1)

The demands of modern society are such that America's public schools must now provide what they have never provided before: a first-rate academic education for nearly all students.

—Phil Schlechty (1997, p. 235)

The history of American education in the second half of the twentieth century is marked by numerous attempts at reform and by increasing public concern. Articles entitled "Crisis in Education," "What Went Wrong with U.S. Schools," and "We Are Less Educated than Fifty Years Ago" may

1

have a contemporary ring, but they were published as early as 1957 and 1958 in *Life* and *U.S. News and World Report*. In that same era, Arthur Bestor (1953) argued in his best seller, *Educational Wastelands*, that citizens should wrest control of the public schools from "educationists" who had "dumbed down" the curriculum. With the launching of Sputnik in 1957, many cited the failure of the public schools as the primary reason that the United States had fallen behind Russia in the race to space. Meanwhile, a spate of university-based curriculum reforms, particularly in mathematics and science, emerged as the preferred strategy for resolving the crisis. A quarter of a century later, the ascendance of Japan as an economic power led critics to conclude that the public schools were responsible for America's fall from its position of unchallenged economic superiority, and a new wave of calls for school reform was issued.

The Rise and Fall of the Excellence Movement

In April 1983 the National Commission on Excellence in Education captured national headlines with its grim assessment of education in the United States. In its report, *A Nation at Risk,* the commission argued that national security was in peril because of substandard education in American public schools. The commission made frequent references to "decline," "deficiencies," "threats," "risks," "afflictions," and "plight." The opening paragraphs of the report set the tone:

> *Our nation is at risk. Our once unchallenged preeminence in commerce, industry, science, and technological innovation is being overtaken by competitors throughout the world. . . . The educational foundations of our society are presently being eroded by a rising tide of mediocrity that threatens our very future as a nation and as a people. . . . If an unfriendly foreign power had attempted to impose on America the mediocre*

*educational performance that exists today, we might
well have viewed it as an act of war. . . . We have, in
effect, been committing an act of unthinking, unilateral
educational disarmament.* (1983, p. 5)

A Nation at Risk served as a catalyst for a flurry of school
improvement initiatives throughout the United States that came
to be known collectively as the Excellence Movement. Within two
years of the report, more than 300 state and national task forces
had investigated the condition of public education in America.
The United States Department of Education (1984) described
the national response to *A Nation at Risk* as "nothing short of
extraordinary" (p. 11), and Secretary of Education Terrell Bell
reported with satisfaction that the arduous work of reform was
"already bearing fruit" (p. 8).

The Excellence Movement offered a consistent direction for
reform. But it was not a new direction. Schools simply needed
to do MORE! Students needed to earn more credits for graduation in courses that were more rigorous and required more
homework. Schools needed to add more days to the school year
and lengthen the school day. Schools needed to test students
more frequently and expect more of teachers both before offering employment and before extending tenure. The reforms of
the Excellence Movement simply called for an intensification of
existing practices. They contained no new ideas.

Five years after the publication of *A Nation at Risk,* President
Reagan hosted a ceremony in the East Room of the White
House to celebrate the school-reform initiatives that the report
had helped to launch. Edward Fiske, the former education edi-
tor of the *New York Times,* was among those in attendance.
Fiske later wrote:

*Leading politicians and educators, as well as those
in the national media who cover education, used the*

occasion to reflect on the accomplishments of school reform. And we came to a startling conclusion: There **weren't** *any.* (1992, p. 24)

The United States Department of Education ultimately came to the same conclusion. In 1990 the agency reported that "stagnation at relatively low levels appears to describe the level of performance of American students" (Alsalam & Ogle, 1990). As the disillusioned undersecretary of education wrote shortly after his resignation, "Despite all of the talk of reform, despite the investment of tons of billions of extra dollars, public education in the United States is still a failure. It is to our society what the Soviet economy is to theirs" (Finn, 1991, p. xiv).

The Unfulfilled Promises of the Restructuring Movement

The demise of the Excellence Movement prompted a new, two-pronged approach to school improvement. The first part of the strategy called for national educational goals and standards. In 1989 President George Bush convened the nation's governors for a summit meeting on education—only the third time in the nation's history that governors had been asked to meet to consider a single topic. (Theodore Roosevelt once called the governors together to discuss the environment; Franklin Delano Roosevelt assembled them to discuss the economy.) The result of the Bush summit was the identification of "Goals 2000"—six national goals for education, which stipulated that by the year 2000:

1. All children in America will start school ready to learn;

2. The high school graduation rate will increase to at least 90%;

3. American students will leave grades four, eight, and twelve having demonstrated competency in challenging subject matter, including English, mathematics, science,

history, and geography, and every school in America will ensure that all students learn to use their minds well, so they may be prepared for responsible citizenship, further learning, and productive employment in our modern economy;

4. U.S. students will be first in the world in mathematics and science achievement;

5. Every adult American will be literate and will possess the knowledge and skills necessary to compete in a global economy and exercise the rights and responsibilities of citizenship; and

6. Every school in America will be free of drugs and violence and will offer a disciplined environment that is conducive to learning. (United States Department of Education, 1994)

Congress later amended this original list to include two more goals:

7. By the year 2000, the nation's teaching force will have access to programs for the continued development of their professional skills and the opportunity to acquire the knowledge and skills needed to instruct and prepare all American students for the next century.

8. By the year 2000, every school will promote partnerships that will increase parental involvement and participation in promoting the social, emotional, and academic growth of children.

In 1991, two years after the Bush summit, the National Center on Education and the Economy joined forces with the Learning Research and Development Center at the University of Pittsburgh to design a national exam system. Then, in 1994, Congress created the National Education Standards and

Improvement Council to review and endorse state and national standards. At about the same time, however, articulating national standards began to become an increasingly political activity. Critics asserted that the standards movement represented a federal takeover of the schools and an attempt to indoctrinate students to the liberal agenda. As a result, when the second Education Summit was held in 1996, the standards movement was transferred from the federal to the state governments, from the White House to the State House. Subsequently, the task of developing national standards was left to professional organizations and curriculum specialists.

While the movement to establish national educational goals and standards advanced, a parallel movement tried to give individual schools more freedom to develop the best methods to achieve those goals. The failure of the Excellence Movement had been widely attributed to the fact that it represented a "top-down" attempt to mandate improvement. Early reform initiatives had tended toward standardization, increased reliance on rules and regulations, and detailed specifications of school practices at the expense of local autonomy. Impetus for the movement had come from elected officials and business. Control was centered in state legislatures. Practitioners had become mere pawns in the movement, and the vast majority of the reform efforts had simply been imposed on them. Ultimately, the paired concepts of establishing national goals and providing local autonomy to achieve these goals seemed to offer a viable alternative to the failed Excellence Movement. National goals could address a national crisis, while job-site autonomy and individual empowerment seemed to be consistent with best practice in the private sector.

This new emphasis on site-based reform came to be known as the Restructuring Movement, a term used so widely and ambiguously that it soon lost any specific, universally understood meaning. Nevertheless, the director of the Center on Organization and Restructuring of Schools noted that comprehensive restructuring typically included some common features: site-based management with meaningful authority over staffing, program, and budget; shared decision making; staff teams with frequent, shared planning time and shared responsibility for student instruction; multi-year instructional or advisory groups; and heterogeneous grouping in core subjects (Newmann et al., 1996).

The Restructuring Movement engendered considerable optimism as it grew to become synonymous with school reform in the early 1990s. The term itself seemed to encompass more than mere innovation or improvement, suggesting instead a comprehensive redesign and systemic transformation of the schools. The simplistic, more-of-the-same approaches of earlier reform movements had apparently been replaced at last by a strategy based on a more realistic assumption: monumental changes were necessary if schools were to successfully respond to the enormous challenges before them.

Another reason the Restructuring Movement generated such hope was the expectation that educators would rush to embrace it. Not only would local educators have greater authority to initiate and oversee changes in their schools, but they would also be given the autonomy to organize and administer programs and facilities. Freed from the shackles of top-down mandates and bureaucratic rules and regulations, teachers and principals could respond creatively to the issues they faced. They could use their knowledge of pedagogy more fully and better serve their students and schools. Resources would be used more efficiently, professional collaboration would flourish, classroom life would be more stimulating, and above all, schools would be demonstrably more effective. As Roland Barth (1991) wrote, "The advent of the restructuring movement brought a sudden confidence that teachers and principals, with the help of parents and students, can get their own schoolhouse in order" (p. 126).

But in spite of the Utopian ideals, the high hopes of the Restructuring Movement have yet to be realized. Studies of the movement's impact to date have consistently found that school practitioners have typically elected to focus on marginal changes rather than on core issues of teaching and learning. When given the opportunity to make decisions for their school site, teachers have opted to focus on peripheral issues that do not directly address the quality of student learning (Newmann & Wehlage, 1995). In fact, teachers in restructured schools seem no more inclined to discuss conditions of teaching and learning than are their colleagues in traditional school structures. As one study concludes:

> *The connections between teacher empowerment and site based management and improved educational processes and outcomes are tenuous at best. . . . It remains to be seen if restructuring leads to radical changes that deeply affect teachers and students or if changes will stop at the classroom door, leaving the teaching-learning process largely unaltered.* (Murphy, Evertson, & Radnofsky, 1991)

Our experience with schools around the country confirms the research finding that the school improvement agendas of restructured schools tend to drift to non-academic, administrative issues. In fact, faculties demonstrate a fairly predictable pattern in their consideration of school improvement issues. First, they focus on student discipline: How can we get the students to behave better in our school? Then they tackle parental involvement: How can we get parents to accept greater responsibility for their child's learning? Finally, they address faculty morale:

How can we ensure that the adults who work in our school feel good about their working conditions?

Certainly student discipline, parental involvement, and staff morale are important issues and should be a part of a school's comprehensive improvement effort. But it is imperative that these initiatives also consider what happens in the heart of the school's enterprise—the classroom. Unfortunately, restructuring seems to have left students virtually untouched by the reforms that swirl around, but not within, their classrooms. So the Restructuring Movement, like the Excellence Movement before it, has been unable to make a real difference in the ability of American schools to meet the challenges they face.

Succumbing to Despair

The failure of the Restructuring Movement seems to have led to unprecedented levels of despair about the possibility of school improvement in the United States. Because neither top-down nor bottom-up school reform have proven to be successful, there is a growing tendency to conclude that American schools are simply incapable of transformation. The Consortium on Productivity in the Schools (1995) concludes that schools resist any meaningful change efforts, have changed very little despite all efforts to reform them, and are unable to learn and improve. A review of the research on school innovation led to "the profoundly discouraging" conclusion that "almost all educational innovations fail in the long term" (Perkins, 1992, p. 205). Michael Fullan (1997b) writes that "none of the current strategies being employed in educational reform result in substantial widespread change. . . . The first step toward liberation, in my view, is the realization that we are facing a lost cause" (p. 220). In a 1996 sequel to a book on school change that he had written 25 years earlier, Seymour Sarason lamented the failure of efforts to reform American education and observed that the single greatest change since he had written his first book was "the sense of disillusionment with and disappointment in our schools" (p. 345).

The inability of the Restructuring Movement to achieve the anticipated results has not only discouraged educational theorists, but has also caused some besieged educators to respond to the constant criticism of their schools with growing defensiveness and resignation. According to a recent report on teacher perceptions, most teachers believe that schools are doing as well as possible given the societal problems and lack of parental involvement (Farkas & Johnson, 1996). From the perspective of these teachers, the improvements that must occur for schools to be more effective must be made outside of the school environment. For example, many educators suggest that schools cannot become more productive until students take more responsibility for their learning. According to this argument, *students* must decide whether they will come to school, be attentive, complete their homework, and try to learn. This argument assumes that these decisions are not influenced by what happens at school. Benjamin Levin (1994) is among those who contend that the focus of reform should shift from improving educators and schools to improving the children we send there:

> *Students must do the learning; there is no way around this fact. Whatever schools provide, whatever teachers do, in the end it is the student who must use the resources to acquire skills and knowledge. . . . Every teacher realizes that what happens in a class is fundamentally dependent on who students are, how they make sense of the world, and what they want to do or do not want to do. . . . [E]very educator recognizes that our best laid plans may, and often do, come to nothing in the face of students with different agendas.* (p. 759)

A variation on this theme is to cite the many problems in society that must be solved before schools can become more effective. Forty percent of those living in poverty in the United States are children. This is the highest percentage of any industrialized nation. One of every three babies born in this country is born to a single mother, and 30% of those single mothers are teenagers. Children aged 12 to 15 are the most likely group in America to be the victims of violent crime, and over 4,000 children are murdered each year. By the eighth grade, seven of ten children have consumed alcohol. The youth population of the United States is becoming increasingly fragmented with more students from minority groups and more students who do not speak English, live in broken homes, are disadvantaged in every way, and are subject to violence in the community (Hodgkinson, 1996; Mehlinger, 1995). Some educators argue that they cannot be expected to improve schools until these societal problems are solved. As Mehlinger (1995) contends, "If America's poor children could be provided the same conditions for growing up, including the same quality of schools, as those afforded to middle-class suburban youth, we would have no crisis (in education) at all" (p. 27).

Another response to mounting criticism among members of the education community is to challenge the premise that schools are ineffective. Books such as Berliner and Biddle's *The Manufactured Crisis* (1995), Schneider and Houston's *Exploding the Myths* (1993), and Bracey's *Setting the Record Straight* (1997) have blatantly refuted some of the allegations aimed at public education in the United States and have argued that schools in this country are indeed more effective than ever. Such major professional education associations as the American Association of School Administrators, the Association of Supervision and Curriculum Development, and the National Education Association have distributed the findings of these "revisionist" works and have also encouraged their members to use the findings in defending their efforts.

While these defensive responses on the part of weary educators are entirely understandable, they do nothing to create the conditions that are critical to improving schools. If teachers and principals believe that the impetus for student learning remains outside of their influence and that there is nothing they can do to overcome these external variables, the idea of school improvement will undoubtedly seem futile, if not downright ridiculous! Unfortunately, if educators continue to argue that they cannot be responsible for students' learning until the problems of society are solved, they are essentially saying that they will *never* accept responsibility for their students' learning. If they are content with the assertion that "we are not as bad off as everyone says we are," they will not create organizations capable of continuous improvement.

We are not prepared to accept the conclusion that it is impossible to improve schools. Nor do we believe that improvement can only occur when parents provide schools with a better class of students and society has solved its problems. Although much of the popular criticism of schools has been unfair and unfounded, we do not believe that educators should accept the status quo. Even Gerald Bracey (1997), one of the most ardent defenders of American schools, cautions that his work should not be interpreted to suggest that schools are not in need of significant reform. If future efforts to improve schools are to be more productive than their predecessors, they should address two questions:

1. Why have past school improvement efforts not achieved their intended results?

2. What course of action offers the best hope for those who seek to make their schools more effective?

Why Educational Reform Has Failed to Deliver

The complexity of the task. Changing any organization is difficult, but changing something as complex as the American system of education is an absolutely daunting task. Fifty states operate over 15,000 relatively autonomous school districts through more than 80,000 school board members who employ over 200,000 district administrators, 120,000 principals, and 2.5 million teachers for the 84,000 schools that serve over 43 million students. But the scope of the effort is not the only obstacle to be overcome. Our educational system is fundamentally conservative. As Fullan (1993) writes, "The way that teachers are trained, the way the hierarchy operates, and the way that education is treated by political decision makers results in a system that is more likely to retain the status quo than to change" (p. 3).

Furthermore, while Americans are quick to identify education as a national problem, they consistently express satisfaction with the schools in their own communities (Elam, Rose, & Gallup, 1997). In fact, results from the annual Gallup Poll seem to suggest that educators are conducting their local schools in accordance with community expectations. Effecting change in this amorphous, fundamentally conservative "system," when educators seem fatalistic or defensive and when parents indicate that their schools are serving the community well, has been and will continue to be an incredibly complex, intractable problem.

Misplaced focus. The good news is that there are strategies for school improvement that can make a difference in the effectiveness of schools. The bad news is that neither the Excellence Movement nor the Restructuring Movement focused on these strategies.

Lack of clarity on intended results. Past reform efforts have been characterized by a lack of clarity on intended results. While there has been general agreement that schools should improve, consensus on the criteria that should be used to assess that improvement remains elusive. This inability to articulate the desired results in meaningful terms has led to initiatives that focused on methods and processes rather than on results.

Lack of perseverance. Because schools have been unable to articulate the results they seek, they have become susceptible to following the educational fads *du jour*. As a result of the constant cycle of initiating and then abandoning innovative fads, educators rarely pursue ideas with the diligence and tenacity that is necessary to anchor a change within the school. Overwhelmed by disconnected, fragmented change initiatives that seem to de-scend upon them one after another, teachers often respond to calls for change with jaded resignation. New proposals fail to generate either enthusiasm or opposition from teachers because experience has taught them that "this too shall pass." As one battle-scarred veteran teacher summarized his experience, "Everything has changed, but nothing is different." Phil Schlechty (1997) argues that nothing has been more destructive to the cause of school change than this inability to stay the course.

Failure to appreciate and attend to the change process. Most educators have not been trained in initiating, implementing, and sustaining change. They have moved too quickly, or they have lost momentum by not moving quickly enough. They have thought too big—or too small. They have neglected the process of creating a "critical mass" of support or have failed to proceed because of the mistaken notion that they needed unanimous support before launching an initiative. They have regarded conflict as a problem to avoid rather than an inevitable and valuable byproduct of substantive change. They have failed to anchor the change within the culture of the school. They have considered a change initiative as a task to complete rather than an ongoing process. In short, school practitioners have not learned how the complexities of the change process transform organizations.

Can This School Be Saved?

It is far easier to critique past strategies for improving schools than it is to identify and implement strategies that are more effective. There is, however, an emerging consensus on what pathway offers the best hope for significant school improvement. Researchers from a variety of fields—organizational development, school improvement, teacher preparation, professional development, effective schools, and innovation and change—have all offered remarkably similar models for school improvement. As Milbrey McLaughlin (1995) excitedly proclaimed at a national conference, "We are closer to the truth than ever before."

What is that truth? It is simply this: If schools are to be significantly more effective, they must break from the industrial model upon which they were created and embrace a new model that enables them to function as learning organizations. We prefer characterizing learning organizations as "professional learning communities" for several vital reasons. While the term "organization" suggests a partnership enhanced by efficiency, expediency, and mutual interests, "community" places greater emphasis on relationships, shared ideals, and a strong culture— all factors that are critical to school improvement. The challenge for educators is to create a community of commitment—**a professional learning community.**

So there you have it. Educators seeking to create more effective schools must transform them into professional learning communities. It sounds simple enough, but as the old adage warns, "the devil is in the details." Educators willing to embrace the concept of the school as a professional learning community will be given ambiguous, oftentimes conflicting advice on how they should proceed.

Just how daunting the details can be is illustrated by the following story. When Germany launched its first submarines, Great Britain feared its naval superiority was in jeopardy. An international prize was offered to anyone who could develop a strategic defense to eliminate the threat of the submarine. Mark Twain wired a solution—"Boil the ocean"—and asked that his prize be sent immediately. When an incredulous naval officer asked Twain how he proposed to boil the ocean, Twain replied that he had developed the concept; it was now up to His Majesty's Navy to work out the details! So it has been for those who would reform education.

Concepts are great, but at some point most of us need practical suggestions on applying those concepts to our current situations. This book begins with the premise that schools need to develop into professional learning communities and includes specific steps educators can take to succeed in "boiling their oceans."

Summary

Despite persistent attempts to reform public education, there is little evidence to suggest that schools have become significantly more effective in meeting the challenges that confront them. The Excellence Movement of the 1980s represented a top-down improvement initiative that was based on standardization, increased reliance on rules and regulations, and detailed specifications of school practices at the expense of local autonomy. The Restructuring Movement of the 1990s based its approach to school reform on the premise that the paired concepts of national goals and local, site-based autonomy offered the best hope for genuine change. The failure of these reform initiatives has led to heightened disillusionment with public schools. Educators have become increasingly defensive and often either blame the problems of public education on factors beyond their control or challenge the premise that problems actually exist. While these responses are understandable, they do little to improve the effectiveness of schools.

Past efforts to improve schools have not had the anticipated results for a number of reasons: the complexity of the task, misplaced focus and ineffective strategies, lack of clarity on the intended results, failure to persist, and lack of understanding of the change process. But educators should not succumb to despair. There is growing evidence that the best hope for significant school improvement is transforming schools into professional learning communities. This book provides educators with specific, practical strategies they can use to make that transformation.

Chapter 2

A New Model:
The Professional Learning
Community

*Our decade-long effort to reform U.S. education has
failed. It has failed because it has not let go of an educational vision that is neither workable nor appropriate to today's needs.*

—Seymour Sarason (1996, p. 358)

*In times of drastic change, it is the learners who inherit
the future. The learned usually find themselves beauti-
fully equipped to live in a world that no longer exists.*

—Eric Hoffer (1972, p. 32)

American public schools were originally organized according to the concepts and principles of the factory model,
the prevalent organizational model of the late nineteenth and early twentieth centuries. The professional learning
community is based on an entirely different model. If schools
are to be transformed into learning communities, educators

must be prepared first of all to acknowledge that the traditional guiding model of education is no longer relevant in a post-industrial, knowledge-based society. Second, they must embrace ideas and assumptions that are radically different than those that have guided schools in the past.

By the late nineteenth century, efforts to create schools in the image of the factory had become explicit and purposeful. In *Principles of Scientific Management,* the bible that articulated the concepts of the industrial model, Frederick Winslow Taylor (1911) argued that "one best system" could be identified to complete any task or solve any organizational problem. According to this philosophy, it was management's job to identify the one best way, train workers accordingly, and then provide the supervision and monitoring needed to ensure that workers would follow the prescribed methods. Thus, a small group of people could do the thinking for the entire organization. Workers were regarded as relatively interchangeable parts in the industrial process. Taylor's model demanded centralization, standardization, hierarchical top-down management, a rigid sense of time, and accountability based on adherence to the system. The assembly line embodied Taylor's principles and had helped the United States become the world's industrial giant. Assured that they had discovered the one best way to run an organization, business leaders and politicians argued that schools should adopt a similar model to produce the kinds of workers that industry required.

For the most part, educators needed little prompting. Much enamored with the industrial model, leading educators were enthusiastic about applying its principles to their enterprises. An ardent advocate of the industrial model, William T. Harris was one of the most influential school superintendents in the United States in the late nineteenth century, serving as the president and director of the National Education Association, the president of the National Association of School Superintendents, and the United States commissioner of education. He wrote:

Our schools are, in a sense, factories in which the raw materials (children) are to be shaped and fashioned in order to meet the various demands of life. The specifications for manufacturing come from the demands of the twentieth century civilization, and it is the business of the school to build its pupils according to the specifications laid down. (quoted in Fiske, 1992, pp. 32–33)

Ellwood Cubberly, a professor at Stanford University and one of the nation's foremost educational thinkers of his time, reflected the opinion of his contemporaries when he wrote the following in 1934:

The public schools of the United States are, in a sense, a manufactury, doing a two billion dollar business each year in trying to prepare future citizens for usefulness and efficiency in life. As such we have recently been engaged in revising our manufacturing specifications and in applying to the conduct of our business some of the same principles of specialized production and manufacturing efficiency which control in other parts of the manufacturing world. (p. 528)

The uniformity, standardization, and bureaucracy of the factory model soon became predominant characteristics of the school district. The key was to have the *thinkers* of the organization specify exactly what and how to teach at each grade level and then to provide strict supervision to ensure that teachers did as they were told. Decisions flowed from state boards of education down the ladder of the educational bureaucracy to local school boards, superintendents, and principals. Eventually, decisions would be directed to teachers who, like factory workers, were viewed as underlings responsible for carrying out the decisions of their bosses. Students were simply the raw material transported along the educational assembly line. They would be moved to a station where a teacher would "pour" in mathematics until the bell rang; then they would be moved to the next station where another teacher would "assemble" the nuts and bolts of English until the next bell rang, and so on. Those who completed this 13-year trek on the assembly line would emerge as finished products, ready to function efficiently in the industrial world.

Unfortunately, many of the principles of this factory model still prevail within the structures of American schools. Schools continue to focus on procedures rather than results, following the assumption that if they adhere to the rules—teaching the prescribed curriculum, maintaining the correct class sizes, using the appropriate textbooks, accumulating the right number of course credits—students will learn what they need to know. Less attention is paid to determining whether or not the learning has actually occurred. Instead, schools remain preoccupied with time and design, organizing the class period, school day, and school year according to rigid schedules that must be followed. In many schools, teachers and their opinions are still considered to be insignificant. Above all else, the factory model has established a conservative tradition in American schools. Taylor's concept of the one right system has led to a credo of "get it right—then keep it going." As a result of this philosophy, many educators seem unable to embrace a concept of continuous improvement that has the significantly different credo of "get it right, and then make it better and better and better."

In defense of nineteenth-century educators, the factory model may have indeed served schools well when they were not intended to educate large numbers of students to a high level. In 1893, for example, when the Committee of Ten issued the report that was to shape the high school curriculum for decades, 1893), less than three percent of American students were actually graduating from high school. Even as late as 1950, the majority of students continued to drop out of high school before graduation. In this way, the factory model did indeed function as it was intended by sorting and selecting students. The model continued to work reasonably well as long as dropouts had ready access to unskilled jobs in industry, regardless of their educational level. The number of unskilled jobs in industry has declined significantly, however, and the most enlightened corporations—even many factories—have abandoned this model (Blankstein, 1992).

The factory model is woefully inadequate for meeting the national education goals of today—goals that call for *all* students to master rigorous content, learn how to learn, pursue productive employment, and compete in a global economy. If educators are to meet these challenges, they *must* abandon an outdated model that is contrary to the findings of educational research, the best practices of both schools and industry, and common sense. They *must* embrace a new conceptual model for schools. The issue then becomes identifying the model that offers the best hope for significant school improvement.

The School as a Professional Learning Community

Researchers both inside and outside of education offer remarkably similar conclusions about the best path for sustained organizational improvement. Consider the following findings:

> *Only the organizations that have a passion for learning will have an enduring influence.* (Covey, 1996, p. 149)

> *Every enterprise has to become a learning institution [and] a teaching institution. Organizations that build in continuous learning in jobs will dominate the twenty-first century.* (Drucker, 1992, p. 108)

The most successful corporation of the future will be a learning organization. (Senge, 1990, p. 4)

Preferred organizations will be learning organizations. . . . It has been said that people who stop learning stop living. This is also true of organizations. (Handy, 1995, p. 55)

The new problem of change . . . is what would it take to make the educational system a learning organization—expert at dealing with change as a normal part of its work, not just in relation to the latest policy, but as a way of life. (Fullan, 1993, p. 4)

The Commission recommends that schools be restructured to become genuine learning organizations for both students and teachers; organizations that respect learning, honor teaching, and teach for understanding. (Darling-Hammond, 1996, p. 198)

We have come to realize over the years that the development of a learning community of educators is itself a major cultural change that will spawn many others. (Joyce & Showers, 1995, p. 3)

If schools want to enhance their organizational capacity to boost student learning, they should work on building a professional community that is characterized by shared purpose, collaborative activity, and collective responsibility among staff. (Newmann & Wehlage, 1995, p. 37)

We argue, however, that when schools attempt significant reform, efforts to form a schoolwide professional community are critical. (Louis, Kruse, & Raywid, 1996, p. 13)

Rarely has research given school practitioners such a consistent message and clear sense of direction. But even if educators are persuaded that creating a professional learning community offers the best strategy for school improvement, difficult questions remain. The best way to initiate consideration of these questions is to "begin with the end in mind" (Covey, 1989, p. 95)— that is, to describe the characteristics of a professional learning community, the conduct and habits of mind of the people who work within it, and its day-to-day functioning. A clear vision of what a learning community looks like and how people operate within it will offer insight into the steps that must be taken to transform a school into a learning community.

Characteristics of Professional Learning Communities

1. Shared mission, vision, and values. The *sine qua non* of a learning community is shared understandings and common values. What separates a learning community from an ordinary school is its collective commitment to guiding principles that articulate what the people in the school believe and what they seek to create. Furthermore, these guiding principles are not just articulated by those in positions of leadership; even more important, they are embedded in the hearts and minds of people throughout the school. Mission, vision, and values are so integral to a learning community that each will be discussed in detail in later chapters.

2. Collective inquiry. The engine of improvement, growth, and renewal in a professional learning community is collective inquiry. People in such a community are relentless in questioning the status quo, seeking new methods, testing those methods, and then reflecting on the results. Not only do they have an acute sense of curiosity and openness to new possibilities, they also recognize that the process of searching for answers is more important than having an answer. Furthermore, their search is a collective one.

Ross, Smith, and Roberts (1994) refer to the collective inquiry process as "the team learning wheel" and identify four steps in that process:

1. Public reflection—members of the team talk about their assumptions and beliefs and challenge each other gently but relentlessly.

2. Shared meaning—the team arrives at common ground, shared insights.

3. Joint planning—the team designs action steps, an initiative to test their shared insights.

4. Coordinated action—the team carries out the action plan. This action need not be joint action but can be carried out independently by the members of the team.

At this point, the team analyzes the results of its actions and repeats the four-step cycle.

This process enables team members to benefit from what Senge et al. (1994) has called "the deep learning cycle . . . the essence of the learning organization" (p. 18). Collective inquiry enables team members to develop new skills and capabilities, which in turn lead to new experiences and awareness. Gradually, the heightened awareness is assimilated into fundamental shifts in attitudes and beliefs. Ultimately, it is this ability to examine and modify beliefs that enables team members to view the world differently and make significant changes in the culture of the organization.

3. Collaborative teams. The basic structure of the professional learning community is a group of collaborative teams that share a common purpose. Some organizations base their improvement strategies on efforts to enhance the knowledge and skills of individuals. Although individual growth is essential for organizational growth to occur, it does not guarantee organizational growth. Thus, building a school's capacity to learn is a *collaborative* rather than an *individual* task. People who engage in collaborative team learning are able to learn from one another, thus creating momentum to fuel continued improvement.

On the other hand, team *learning* is not the same as team *building*. The latter focuses on creating courteous protocols, improving communication, building stronger relationships, or enhancing the group's ability to perform routine tasks together. Collaborative team learning focuses on *organizational* renewal and a willingness to work together in continuous improvement processes.

It is difficult to overstate the importance of collaborative teams in the improvement process. Fullan (1993) stresses their importance in *Change Forces*:

> The ability to collaborate—on both a large and small scale—is one of the core requisites of post modern society. . . . [I]n short, without collaborative skills and relationships it is not possible to learn and to continue to learn as much as you need in order to be an agent for social improvement. (pp. 17–18)

4. Action orientation and experimentation. Professional learning communities are action oriented. Members of such organizations turn aspirations into action and visions into reality. Not only do they act; they are unwilling to tolerate inaction. They recognize that learning always occurs in a context of taking action, and they believe engagement and experience are the most effective teachers. Even seemingly chaotic activity is preferred to orderly, passive inaction.

An important corollary of the action orientation is a willingness to experiment—to develop and test hypotheses. Members of professional learning communities are often asked to develop, test, and evaluate theories. They reflect on what happened and why, develop new theories, try new tests, evaluate the results, and so on. This willingness to experiment is accompanied by a tolerance for results that may be contrary to what was anticipated. While traditional organizations tend to brand such experiments as failures and then seek to assign blame, learning organizations consider failed experiments to be an integral part of the learning process—opportunities to learn and then begin again more intelligently.

5. Continuous improvement. A persistent discomfort with the status quo and a constant search for a better way characterize the heart of a professional learning community. Continuous improvement requires that each member of the organization is engaged in considering several key questions:

1. What is our fundamental purpose?

2. What do we hope to achieve?

3. What are our strategies for becoming better?

4. What criteria will we use to assess our improvement efforts?

A commitment to continuous improvement is evident in an environment in which innovation and experimentation are viewed not as tasks to accomplish or projects to complete, but as ways of conducting day-to-day business, *forever*. Members of a professional learning community recognize and celebrate the fact that mission and vision are ideals that will never be fully realized, but must always be worked toward. In short, becoming a learning community is less like getting in shape than staying in shape—it is not a fad diet, but a never-ending commitment to an essential, vital way of life.

6. Results orientation. Finally, a professional learning community realizes that its efforts to develop shared mission, vision, and values; engage in collective inquiry; build collaborative teams; take action; and focus on continuous improvement must be assessed on the basis of *results* rather than *intentions*. Unless initiatives are subject to ongoing assessment on the basis of tangible results, they represent random groping in the dark rather than purposeful improvement. Peter Senge (1996) notes that "the rationale for any strategy for building a learning organization revolves around the premise that such organizations will produce dramatically improved results" (p. 44).

The School as a Professional Learning Community: A Scenario

How would these characteristics of learning communities affect daily operation of a school? Consider the following scenario, which illustrates the professional learning community at work:

> Connie Donovan approached her first teaching assignment with all the anxiety and nervous trepidation of any first-year teacher. She had been assured during her interview that her new school operated as a learning community that valued teacher collaboration. Nevertheless, the memory of her roommate's introduction to the teaching profession the year before was still fresh in her mind. Poor Beth had been assigned to teach one of the most difficult remedial courses in her school—classes filled with students who had failed the course in the past due to a variety of problems. Her orientation had consisted of a review of the employee manual and an overview of the teacher's contract by the principal on the morning of the day before students were to arrive. Then she was given the key to her room, the teacher's edition of the textbook, and her class roster. The following day, she faced her 135 stu-

dents for the first time. Her nine weeks of training as a student teacher had not prepared her for the difficulties she encountered, and there was no support system to help her. She did not know how to respond to student misbehavior and apathy, and she had told Connie tearfully that she felt she was losing control of her class. Connie had watched Beth work far into the night, preparing lessons and grading papers, but each week Beth only seemed to become more discouraged and overwhelmed. Weekends offered no respite. Beth's teaching position had been contingent upon her willingness to serve as cheerleading sponsor, and Friday nights and Saturdays were spent supervising cheerleaders. By March, she had decided that she was not cut out for teaching. She dreaded each day and frequently called in sick. By the end of the year, she had admitted to Connie that she felt like she was hanging on by her fingernails.

Knowing this story as she did, Connie was relieved to get a phone call that summer from Jim, a veteran member of the faculty of her new school. Jim had participated on the committee that had interviewed her for the position. He congratulated her on her appointment to the social studies department, explained that he would be serving as her mentor during her first year, and invited her to lunch to make introductions and answer any questions she might have. Her anxiety diminished somewhat when Jim told her that the school provided two full days of orientation and another three days for the faculty to work together before students arrived.

The new teacher orientation was nothing like what Beth had described. After introductions, the principal spent the morning explaining the history of the school. She carefully reviewed the school's vision statement, pointing out that it had been jointly developed by the faculty, administration, community members, and students. She explained that the statement described what the school was striving to become, and she highlighted recent initiatives that the school had begun in its effort to move closer to the ideal described in the vision. She then divided all the new teachers into small groups and asked them to identify any points of the vision statement that they felt needed clarification. The emphasis the principal gave to the vision statement made it clear to Connie that it was a major focus for the school.

Connie spent the afternoon with her department chairman and Jim. Together they provided Connie with an overview of the entire scope and sequence of the social studies department's curriculum. They also provided her with course descriptions that teachers had developed for each course, and they reviewed the essential outcomes all students were expected to achieve in the courses she was teaching. They explained further that these outcomes had been determined collectively by the teachers after considerable discussion and a lengthy review of the state's goals in social studies, the report on student achievement in social studies by the National Assessment of Educational Progress, and the curriculum standards recommended by the National Council for the Social Studies and the National Center for History in the Schools. Finally, they reviewed the vision statement for the department that the teachers themselves had developed. They discussed the department's improvement goals and priorities and demonstrated to Connie how she might use the department's common files in her own planning and assessment activities.

On the second day of orientation, the principal introduced the president of the teachers' association, who distributed and explained the faculty value statements. These statements had been developed by the faculty to give direction to the daily work of teachers. The association president pointed out the link between the value statements and the school's vision and explained that every group in the school—the Board of Education, administration, support staff, students, and parents—had articulated similar statements of the commitments they were prepared to make to improve the school.

The rest of the morning was spent hearing from representatives of the different support services available to teachers—the deans, the director of the media center, the technology coordinator, the pupil personnel department, the special education department, and the tutors from the resource centers. Each speaker emphasized that his or her function was to help teachers. That afternoon, Connie's mentor helped her set up her classroom, asked what she hoped to accomplish on the first day and during the first week of class, and offered a few suggestions based on her response.

When the entire faculty arrived the next day, Connie was surprised to see that the morning was devoted to a celebration of the start of the school year. At the opening meeting, the principal announced milestones—weddings, births, engagements, advanced degrees, and other important events that faculty members had experienced over the summer. Each announcement was met with warm applause by the faculty. The principal then stressed several themes from the vision statement and reminded teachers of the priorities they had established for that school year. Each new faculty member was introduced to the group by his or her mentor and then given a faculty T-shirt. The rest of the morning was spent enjoying a festive, schoolwide brunch, complete with skits and entertainment presented by members of the faculty and administration. Connie was surprised and pleased to learn that this back-to-school celebration was an annual tradition planned and orchestrated by a faculty committee.

That afternoon, the teachers split into teaching teams to discuss how the team would handle its responsibilities. Every teacher in the school had been appointed as a member of one or more teaching teams. Connie was a member of an interdisciplinary team that included an English teacher and a science teacher. Together the three of them would be responsible for 75 students. These students were assigned to Connie and her two colleagues for a three-hour block every day and would remain with the same three teachers for two full years. Connie was excited about this assignment. She believed in the benefits of an integrated curriculum. She felt that the long-term relationships with students would be beneficial, and she welcomed the idea of working closely with two colleagues who shared the same students. She was also enthusiastic about the fact that the teachers were free to schedule the three-hour block as they saw fit. Free from the limits of a 50-minute period, Connie thought she could offer some interesting simulations and mock trials for her students. She spent the rest of the day working with her colleagues to strengthen their first interdisciplinary unit. She appreciated the fact that they solicited her opinion and were receptive to her questions.

On the next day, Connie worked with her other team— the United States history team. All teachers responsible for teaching the same course were members of a team for that course. The teams developed common course descriptions, articulated the essential outcomes for the course, established the criteria for assessing the quality of student work, and developed common assessment instruments. The history team spent considerable time reviewing and grading ex-amples of essays that students had written the year before. Connie found this practice particularly helpful in both understanding what the department emphasized and identifying the criteria for evaluating student work. By the end of the morning, the teachers were very consistent in the way they applied the departmental criteria to grading student work.

That afternoon the team analyzed student performance according to the common assessment instruments from the previous year, identified areas where students did not meet the desired proficiencies established by the team, and discussed strategies for improving student performance. The discussion helped Connie understand what students were to accomplish, how they were to be assessed, and where they had experienced difficulties in the past. She found the discussion to be invaluable. She spent part of the third day of teacher preparation working with her teams and discussing with her mentor a few ideas she planned to use in her opening comments to students the next day. Finally, she spent the rest of her day examining profiles of her new students.

Once the school year was underway, the new teachers continued to meet at least once each month for ongoing orientation. Sometimes teachers with particular interests or skills would talk to the group on activities in their classes. One of these sessions helped Connie solve a problem she was having structuring individual accountability into cooperative learning activities. Other times, the principal provided new teachers with an article or case study and asked them to react to the item in their personal journals. These reflections then became the basis for the group's discussion. The sessions always included an opportunity to ask questions. As the year progressed, Connie found that her meetings with the other new teachers helped her develop a sense of camaraderie and shared experience with them.

By the third week of school, Connie had become concerned about one of her history students who seemed unwilling to work. Although he was not disruptive, Matthew seemed detached in class and rarely turned in any work. Connie spoke to him after class one day to express her concerns and to discuss possible ways of engaging him in the classroom activity. When the conference failed to bring about any change, Connie discussed the problem with Jim. He suggested alerting Matthew's student support team (SST). Connie learned that teachers were not the only ones in the school to work in teams. A counselor, dean, and social worker also shared responsibility for the same group of students. When Connie explained her concerns to Matthew's counselor, the SST decided to seek information from all of his teachers. It soon became evident that the behavior pattern that Matthew demonstrated in Connie's classroom was evident in all of his classes. The SST decided it was time to convene a parent conference to review Matthew's status both with his parents and teachers. At the conference, the teachers jointly developed strategies that would enable Matthew's parents to be aware of his assignments. The parents promised to monitor their son carefully to ensure he would keep up with his work.

Jim trained Connie in the school's approach to classroom observation and teacher evaluation before the department chairman and principal began the formal process with her. She became comfortable having Jim observe her teaching and found her debriefing sessions with him to be very helpful. He explained that all the mentors had been trained in analyzing teaching and providing constructive feedback.

Connie expected the principal to be more directive in the teacher evaluation process and anticipated she would receive some kind of rating at the conclusion of her conference with the principal. She was wrong on both counts. The principal asked probing questions: Why did you decide to teach this content? How does it fit with the major outcomes of the course? How did you know students had the prerequisite knowledge and skills to be successful in this unit? Why did you use the instructional strategies you selected? How do you know if students achieved the intended outcomes? What patterns do you see in your teaching? What worked and what did not work in this lesson? If you were to teach this lesson again, would you do anything differently? By the end of the conference, Connie realized that she had done most of the talking and that the principal was simply providing prompts to encourage her to reflect on and articulate her conclusions about her teaching.

Connie was surprised to discover the number of action research projects in progress in her department. For example, teachers were divided on the question of ability grouping. Some argued that remedial classes created a climate of low expectations and were harmful to students. They called for students to be grouped heterogeneously. Others argued that remedial classes offered the best strategy for meeting the special needs of students who had experienced trouble with social studies in the past. The teachers subsequently agreed to put their respective theories to the test. Remedial students were randomly assigned either to heterogeneous classes or to remedial classes, and the teachers agreed on the assessment strategies they would use at the end of the year to see which approach was more effective. In another project, some teachers volunteered to increase their class size by 25% in order to reduce their teaching assignment from five sections to four, thus leaving more time for joint planning. Once again, teachers in the experimental and traditional classes agreed on the criteria they would monitor to determine the effectiveness of each approach.

Connie learned that action research was not limited to her department; in fact, each department had various action research projects underway. She also learned that the school had established a special entrepreneurial fund offering teachers opportunities to develop grant proposals for projects to improve the school. After a review by a faculty committee to determine which proposals offered the greatest promise, the school board provided funding for the implementation of those proposals. It was obvious to Connie that experimentation played an important part in the culture of her new school.

Reflection and dialogue were also essential to the workings of the school. For example, all teachers benefited from peer observation. Teachers created reading clubs that reviewed and discussed books and major articles on teaching and learning. Faculty members participated in a portfolio development project based on the criteria identified by the National Board of Professional Teaching Standards. Department meetings typically opened with a teacher sharing a strategy or insight with colleagues and then responding to questions. Connie was impressed with the lively give and take of these discussions. She noticed that teachers felt comfortable probing and challenging one another's thinking.

It was soon very evident that ongoing professional growth was expected at this school. The district offered three different areas of concentration—authentic assessment, student-centered learning, or multiple intelligences. Teaching teams agreed to pursue one of these three professional development initiatives for at least three years. Connie's interdisciplinary team had already opted for authentic assessment. Each school year, five half-days and two full days had been set aside for concentrated focus on these topics.

The faculty members had committed themselves to making a concerted effort to integrate technology into the curriculum. They had agreed to adjust other budget areas in order to fund a full-time technology trainer. This trainer not only offered a regular schedule of technology classes for all staff during their preparation periods; she also provided one-on-one, just-in-time training when individual staff members identified a need. With the trainer's help, Connie learned to log onto a social studies teachers' group on the Internet. She enjoyed asking a question and soliciting ideas from colleagues around the world.

Each teacher in the school was asked to develop an individualized professional growth plan in an area of special interest. Connie decided to focus on effective questioning strategies and worked with her department chairman to develop a plan for investigating the topic. The chairman provided her with articles summarizing the research on questioning strategies, and the principal recommended that she observe several teachers who were particularly skilled in questioning. During the next several weeks, Connie implemented some of the strategies she had either read about or observed firsthand. She also requested feedback on her questioning techniques from Jim after he had observed her teaching.

In addition, the district offered a series of workshops and courses that were tied to district goals. Most of these classes were taught by local teachers or administrators. Connie took the course on questioning strategies as well as a series of courses on classroom management, and she received credit on the salary schedule for doing so. The district not only encouraged teachers to be active in their professional organizations, it also contributed toward the membership fee of approved organizations. Connie joined both the National Council of Social Studies Teachers and its state affiliate. The principal, department chairman, and Connie's colleagues frequently distributed copies of journal articles that they found interesting, and team and department meetings were often devoted to the discussion of the ideas in those articles. The district also published its own professional journal once each year, comprised exclusively of articles written by teachers in the district.

The district's partnership with a local college served as another stimulus for reflection and productive interchange. Undergraduate students in education were frequent observers and often served as teacher aides in the school. They had many questions after they observed a class. University staff often advised teachers in setting up action research projects. School staff reciprocated by participating in the research of the university. Professors frequently taught units in the high school, and many of the undergraduate and graduate education courses were team-taught by university staff members and a teacher from the district. Late in the year, Connie was invited to share reflections on her experience as a first-year teacher with a class of college students as they prepared for their student teaching assignments.

Connie had been surprised when, shortly after she had accepted her teaching position, the personnel office asked her to complete a survey on her experience as a teaching candidate. As the year went on, she realized that surveys soliciting feedback were frequently used throughout the district. The principal and department chairpersons distributed surveys to the staff for feedback on their performance. Teachers could choose from a variety of survey instruments that gave students the opportunity to comment on the teacher and the class. All seniors were asked to complete a survey reflecting on their high school experience, and the school conducted a phone survey of randomly selected students one year and five years after their graduation to assess their high school experience and to determine their current status.

Parents were surveyed annually to determine their impressions of the school, and the principal and members of the school board participated in neighborhood coffees throughout the district to seek feedback and answer questions from members of the community. Teachers completed annual surveys for assessing the school's improvement efforts and identifying areas for improvement. They also completed self-evaluation forms on how effectively their teams functioned. It was clear that seeking and considering feedback on performance was the norm both within the school and throughout the district.

Connie considered her common planning time with the members of her interdisciplinary team and several members of her history team to be her most valuable resource. The members of the interdisciplinary team used some of their time to refine integrated curriculum units and to discuss how to apply what they were learning about authentic assessment. Much of this time was spent discussing the students they had in common, identifying individuals who seemed to be having problems, and developing unified strategies for helping those students. Because the history team did not share the same students, its discussions focused more on ideas for teaching particular units and assessing students' understanding in general.

At the end of the semester, Connie worked with her teams to analyze the results of student performance on the common comprehensive assessments the teams had developed. First, they compared the students' achievements to the anticipated proficiency levels the teams had set. Then they compared the results to their longitudinal study of past student performance. They identified areas of concern and then brainstormed steps that they might take to improve the level of student achievement. Finally, they wrote a brief summary of their analysis and improvement plan and sent copies to the principal and their department chairpersons.

Connie felt there was never enough time to do everything that was required, but she appreciated the efforts the school had made to provide teachers with time to plan, reflect, and collaborate. In addition to the teacher planning days at the start of the year, the five half-days and three full days set aside for professional development, and the common preparation periods allocated for teaching teams, teachers were given two hours every two weeks for planning and conferencing. This was possible because a few years earlier the faculty had agreed to extend the school day by 10 minutes each day in exchange for a two-hour block every other Wednesday when teachers could work together on joint projects. The principal emphasized the importance of teacher collaboration by assuring her faculty that she would provide substitutes for any team that needed more time to complete its work. She also had an enlisted corps of parent volunteers who would substitute for this purpose as needed.

That spring, teaching teams were invited to develop proposals for summer curriculum projects. The proposal form called on each team to describe what it wanted to accomplish, how the project was related to departmental and school visions, and what the project would produce. Connie's interdisciplinary team submitted a proposal for creating two units that linked American literature, United States history, and scientific principles. After their plan was approved by the faculty committee that reviewed project proposals, the team members coordinated their calendars to find a week during the summer break when everyone would be available.

On three different occasions during the year, Connie participated in small-group discussions on proposals developed by different school improvement task forces. The task forces—composed of teachers, parents, and students—were convened to generate strategies for addressing priorities that had been identified by the school. One task force submitted a proposal to increase student participation in co-curricular activities. Another offered strategies for teaching students to accept increasing responsibility for their learning as they advanced from their freshman to senior years. The third proposed a systematic way of monitoring each student's academic progress and responding to any student who was in danger of failing. Each proposal included the criteria with which the long-term impact of its recommendations should be assessed. Connie learned that every teacher in the school was expected to participate in these improvement task forces from time to time, and that one of the primary responsibilities of each task force was to build a consensus in support of its recommendations. It became apparent that proposals often had to be revised several times before that consensus could be reached.

At the end of the school year, Jim asked Connie to reflect on her overall experience. She acknowledged that not every lesson had gone well and that there had been days when she was frustrated and perplexed. Teaching had turned out to be much more difficult and complex than she had ever imagined. She had expected that her enthusiasm for history would be contagious and that her students would learn to love the subject just as she had. She now had to acknowledge that some did not seem to care for history at all, and she wondered why she had been unable to generate their enthusiasm. She had been certain that she would be able to reach *every* student, and when one of her students elected to withdraw from school saying, "This school sucks!" she questioned why she had been unable to connect with him. She admitted she did not understand where her responsibility for student learning ended and the student's began. She often asked herself if she were doing too much or not enough to help each student succeed in her class.

She had been quite certain she knew all the answers when she decided to become a teacher, but as she worked through her first year of actual experience, she felt as though she had more questions than answers. It was not until the second semester that she came to realize that good teaching is driven by such questions. She gradually came to a clearer understanding and appreciation of the section of the school's vision statement that said, "We will be a school that is noted for two characteristics: our commitment to promoting the success of every student and our continuous discontent with the immediate present." In her school, the process of searching for answers was more important than actually having answers.

It was clear that every teacher was called on to ask him- or herself each day, "How can I be more effective in my efforts to be a positive influence in the lives of the students entrusted to me?" Yet, it was equally clear that teachers were never to conclude that they had arrived at *the* definitive answer to any fundamental question. The year had been exhilarating and exhausting, fun and frustrating, but at its end, despite all of the unanswered questions, Connie was certain of one thing—her life would be spent teaching!

The experience described above could not occur in a school that continues to operate according to the principles of the industrial model. Connie's school offers a fundamentally different model based on significantly different assumptions, beliefs, and behaviors. The challenge of implementing this model is determining how schools can initiate and sustain a change process that transforms their traditional culture so that they can function as professional learning communities.

Summary

The assumptions that have guided the operation of schools since the late nineteenth century were based on the factory model and its reliance on centralization, standardization, hierarchical top-down management, a rigid sense of time, and accountability based on adherence to the system. That model is no longer valid in a post-industrial, knowledge-based society. Researchers both inside and outside of education have arrived at the same conclusions regarding a new model that offers the best hope for stimulating significant improvement in the ability of schools to achieve their objectives. This model requires schools to function as professional learning communities characterized by a shared mission, vision, and values; collective inquiry; collaborative teams; an orientation toward action and a willingness to experiment; commitment to continuous improvement; and a focus on results. The scenario that ends the chapter describes how a school organized as a professional learning community might function during the course of a typical school year.

Chapter 3

The Complexity of the Change Process

The issue is not that individual teachers and schools do not innovate and change all the time. They do. The problem is with the kinds of changes that occur in the educational system, their fragile quality, and their random and idiosyncratic nature.

—The Consortium on Productivity in the Schools
(1995, p. 23)

We are wise to believe it is difficult to change, to recognize that character has a forward propulsion which tends to carry it unaltered into the future, but we need not believe it is impossible to change. . . . We create ourselves. The sequence is suffering, insight, will, action, change.

—Allen Wheelis (1973, pp. 101–102)

Those who review the research for help on how to implement and sustain a successful change process are likely to become confused. Consider the following explanations that have been offered for the failure of school reform initiatives:

- The change moved too fast—people were overwhelmed.

- The change moved too slowly—people lost their enthusiasm.

- The change lacked strong leadership from the principal.

- The change relied too heavily on the leadership of a strong principal.

- The change was too big and attacked too much at once—people change incrementally, not holistically.

- The change was too small—organizations need a more aggressive, comprehensive shake-up.

- The change was top-down without buy-in from the faculty.

- The change was bottom-up without the support of the central office or administration.

- Gains were celebrated too soon, and the sense of urgency was lost.

- Gains were not recognized and celebrated, and the initiative lost momentum.

- Schools were unwilling to change—they were steadfastly committed to the status quo.

- Schools embraced every change that came along and careened from fad to fad.

- Leaders failed to develop a critical level of support before initiating change.

- Leaders mistakenly insisted on overwhelming support as a prerequisite for initiating change; this stipulation ensured implementation would never occur.

Each of these observations can, of course, be a valid assessment of the failure of a change initiative. Yet the paradoxes they present fail to offer guidance on overcoming obstacles to substantive innovation. What is the answer then? What must educators understand about the change process if they are to transform their schools into learning communities?

Both research and practice offer one inescapable, insightful conclusion to those considering an improvement initiative: **change is difficult.** After more than a decade of efforts to help schools reform according to the principles of the Essential Schools Movement, a weary Ted Sizer admitted, "I was aware that it would be hard, but I was not aware of how hard it would be" (1996, p. 1). The complexity and difficulty of change is a fact that cannot be overstated.

One of the most damaging myths that aspiring school administrators often learn is that the change process, if managed well, will proceed smoothly. That myth amounts to little more than a cruel hoax, an illusion that encourages educators to view problems and conflict as evidence of mistakes or a mismanaged process rather than as the inevitable byproducts of serious reform. Seymour Sarason (1995) tried to expose that myth when he wrote:

> *The decision to undertake change more often than not is accompanied by a kind of optimism and rosy view of the future that, temporarily at least, obscures the predictable turmoil ahead. But that turmoil can not be avoided and how well it is coped with separates the boys from the men, the girls from the women. It is . . . rough stuff. . . . There are breakthroughs, but also brick walls* (p. vii).

Those who seek to initiate substantive change must recognize that an existing system with a well-entrenched structure and culture is already in place. In general, those working within that system will always resist, always fight to preserve the system. The fragmented, piecemeal approach to change that characterizes most school reform lacks the power and focus needed to overcome that resistance.

Thus, change is a complex and formidable task that is certain to be accompanied by pain and conflict. Many argue that pain is an essential element for initiating change, that the familiar status quo is always preferable to change until the traditional way of doing things results in considerable discomfort to those in the organization. We contend that a learning community can foster constant exploration of change as part of its culture rather than as a response to pain. But that does not mean discomfort either can or should be avoided. The change process is necessarily filled with uncertainty, anxiety, and problems—conditions that are certain to lead to conflict. In fact, the absence of problems and conflict, particularly in the early stages of change, suggests that the initiatives are superficial rather than substantive. As Michael Fullan (1993) has emphasized, "**Conflict is essential** to any successful change effort" (p. 27).

Attempts to persuade educators to participate in reform by assuring them that change will be easy are patently dishonest. Principals and teachers should be advised, and should acknowledge, from the outset that transforming their schools from the industrial model to learning communities will be difficult, regardless of how carefully they plan and how skillfully they manage the process. Still, they can make their efforts to change more effective by learning important lessons from the common mistakes others have made when they initiated the change process.

Common Mistakes in the Change Process

John Kotter (1996) of the Harvard Business School has identified the eight most common mistakes in the change process:

1. **Allowing too much complacency.** Kotter contends that the biggest mistake people make when trying to change organizations is to plunge ahead without establishing a high enough sense of urgency (p. 4). This is a fatal error because change efforts always fail when complacency levels are high.

2. **Failing to create a sufficiently powerful guiding coalition.** Individuals working alone, no matter how competent or charismatic they are, will never have everything that is needed to overcome the powerful forces of tradition and inertia. A key to successful change is creating first a guiding coalition and ultimately a critical number of people within the organization who will champion the change process together.

3. **Underestimating the power of vision.** Vision helps to direct, align, and inspire the actions of the members of an organization. Without the clear sense of direction that a shared vision provides, the only choices left to individuals within an organization are to "do their own thing," to check constantly with supervisors for assurance about the decisions they must make, or to debate every issue that arises.

4. **Undercommunicating the vision by a power of 10.** Without credible communication, and a lot of it, change efforts are doomed to fail. Three types of errors are common. In the first, leaders underestimate the importance of communicating the vision. They mistakenly believe that sending a few memos, making a few speeches, or holding a few meetings will inform people in the

organization of the change and recruit them to it. A second mistake is divided leadership. While the head of the organization articulates the importance of the change, other leaders in the organization may tend to ignore it. The third mistake is incongruency between what key leaders say and how they behave. Strategies to communicate vision are always ineffective if highly visible people in the organization still behave in ways that are contrary to the vision.

5. **Permitting structural and cultural obstacles to block the change process.** Organizations often fail to address obstacles that block change. These obstacles typically include (a) structures that make it difficult to act, (b) in-sufficient training and support for people who are critical to the initiative's success, (c) supervisors who do not endorse the change, and (d) information and reward systems that are not aligned with the new vision. Simply declaring a new vision is not sufficient. The organization must make every effort to remove the structural and cultural barriers that threaten to impede the implementation of that vision.

6. **Failing to create short-term wins.** Change initiatives risk losing momentum if there are no short-term goals to reach and celebrate. Most people will not "go on the long march" unless they see compelling evidence within a year that the journey is producing desirable results. Creating short-term wins requires establishing goals, identifying performance criteria, achieving the goals, and then publicly celebrating the results.

7. **Declaring victory too soon.** There is also a difference between celebrating a win and declaring victory. Until change initiatives become anchored in the culture, they are fragile and subject to regression. Handled properly,

the celebration of short-term wins can give the change initiative the credibility it needs to tackle bigger, more substantive problems. Handled improperly, this celebration can contribute to the complacency that is lethal to the change process.

8. **Neglecting to anchor changes firmly in the culture.** Change sticks only when it is firmly entrenched in the school or organization's culture, as part of "the way we do things around here" (see Chapter 7). As Kotter concludes, "Until new behaviors are rooted in social norms and shared values, they are always subject to degradation as soon as the pressures associated with a change effort are removed" (p. 14).

These eight common mistakes represent potential minefields for those attempting to traverse the perilous path of transforming a school from its industrial traditions into a learning community. Any one of them can destroy the change process. The critical question thus becomes, "What strategies can a school use to avoid these mistakes as it initiates a change process?"

Creating a Learning Community—Where Do We Begin?

Kotter's contention that successful change initiatives require a sense of urgency can, of course, be troubling for those who are considering school reform. Most educators simply do not seem to respond to warnings of impending doom. The rhetoric of *A Nation at Risk* was, after all, an explicit attempt to alert America to an alleged national crisis, and yet it failed to evoke much response from teachers and principals. Currently, both disparaging critics and critical friends of education warn that public schools are in peril. The chairman of IBM blasts public education as a "bureaucratic monopoly" that has been given one last chance to save itself before being "abandoned across the board" (Gerstner et al., 1994, p. 22). And after 10 years of research on the relationship between the public and its schools, the president of the Kettering Foundation made the following conclusion: "The research forces me to say something I never thought I would say—or even think. The public school system, as we know it, may not survive into the next century" (Matthews, 1997, p. 741). Phil Schlechty (1997) is among the reformers who warns educators that unless they move quickly to transform their schools in dramatic ways, "public schools will not be a vital component of America's system of education in the twenty-first century" (p. xi). Nearly one in four Americans, when questioned on whether public education can ever be reformed, believes that finding alternatives to public education is preferable to further reform efforts (Elam, Rose, & Gallup, 1997). Yet, in spite of such urgent messages, there is little evidence to suggest that contemporary educators recognize a pressing need for change.

Many contend that it is impossible to create a sense of urgency in school administrators and teachers, and they point to a history of failed reforms to support their contention. As the argument goes, there is virtually nothing that can be done to shake educators from their complacency and convince them of a critical need for change because public schools represent virtual monopolies in most communities, compulsory attendance laws assure schools of a captive audience, and many teachers are protected by tenure and seniority laws that seem to give them lifetime job security. Most of the present-day calls for school choice, charter schools, open enrollments, and the abolition of tenure reflect the argument that, under current conditions, there is virtually no motivation for educators to take any change initiative seriously. Proponents of these alternatives contend that unless schools feel "the spur of the market," they will never change (Gerstner et al., 1994, p. 85).

Is a sense of urgency a prerequisite for change? If so, is it possible to shake off the prevailing complacency and create that sense of urgency among the personnel in public schools? Can this be accomplished even in schools with good reputations and evidence of widespread community support? The answer to these questions is a reverberating *yes*. "Urgency" need not be the equivalent of "crisis" or "panic." Certainly a struggle for survival can generate a feeling of urgency, but that feeling is likely to be short-lived. Motivation for change will last only until the crisis is averted. More enduring catalysts for change are a powerful sense of purpose, a widely shared vision of what an organization might become, and a collective commitment to act in a way that will make that vision a reality. A culture of continuous improvement does not require a persistent state of panic. Schools can certainly become organizations that are characterized by a consistently high state of urgency and the absence of complacency if they are guided by a compelling picture of a future that is clearly superior to the status quo. The concept of the professional learning community can provide that compelling picture.

Summary

Managing the change process requires the ability to operate within a myriad of paradoxes. Those who attempt to transform their schools into professional learning communities should recognize that change is difficult but not impossible. They must be prepared for the anxiety, the discomfort, and the ongoing conflict that always accompany change initiatives, particularly in the early stages of the process. According to Kotter (1996), the most common mistakes in the change process include:

1. Allowing too much complacency.

2. Failing to create a sufficiently powerful guiding coalition.

3. Underestimating the power of vision.

4. Undercommunicating the vision by a power of 10.

5. Permitting structural obstacles to block the change process.

6. Failing to create short-term wins.

7. Declaring victory too soon.

8. Neglecting to anchor changes firmly in the culture.

Some contend that schools will never change unless those within them feel a sense of urgency. These critics call for dooms-day strategies that threaten the very existence of public education. But while such a struggle for survival can generate a feeling of urgency, that feeling is likely to last only until the crisis has passed. A more enduring catalyst for change is a compelling picture of what the school might become—one that projects positive images and practical alternatives that are clearly superior to the status quo. The concept of the *professional learning community* can provide that picture.

Chapter 4

Building the Foundation of a Professional Learning Community: Mission and Vision

The most important question in any organization has to be "What is the business of our business?" Answering this question is the first step in setting priorities.

—Judith Bardwick (1996, p. 134)

There is no more powerful engine driving an organization toward excellence and long-range success than an attractive, worthwhile, and achievable vision of the future, widely shared.

—Burt Nanus (1992, p. 3)

I magine that the school as a professional learning community rests on a foundation of four building blocks or pillars that support the school and give direction to the people within it. Each of these building blocks takes its shape and form from the answer to a specific question addressed to the people in the school. If these people all take the time to consider the questions, engage in deep discourse about them, and reach consensus on how the questions are to be answered, the foundation of a learning community will have been established. Much work will remain, but the reconstruction work will have the benefit of a solid foundation.

The First Building Block: Mission/Purpose

Why **do we exist?** The mission question challenges members of a group to reflect on the fundamental purpose of the organization, the very reason for its existence. The question asks, "Why do we exist?" "What are we here to do together?" and "What is the business of our business?" The focus is not on how the group can do what it is currently doing better or faster, but rather on why it is doing it in the first place. Addressing this question is the first step in clarifying priorities and giving direction to everyone in the organization.

Mission statements are nothing new to schools. Many states have passed legislation that requires schools to have a mission statement. Even in states without this legislative mandate, mission statements for local schools or school districts are commonplace. A cursory review of these statements reveals that they sound much the same. The generic mission statement for North American schools solemnly proclaims:

> *It is the mission of our school to help each and every child realize his or her full potential and become a responsible and productive citizen and life-long learner who is able to use technology effectively and appreciate the multi-cultural society in which we live as we prepare for the challenges of the twenty-first century.* (DuFour, 1997a).

The similarity of mission statements is not necessarily a cause for concern. Whether their schools are in Miami or Vancouver, the province of Ontario or the state of California, educators seem to acknowledge that schools serve a common purpose—to help every child lead a successful and satisfying life and make a contribution to community and country. This idea of success for every student so eloquently articulated in mission statements across the country is closely linked to another affirmation that "we believe all kids can learn." In fact, that phrase has become something of a cliché, a mantra chanted unthinkingly by educators across the country. Few contemporary teachers or principals would challenge this assertion that all children are capable of learning. In fact, answers to the question, "Do you believe all kids can learn?" reveal very little about the beliefs, expectations, or practices of the educators in a given school. The more relevant and useful questions to ask when trying to build a shared sense of purpose are:

1. If we believe all kids can learn, exactly what is it that we will expect them to learn?

2. If we believe all kids can learn, how do we respond when they do not learn?

Below are descriptions of four schools that operate under very different assumptions. Even though the educators within these schools would contend that they believe "all kids can learn," they would respond to students who are *not* learning in significantly different ways.

We believe all kids can learn . . .

. . . based on their ability. The extent of students' learning is determined by their innate ability or aptitude. This ability is relatively fixed, and as teachers, we have little influence over the extent of student learning. It is our job to create multiple programs or tracks that address these differences in ability in our students and then to guide students to the appropriate program. This ensures that students have access to the proper curriculum and an optimum opportunity to master material appropriate to their abilities.

. . . **if they take advantage of the opportunity to learn.** Students can learn if they choose to put forth the effort to do so. It is our job to provide students with this opportunity to learn, and we fulfill our responsibility when we attempt to present lessons that are both clear and engaging. In the final analysis, however, while it is our job to teach, it is the student's job to learn. We should invite them and encourage them to learn, but we should also honor their decision if they elect not to do so.

. . . **and we will accept responsibility for ensuring their growth.** Certainly it is our responsibility to help each student demonstrate some growth as a result of his or her experience in our classrooms. But the extent of that growth will be determined by a combination of the student's innate ability and effort. It is our job to create a warm, inviting classroom climate and to encourage all students to learn as much as possible, but the extent of their learning depends on factors over which we have little control.

. . . **and we will establish high standards of learning that we expect all students to achieve.** It is our job to create an environment in our classrooms that engages students in academic work that results in a high level of achievement. We are confident that with our support and help, students can master challenging curricula, and we expect them to do so. We are prepared to work collaboratively with colleagues, students, and parents to achieve this shared educational purpose (DuFour, 1997a).

While educators in all four of these schools would contend that they believe every student can learn, they will respond to students who are not learning in fundamentally different ways.

The first school views failure to learn as an indication that the student lacks the ability or motivation to master the content. Based on this assessment, the school offers a less rigorous program as the solution. The second school considers failure an important part of the learning process. Students who do not put forth the necessary effort to succeed here must be taught that they are responsible for their own decisions. To ensure that this important lesson is learned, teachers must allow students to fail. The third school is prepared to accept responsibility for helping each student demonstrate *some* growth but is unwilling to establish high standards for all students. Here, too, the faculty members contend that they have little influence over the extent of an individual's learning.

These responses are entirely acceptable in a system that believes its primary purpose is to sort and select students according to their abilities and/or willingness to master particular curriculum challenges. That approach might have been effective in the Industrial Age when students had ample opportunities to pursue occupations that did not require intellectual ability. In today's Information Age society, however, educators must operate from the premise that it is the purpose of schools to bring *all* students to their full potential and to a level of education that was once reserved for the very few. Clearly then, it is only the fourth school in the above scenario that offers a viable, modern-day response to students who are not learning.

If such an all-encompassing mission is to be accomplished, clarity of purpose and a willingness to accept responsibility for achieving that purpose are critical. From 1990 to 1995, the Center on Organization and Restructuring of Schools conducted a comprehensive, longitudinal study of school improvement initiatives. The center analyzed data from more than 1,500 elementary, middle, and high schools throughout the United States and conducted field research in 44 schools in 16 states. One of the significant findings of that study was that the most successful schools function as professional communities "in which teachers pursue a clear shared purpose for all students' learning, engage in collaborative activity to achieve that purpose, and take collective responsibility for student learning" (Newmann & Wehlage, 1995, p. 30).

The lesson of that study is an important one for principals and teachers who hope to develop their capacity to function as facilitators in professional learning communities. They must go beyond the clichés in examining their current beliefs or assumptions about the mission of education. They cannot be content with a half-hearted affirmation of their belief that all students can learn. Instead, they must challenge themselves to answer the tougher questions that address the very heart of the purpose of schooling: What is it we expect our students to learn, and how will we fulfill our collective responsibility to ensure that this learning takes place for *all* of our students? Mission statements that do not answer these questions will contribute very little to the creation of a learning community.

The Second Building Block: Vision

What **do we hope to become?** Whereas mission establishes an organization's purpose, vision instills an organization with a sense of direction. It asks, "If we are true to our purpose now, what might we become at some point in the future?" Vision presents a realistic, credible, attractive future for the organization—a future that is better and more desirable in significant ways than existing conditions. It offers a target that beckons (Bennis & Nanus, 1985). An effective vision statement articulates a vivid picture of the organization's future that is so compelling that a school's members will be motivated to work together to make it a reality.

It is difficult to overstate the importance of collective vision in the establishment of a learning organization. Vision has been described as "essential" to a successful change process (Kotter, 1996, p. 68), and Peter Senge (1990) contends that "you cannot have a learning organization without shared vision" (p. 209).

But the development of shared vision has been particularly troublesome for educators. Reformers and critics of education have bombarded teachers and principals with countless (and often conflicting) images and ideas about how schools should function and the purposes they should serve. For example, consider some of the following debates raging in public education.

- Schools must demand more of students—more courses for graduation, more days in the school year, more homework, and greater mastery of more content.

   No, "less is more": schools should remove content from the curriculum and focus instead on teaching children *how* to learn.

- Strong principals are the essential prerequisite of effective schools.

   No, the principalship should be abolished in favor of faculty committees.

- Schools exist to instill and develop essential core values in students.

   No, schools must focus on teaching basic competencies and leave the task of teaching values to the family.

- The school curriculum should transmit the traditional academic content that comprises the "cultural literacy" of an educated person.

   No, the school curriculum should concentrate on developing "process skills" and recognize that content is secondary.

- Teachers must be empowered if schools are to become more effective.

  No, teachers' unions with too much power represent the single biggest obstacle to meaningful school improvement. (DuFour, 1997b, p. 56).

Bombarded by this cacophony of mixed signals and anxious to be all things to all people, educators have often resorted to vision statements filled with sweeping generalities. But even this strategy has failed to result in consensus as groups have challenged what were assumed to be irrefutable, morally impeccable goals. Such seemingly uncontroversial statements as "We will teach our students to be critical thinkers" or "We will promote the health and well-being of each student" have generated vocal opposition in communities around the country.

So the lack of a compelling vision for public schools continues to be a major obstacle in any effort to improve schools. Those who hope to develop a school's capacity to function as a learning community cannot overlook the importance of this critical building block in achieving that goal. Until educators can describe the ideal school they are trying to create, it is impossible to develop policies, procedures, or programs that will help make that ideal a reality. In the indisputable logic of the great Yankee philosopher, Yogi Berra, "If you don't know where you are going, you probably aren't going to get there."

Creating a Vision of a Learning Community

Although there are a variety of ways to develop a written vision statement for a learning community, relatively few of them actually result in the ownership of that vision. Bryan Smith offers five scenarios for implementing a vision within an organization:

1. *Telling.* The boss assumes that he or she knows what the vision should be and announces it to the organization

in the grand dictatorial tradition: "It's my way or the highway."

2. *Selling.* The boss assumes that he or she knows what the vision should be and attempts to persuade members of the organization before proceeding.

3. *Testing.* The boss has an idea about what the vision should be but seeks reactions from those in the organization to help him or her refine and redesign the vision before proceeding.

4. *Consulting.* The boss puts together a representative committee of members of the organization and encourages it to develop a vision for his or her review and approval. The boss then reserves the right to accept or ignore the recommendations.

5. *Co-creating.* The boss and members of the organization, through a collaborative process, build a shared vision together (in Senge et al., 1994, p. 314).

This co-creating strategy is perhaps not the most efficient way to develop a written vision statement, but it is certainly the strategy most likely to result in the shared vision critical to a learning community. A vision will have little impact until it is widely shared and accepted and until it connects with the personal visions of those within the school. Building a shared vision is the ongoing, never-ending, daily challenge confronting all those who hope to transform their schools into learning communities. The key to meeting that challenge is not to impose a vision on an unwilling faculty, but rather to help faculty members identify common causes, interests, goals, and aspirations. Instead of saying, "Listen to me, I have decided what we must become," the leader of a learning community uses an approach that says, "I have listened to you, and this is what I heard you say that you want for yourselves and for our students."

The process that is used to develop a vision statement can foster the pervasive support and endorsement that make such a statement an effective instrument for change. The most important question to ask in guiding the process is, "Will this strategy foster widespread ownership?" It is not enough to have people agree with someone else's statement. They should feel as though they have played an integral part in formulating that statement. Adherence to the principle of fostering widespread ownership offers direction in responding to other key questions about the vision-building process.

Should the Vision Be Written at the District or School Site Level?

Districts have a legitimate interest in ensuring that students have comparable educational experiences, regardless of the particular school they attend. To promote that consistency, districts often centralize curricula, textbooks, processes, and procedures. Many districts have applied this same principle to writing vision statements. The central office may coordinate a committee representing its schools and challenge them to develop a vision statement that applies to all schools. Even if this process is based on a sincere and concentrated effort to include input from all teachers in each school, most teachers will view the process as a central office activity that has little relevance to them. Far too many vision statements are proudly displayed in the district office, but provide little direction for the daily work of the district's schools. Conversely, ignoring the question of vision at the district level and allowing each school to develop a vision as if it were an independent entity, separate from all the other schools in the district, can result in schools that move in very different directions. The schools of a district should have the benefit of common guiding principles. The district office is ideally positioned to initiate processes to develop district-wide principles.

The best way to prepare a vision statement is to be sure that both the district and the individual school play a major role in its development. The district should initiate discussion by bringing together representatives of each school. These representatives, in turn, should be specifically charged to involve their colleagues in discussions of what the district's schools should strive to provide for the community as a whole. Once this common district statement has been developed, it should be reviewed and endorsed by each school. Then the personnel in each school should be asked to develop their own statements of what they hope their individual schools will become. These statements should also be consistent with the district's vision for *all* of its schools. In short, the district should provide an umbrella statement that gives direction to all of its schools, but should also ask each school to develop its own answer to the question, "What do we hope to become?" The response should be congruent with the district statement. This strategy offers the best hope for both consistent direction throughout a school district and teacher ownership of the final product.

Should the Process Be Limited to School Personnel?

Although some schools have limited their discussion to the people at the school site, a process that also includes representatives of parents, community members, area businesses, and students is preferable for three reasons. First, each of these groups offers a different perspective, a way of viewing the school that will be somewhat different than those employed within it. Marcel Proust once wrote that "the real art of discovery consists not in finding new lands, but in seeing with new eyes." If educational personnel are to discover new ways to conduct their business, the "new eyes" that students and those outside of the school can contribute to the task provide a valuable resource that should be used.

Second, each of these groups represents a "customer" of the school. Feedback from customers about their experiences and expectations can serve as a powerful catalyst for change.

Third, significant and substantive change initiatives are likely to generate conflict at some point in their implementation. If representatives of parents, the community, businesses, and students have been involved in the change process, if they have indeed endorsed the new direction and feel ownership in it, they can become powerful advocates for change in times of conflict. Conversely, if these constituencies have been left out of the process, teachers and principals are typically left to fend for themselves when conflict arises. While it is true that the greatest challenge of creating a professional learning community must be met by the personnel within a school, those people can increase their likelihood of success if they include their customers in the process.

There are two strategies for engaging parents, community members, business representatives, and students in the process of developing a vision statement. In the first strategy, representatives of each group serve as part of a larger task force that also includes teachers and administrators. Each member of the task force is responsible for soliciting feedback from his or her constituents and reporting it back to the full task force. For example, task force representatives could be asked to have their colleagues consider the question, "In what ways would we like our school to be significantly different five years from now than it is today?" Parents on the task force can host informal neighborhood coffees to solicit feedback from other parents. Community members can lead discussions at the local meetings of the Rotary, Lions, and Elks clubs. Business representatives might host similar discussions at local Chamber of Commerce meetings or could convene a business round table on the subject. Student representatives can solicit the ideas of their classmates in each homeroom. Finally, each group takes responsibility both for reporting the results of their inquiry to the full task force and for sharing drafts of vision statements with their constituents for feedback.

Another strategy calls for each group to submit more formalized surveys reflecting their own assessment of the school's strengths, weaknesses, and preferred direction. Focus groups then delve into the results of the survey more closely and provide the insight that can often be gained only through dialogue. Finally, the results of that discussion are shared with the task force charged with writing the vision statement.

Informed Decisions Require Informed Groups and Individuals

Advocates of site-based management sometimes forget that giving those at the school site the authority to make decisions without providing them with adequate information to identify and assess alternatives simply gives local schools the ability to make uninformed decisions more quickly. A professional learning community will *always* begin its exploration of an issue by gathering relevant background information and compiling the best thinking on that issue.

One district began its development of a vision statement by convening an oversight committee to identify relevant materials that should be available to all participants in the vision-building process. The committee assembled the following:

- A historical timeline of the district.

- A brief history of the district and a summary of major trends in that history.

- A chronology of the district's enrollment, assessed valuation, and facilities.

- Copies of the vision and values statements that had been developed by the district in the past.

- Identification and analysis of external and internal factors impacting the district.

- Findings of visitation teams that had evaluated the school for accreditation purposes.

- Longitudinal achievement data.

- Community survey results.

- Readings on national demographic trends, research on effective schools, and recommendations from various commissions on school reform.

Operating from a Research Base

A critical element of the background material that should be provided in the vision development process is the research on what we know about effective schools and school improvement processes. Before trying to decide on the kind of school they hope to create, educators should ask the question, "What does research tell us about good schools and successful improvement initiatives?" The following descriptors will serve as useful examples of the kinds of information that should be made available to those who are developing a vision statement.

Synthesis of Research on Indicators of a Productive School Culture

Georgiades et al. (1983)

A. *Predispositions*

1. Student-centered orientation

2. Improvement orientation

3. Success orientation: high expectations

B. *Collaborative Work Behavior*

C. *Professional Productivity*

1. Strong knowledge base supported by staff development

2. Sense of group goals and commitments

3. Staff is focused, involved, and concerned

Synthesis of Research on the Characteristics of Effective Schools

Lezotte (1997)

A. *Safe and Orderly Environment*
There is an orderly, purposeful, businesslike environment that is conducive to learning without being oppressive. Students work together cooperatively, respect human diversity, and appreciate democratic values.

B. *Climate of High Expectations for Success*
The staff demonstrates its belief that all students can attain mastery of essential school skills. Teachers develop and implement a wide array of varied strategies to ensure that students achieve mastery. The school responds to and helps students who do not learn.

C. *Instructional Leadership*
The principal is an instructional leader who communicates the school's mission to students, teachers, and the community. However, leadership is widely dispersed, and the principal serves as a leader of leaders—a coach, a partner, and a cheerleader.

D. *Clear and Focused Mission*
The staff understands and is committed to the school's mission, instructional goals, and priorities. Staff members

design and deliver a curriculum that goes beyond low-level skills and responds to the need for higher levels of learning for all students.

E.   *Opportunity to Learn and Student Time on Task*
A significant amount of classroom time is allocated to instruction in essential skills. The school is willing to declare that some things are more important than others and to abandon some less important areas of content in order to have enough time for material that is valued more.

F.   *Frequent Monitoring of Student Progress*
Student progress is measured frequently through a variety of assessment procedures. Teachers recognize the need to align what is taught and what is tested. There is less emphasis on standardized, norm-referenced, paper-pencil tests and more on authentic, curricular-based, criterion-referenced measures of student mastery.

G.   *Home-School Relations*
Parents understand and support the school's mission and play an important role in achieving the mission. There is enough trust and communication between teachers and parents to enable parents to serve as full partners in working toward the mutual goal of providing children with a high-quality education.

Characteristics of Effective Schools

Purkey and Smith (1983)

A.   *Structural Variables*

1. School site management

2. Strong leadership

3. Staff stability

4. Curriculum articulation and organization

5. Staff development

6. Parental involvement and support

7. Schoolwide recognition of academic success

8. Maximized learning time

9. District support

B. *Process Variables*

1. Collaborative planning and collegial relationships

2. Sense of community

3. Clear goals and high expectations that are commonly shared

4. Order and discipline

Successful School Restructuring

Newman and Wehlage (1995)

Characteristics of schools that can link restructuring initiatives with improved student learning include the following:

A. Schools' focus is an agreed upon vision of what students should learn.

B. Schools' teaching requires students to think, develop in-depth understanding, and apply academic learning to important, realistic problems.

C. Teachers in schools that function as professional learning communities:

1. Are guided by a clear, commonly held, shared purpose for student learning;

2. Feel a sense of collective responsibility for student learning; and

3. Collaborate with one another to promote student learning.

D.   Schools have external supports that:

1. Set high standards for student learning;

2. Provide sustained, schoolwide staff development; and

3. Encourage increased autonomy at the school site.

Assessing the Present, Envisioning the Future

Another strategy for sharpening the thinking of those developing the vision statement is to ask them to examine and evaluate research and observations that are critical of standard school practices. For example, completing the exercise presented on the following three pages can provide the different perspective and "new eyes" that can lead to greater insight on the changes a school might consider.

Current Reality versus Our Future Ideal

An important step in creating a learning organization is making an honest assessment of the current conditions in your school. The following survey includes conclusions presented by different researchers who have examined conditions in schools across the country. To assess the current reality of your school, use the following scale to rate each statement in terms of how well it describes conditions in your own school.

     1–3   We are not at all like this.

     4–7   We are somewhat like this.

     8–10   We are very much like this.

I.   Schools and Change

____   Schools are not organized to respond to the needs and interests of students. They are bureaucratic monopolies that rely on a captive audience for their customers. There are few incentives—and fewer rewards—to improve.

____   The issue is not that individual teachers and schools do not innovate and change all the time. They do. The problem is that the change is unproductive, focusing on the margins of practice rather than on the core of teaching and learning.

____   From the perspective of teachers, much of school life is an endless cycle of first implementing and then abandoning new initiatives. Teachers are left with the impression that no one in the system really understands why change is occurring.

____ For teachers, the concept of change becomes a matter of coping with management's tendency to introduce and then abandon educational fads.

II.   Teaching

____ Teachers believe that it is their job to teach and the student's job to learn. Thus, they are responsible for teaching but not for student learning.

____ Typical classroom instruction is dominated by "teacher talk." Teachers work very hard, and students sit passively and watch them work.

____ Teachers work in isolation. There is little opportunity for serious professional interaction in which teachers share ideas, observe each other teaching, or assist each other in professional development activities.

III.   Curriculum

____ The typical school curriculum is overloaded with trivia. Schools cannot do what they *should* be doing as long as they continue to do what they *are* doing.

____ There is typically no uniform school curriculum. Students studying the same subject with different teachers in the same school often learn vastly different content and have vastly different experiences.

____ Subjects are taught in isolation. Teachers make little effort to connect content from different subjects into a meaningful conceptual framework.

____ Schools typically have no meaningful curricular goals. They focus on means (materials, programs, instructional arrangements, etc.) rather than on ends—student outcomes.

____ Because they are unclear on the outcomes they are trying to achieve, schools are typically unable to offer valid evidence that they are accomplishing their intended purpose (i.e., student learning).

____ Teachers have not worked collectively to identify the criteria by which they will assess student work.

____ The inability to establish a results orientation means that the procedures for continuous improvement do not exist in schools.

IV.   Structure

____ Schools have no structure. They are simply convenient locations for a bunch of individual teachers, like independent contractors, to come together to teach discrete groups of students.

____ Schools have no infrastructures to support teacher collaboration in addressing schoolwide problems. Teachers, like their students, carry on side by side in similar, but essentially separate, activities.

____ Schools are structured as top-down bureaucratic hierarchies that rely heavily on rules for teachers, who can ignore much of the top-down direction when they are behind their own classroom doors.

Once the members of a learning community have reviewed relevant background information and research findings, they can begin to describe the school they are trying to create. To facilitate this process, Charlotte Roberts recommends asking teachers to project themselves five years into the future. They are to imagine that they have been spectacularly successful in creating a school that functions as a professional learning community (in Senge et al., 1994, pp. 337–338). Teachers are then challenged to describe the school as if they were actually seeing it. Questions teachers might consider in this process include the following:

1. What is our purpose?

2. How are we behaving?

3. How do we treat each other?

4. How do we treat our students?

5. How are we interacting with parents and the community?

6. What makes our school a great place to work?

7. How have we measured our progress?

Similarly, Roberts and Smith (Senge et al., 1994, p. 208) suggest using the following types of questions to guide the vision development process:

1. What would you like to see our school become?

2. What reputation would it have?

3. What contribution would it make to our students and community?

4. What values would it embody?

5. How would people work together?

Next, Roland Barth (1990) recommends having teachers complete the following statements to help them articulate a vision:

1. When I leave this school, I would like to be remembered for . . .

2. I want my school to be a place where . . .

3. The kind of school I would like my own child to attend would . . .

4. The kind of school I would like to teach in would . . . (p. 148)

Other questions might include:

1. Envision our school five years from now. In what significant ways would you like it to be different than it is today?

2. What could we accomplish in the next five years that would make us proud?

3. Describe a school that functions as a model of a professional learning community. What are its key characteristics? How is it functioning?

Whatever prompt is used to help the faculty discuss the kind of school it is trying to create, each staff member should be given the opportunity to respond. The following process represents one practical strategy to ensure that everyone has an opportunity to discuss his or her hopes and aspirations for the school.

1. Each staff member is given a pad of Post-it™ notes.

2. Each staff member thinks of what he or she hopes the school will become and writes one descriptor or idea per Post-it™ note.

3. Staff members are arranged into groups of five or six.

4. Each group is given a big piece of chart paper, and group members post their notes on the paper.

5. Members of each group read each note on their chart paper.

6. Each group arranges the notes into categories or classifications.

7. Each group writes a statement that best describes its collective vision for that category or classification.

8. A writing committee collects the statements from each group and develops a draft of a vision statement based on the common trends and themes that have been identified by all the groups.

9. The draft is shared with the entire staff, and each small group critiques the draft and proposes revisions, additions, and deletions.

10. The writing committee reviews the revisions, meets with each small group to clarify any confusion about its recommendations, and makes changes as it deems appropriate.

11. A second draft of the statement is presented to the entire staff for review and discussion.

12. Every staff member is asked if he or she believes the statement is meaningful and, if not, what changes could be made that would make it more meaningful.

13. Every staff member is asked if he or she could "own" the statement.

This process presents a constant challenge of building consensus and unity without paying the price of compromises that diminish either the substance or the clarity of the vision statement. Disagreements should not be glossed over. When they occur, individuals should be invited to present the assumptions behind their reasoning in order to see if there is a way to resolve differences and to identify common ground. Every staff member should have the opportunity to present his or her point of view and should be given serious consideration. Respect for differences of opinion must always be nurtured.

While the goal of reaching consensus should never be used to squelch discussion and debate, differences of opinion should not be used as an excuse for inaction. Consensus does not mean unanimity, and schools that believe every staff member must be an enthusiastic proponent of a new vision statement may be setting a standard that is impossible to meet. When everyone has had the opportunity to express his or her ideas, and the will of the group is evident to all (even to those who might oppose it), the faculty *has* reached a consensus and should be prepared to move forward with everyone's support. If the vision is widely shared, sufficiently compelling, and results in recognizable improvements, even those who were initially skeptical will be inclined to support it in time.

Evaluating the Vision Statement

Here are two sets of guidelines that can be used to assess vision statements.

Kotter (1996) contends that effective visions are:

- Imaginable—they convey a picture of what the future will look like.

- Desirable—they appeal to the long-term interests of stakeholders.

- Feasible—they comprise realistic, attainable goals.

- Focused—they are clear enough to provide guidance in decision making.

- Flexible—they are general enough to allow for individual initiative and changing responses in light of changing conditions.

- Communicable—they are easy to communicate and explain.

Nanus (1992) offers the following questions that can help evaluate a vision statement:

1. To what extent is the vision statement future-oriented?

2. To what extent is it likely to lead to a clearly better future for the organization?

3. To what extent does it fit with the organization's history, culture, and values?

4. To what extent does it set standards of excellence and reflect high ideals?

5. To what extent does it clarify direction?

6. To what extent does it inspire enthusiasm and encourage commitment?

7. Is it ambitious enough?

The Longevity of a Vision Statement

Organizations have addressed the longevity of their vision statements in very different ways. Some contend that in the age of the information explosion, the world is so fast-paced and ever-changing that a new vision statement should be adopted frequently, perhaps annually. Others view their vision statements as timeless works that will last for the ages. We believe that the preferred approach is to sustain a focus on a particular vision statement for an extended period of time—five to seven years.

While it is true that we live in ever-changing conditions, it is equally true that substantive change is difficult. As Adam Urbanski (1997) notes, "Real change is real hard." Making the changes necessary to advance a vision will not happen overnight, and results may not be immediately apparent. If a vision is a target that beckons, a school has a much greater likelihood of hitting a target that is stationary for a number of years than one that is constantly moving. But a vision statement should not be static; it should not be enunciated once and for all time. Because the task of clarifying and pursuing any vision leads to new interactions and insights, the vision-building process should be somewhat open-ended. As Nanus (1992) writes:

> *Vision plays an important role . . . throughout the organization's entire life cycle. . . . Sooner or later the time will come when an organization needs redirection or perhaps a complete transformation, and then the first step should always be a new vision, a wake-up call to everyone involved with the organization that fundamental change is needed and is on the way.* (p. 9)

Once a school has been working toward its vision for five to seven years, its staff should consider key questions, such as the following:

- Has current research given us new insights into how schools can fulfill their missions most effectively?

- Have there been significant changes in the internal and external factors affecting our school?

- Is the school described in our vision statement still the school we want to create?

Educators who recognize that school improvement is a continuous process will certainly realize that this process must include periodic reformulation of any vision statement.

Benefits of a Clear, Shared Vision

A faculty that works to develop a clear, shared vision of the school they are attempting to create will benefit from the process in a number of ways.

Shared vision motivates and energizes people. When people can connect their daily tasks with larger goals and collective purposes, they are more likely to think their work is meaningful. Commitment and meaning will help sustain the effort and energy needed for the difficult work of implementing change.

Shared vision creates a proactive orientation. Schools tend to be reactive, problem-driven organizations. If a problem arises, the school attempts to restore the status quo. Shared vision enables a school to move from this reactive orientation to a proactive outlook that is focused on creating a new future.

Shared vision gives direction to people within the organization. When educators have a clear sense of the purpose, direction, and the ideal future state of their school, they are better able to understand their ongoing roles within the school. This clarity simplifies the decision-making process and empowers all members of the staff to act with greater confidence. Rather than constantly checking with their bosses for approval, employees can simply ask, "Is this decision or action in line with the vision?" and then act on their own.

Shared vision establishes specific standards of excellence. A shared vision articulates standards of excellence, benchmarks by which individuals can measure their work.

Shared vision creates a clear agenda for action. Most important, a shared vision creates an agenda for action. A vision statement enables a faculty to assess current policies, practices, programs, and performance indicators and then to identify discrepancies between the existing conditions in the school and those described in the vision statement. Until a school has clarified what it is trying to become, attempts to improve it will represent only random lunges in the dark. A vision statement provides the essential bridge between the current reality of the school and what it hopes to become in the future.

Examples of vision statements developed by different schools are offered in Appendix A, but readers who simply consider using one of these statements in order to accelerate their school improvement initiative will have missed the major point. The product, the statement itself, is not nearly as important as the process. If a vision statement is adopted, but not developed, by a school's staff, its words will probably mean little or nothing at all to the staff. It is only when the teachers and constituents who develop the statement find meaning and ownership in its words that a vision statement will have an impact. This impact lies not in the eloquence of its statement, but in the meaning and direction it gives to the people in the school who developed it.

Other critical variables in the impact of a vision statement include the extent of its use in the daily operation of the school and the effectiveness with which its importance is communicated throughout the school. Chapter 6 addresses these issues.

Summary

The first step in establishing the foundation of a professional learning community is to clarify the mission or purpose of the school. The typical mission statement for schools proclaims the belief that all students can learn and acknowledges that the school has been established primarily to ensure that this learning takes place. However, the assertion that all students can learn is meaningless unless the faculty is prepared to wrestle with two very significant questions:

1. What is it we expect all students to learn?

2. How will we respond when they do not learn?

Without a resolution of these crucial questions, mission statements will contribute little to the creation of a professional learning community.

The second step in laying the foundation of a professional learning community is to address the issue of vision. If a change initiative is to produce the desired results, educators must be able to describe the results they seek. A shared vision provides them with a compelling, realistic picture of the school they are trying to create. Effective vision statements are:

- based on relevant background information and research

- desirable, feasible, and credible

- focused on clarifying direction and priorities

- easy to communicate

- developed through a collective process that promotes widespread ownership

Effective vision statements motivate and energize people. They create a proactive organization that is focused on the future, and they give direction to people within the school. They establish standards, and they create an agenda for action as the faculty identifies discrepancies between the reality of their school and the school they have described in their vision statement. The shared vision must be used to guide the daily operation and improvement initiatives of the school, and its importance must be communicated constantly.

Chapter 5

Building the Foundation of a Professional Learning Community: Values and Goals

Values are the link between emotion and behavior, the connection between what we feel and what we do. . . . With everything changing around us we need something unchanging . . . to hang on to. . . . Values are our moral navigational devices.

—James Champy (1995, p. 78)

Every shared vision effort needs not just a broad vision, but specific realizable goals—milestones we expect to reach before too long. Goals represent what people commit themselves to do.

—Senge et al. (1994, p. 303)

Mission and vision represent the first two of the four building blocks of a successful learning community. Once a faculty has resolved the critical questions of what it wants all students to learn, how it will respond when they do not learn, and what it wants its school to become, the entire school community must turn its attention to the issues of shared values and goals.

The Third Building Block: Values

How **must we behave in order to make our shared vision a reality?** While a mission statement asks the school to consider *why* it exists, and a vision statement asks *what* it might become, a statement of core values asks people to clarify *how* they intend to make their shared vision a reality. In the context of organizational development, the values question represents the essential ABCs of school improvement because it challenges the people within that organization to identify the specific attitudes, behaviors, and commitments they must demonstrate in order to advance toward their vision.

Research findings from both business and educational settings consistently cite the identification, promotion, and protection of core values as critical elements in ensuring the success of any improvement initiative. The significance of shared values emerges as a prominent theme in the literature on organizational effectiveness (Enz, 1986). Analysts describe it as the essential ingredient in excellent companies (Deal & Kennedy, 1982; Peters & Waterman, 1982) and as "the most important structural element" in any enterprise (Champy, 1995, p. 77). "Creating a community of shared values" has been identified as the fundamental leadership function in contemporary organizations (Lezotte, 1997, p. 74), and a study of leaders of the best performing organizations reveals that they "define their jobs in terms of identifying and constantly communicating commonly held values" (Heskett & Schlessinger, 1996, p. 112). The clarification and promotion of values have been cited as key factors both for effective schools (Sergiovanni, 1984) and for successful principals (Deal & Peterson, 1990). As one study of improving schools (Louis, Kruse, & Marks, 1996) concludes, "Clear shared values and norms, collectively reinforced, increase the likelihood of teacher success" (p. 181).

The message is consistent and clear. Learning organizations are not content merely to describe the future they seek; they also articulate and promote the attitudes, behaviors, and commitments that must exist to create that future. Therefore, when faculty members have reached consensus on the vision of the school they are trying to create, they must then focus on reaching consensus on the shared values they intend to promote and protect.

One way to approach this task of identifying shared values is to create a representative task force and challenge its members with the following responsibilities:

1. Carefully review the school's vision statement.

2. Identify the attitudes, behaviors, and commitments that must be demonstrated by the group in order to move the school closer to this vision.

3. Develop a draft of a statement of these attitudes, behaviors, and commitments, limiting it to no more than 10 statements.

4. Arrange small-group meetings with colleagues to present task force findings, solicit feedback, and answer questions.

5. Revise initial draft as appropriate.

6. Continue small-group meetings and revisions until there is a strong consensus for the statements.

7. Present your findings to the entire staff and obtain its endorsement of the final product.

One faculty that completed this process developed the following statement:

> *In order to advance our shared vision of an exemplary school, we will:*
>
> - *Provide an inviting classroom environment for students—an environment with clear expectations, consistent consequences, and specific, articulated, academic goals.*
>
> - *Help all students achieve the intended outcomes of the curriculum by addressing their individual needs and learning styles.*
>
> - *Use methods of assessment that enable us to monitor the learning of individual students.*
>
> - *Collaborate with one another and our students so that we can achieve our collective goals more effectively.*
>
> - *Demonstrate our commitment to ongoing professional development and continuous improvement.*
>
> - *Promote a positive school climate by modeling the qualities and characteristics that we hope to instill in our students.*
>
> - *Involve parents in the education of their children by keeping them informed of student progress and offering suggestions for assisting their students.*

Teachers at another school developed the following guidelines for their decisions and behaviors:

> *We will identify the essential outcomes for each grade level and help each student to achieve those outcomes.*

We will teach for understanding, frequently assessing students' understanding and providing a variety of opportunities for students to demonstrate mastery.

We will work collaboratively in developing instructional strategies, designing methods of assessment, and advancing the vision of the school.

We will involve the parents and the community at-large in the learning process by creating shared learning experiences.

We will model the life-long learning and commitment to high-quality work that we hope to develop in our students.

We will monitor the results of our individual and collective efforts and use evidence of results to guide our processes of continuous improvement.

The task of developing value statements should not fall exclusively to teachers. Each constituent group that makes up a school can make a significant contribution to advancing the school's vision if that group articulates and fulfills its own set of commitments. Therefore, every group within the school community should complete an exercise that identifies value statements for that group. The statements developed by the board of education and administration, support staff, students, and parents at one school district that completed this process are offered below as an example:

Board/Administrative Leadership Team
Value Statements

The Leadership Team of this District is committed to placing the education and well-being of each student above all other considerations. Toward that end, it has identified the values listed below to guide the policies, procedures, programs, priorities, and day-to-day decisions of the District and its personnel. The Team will observe, promote, and protect these values. It will also acknowledge and address behaviors that are inconsistent with the District's vision and goals.

We will model and promote the behaviors called for in the District Vision Statement. These behaviors include, but are not limited to, open and effective communication, collaborative problem solving and decision making, high expectations for achievement, commitments to life-long learning and continuous improvement, and a work ethic that reflects the importance of our mission.

We will recruit and retain individuals who are best suited to advancing the vision and goals of the District, and we will create conditions which support their ongoing professional growth.

We will facilitate the development of curricular and co-curricular programs which result in high levels of student engagement, reflect student needs and interests, integrate technology when appropriate for achieving program goals, and enable students to understand and appreciate diverse cultures.

We will develop and implement policies, programs, and procedures to monitor and support collective achievement and individual student success.

We will develop and implement policies, programs, and procedures which result in students assuming increasing responsibilities for their learning, decisions, and actions.

We will recognize and celebrate the efforts and achievements of the members of the school community.

We will fulfill our responsibilities for good stewardship by managing the District's resources in a manner that addresses the needs of the community, builds community support, and establishes community partnerships.

Support Staff Value Statements

Although we have diverse responsibilities as members of the support staff, each of us is in a position to help our school achieve its mission of success for every student. Furthermore, in fulfilling our respective responsibilities, we share common commitments. These include the following:

We will support the collective effort to create the school described in the school's Vision Statement.

We will continue to develop and support positive relationships with our colleagues, our students, and our community.

We will approach every situation with an open mind and a commitment to continuous improvement.

We will participate in effective communication throughout the school and community.

We will promote a safe and nurturing environment that is conducive to the academic and social growth of each individual student.

We will model:

- A commitment to life-long learning.

- Appreciation for cultural diversity.

- Pride and ownership in the school.

Guiding Principles for Parents

We recognize that as our children's first and most influential teachers, we can promote their success and contribute to an excellent school if we make and fulfill the following commitments:

We will establish high expectations for our students. We will not accept minimum effort or indifference to quality work.

We will know what is expected in each of our student's classes and communicate with teachers when we have a question or concern.

We will insist on good attendance.

We will provide a quiet time and place in our home for study.

We will insist that our students accept responsibility for their learning and conduct.

We will model the importance of life-long learning.

Guiding Principles of the Student Code of Conduct

For over 30 years, the students of this school have been building a tradition of excellence. As current students, we can help contribute to that tradition and increase the likelihood of our personal success if we:

1. Accept responsibility for our education, decisions, and actions.

2. Act in a way that best represents our school, parents, community, and self to promote a safe, healthy environment in which to learn.

3. Are active in the school and community.

4. Maintain a balance between academics, co-curricular activities, and community projects, and continually give our best effort to each.

5. Support our fellow students and their activities.

6. Respect cultural diversity, individuality, and the choices and rights of others.

The lists provided above are intended to serve as examples, not as models. Each school must identify and endorse commitments that support its own, unique vision statement. There are, however, several important criteria to keep in mind when developing value statements.

Keep them few in number. The longer the list of statements, the less likely it is to be remembered by the group. The statements are intended to influence behavior. Forty-seven value statements may make for stirring reading, but it is unlikely that they will be effective in guiding the day-to-day decisions and actions of the people in a school. Each respective constituency of a school should be able to get by with 10 or fewer value statements.

Link the statements directly to the vision statement. The importance of linking vision and values cannot be overstated. Drafting values should not be viewed as an independent activity, but rather as the first step in support of the vision statement. The question is not, "What are appropriate value statements for teachers in general?" but "What are the specific commitments that we must make in order to move our school closer to the desired future we have identified?"

Be direct. Because value statements are intended to give direction, they are most effective when they are explicit. While a statement such as "We will recognize the spark of divinity that flows from the soul of every child" may be morally impeccable, it does not describe the specific behavior that personnel are to demonstrate. "We will work collaboratively in developing instructional strategies, designing methods of assessment, and advancing the vision of the school" is a much more effective value statement because it carries explicit expectations regarding how teachers will conduct their business.

Focus on behavior, not beliefs. Many schools choose to develop statements of beliefs instead of value statements that articulate desired attitudes, behaviors, and commitments. There are several problems with such an approach. First, belief statements do not prescribe specific action. In addition, the fact that schools endorse the same belief statement, such as "all students can learn," does not mean they will respond consistently to students who fail to learn. The goal is to provide clear direction, and belief statements will not help a school meet that goal. Second, belief statements do not effectively assign responsibility. A teacher may heartily endorse the statement, "We believe our school should provide students with a safe and orderly learning environment," but he or she may also conclude that the administration is exclusively responsible for ensuring this environment. The statement, "We will help to provide an orderly environment that is conducive to learning" more effectively assigns mutual responsibility. Finally, it is much more difficult to monitor the presence of beliefs than it is to monitor the presence of behaviors. While asking the question, "What do you believe?" could provide interesting answers that are worthy of consideration, finding shared answers to the question, "What are you prepared *to do* in support of those beliefs?" will be much more effective in advancing school improvement. As Senge et al. (1994) advises, "Values are best described in terms of behavior: If we operate as we should, what would an observer see us doing?" (p. 302).

Focus on ourselves rather than others. An interesting phenomenon inevitably occurs whenever a group is brought together to identify what can be done to improve a school. Each group is enthusiastic about generating a long list of the steps that *other* groups must take to improve the school. Administrators have little difficulty identifying the attitudes, behaviors, and commitments that teachers should demonstrate; parents can describe what administrators should do; and students can articulate what teachers and administrators should do. And so it continues.

Our work with an elementary school faculty provided a dramatic illustration of this point. Teachers enthusiastically developed a list of what needed to be done in order to help their school become a more collaborative learning community—only to discover at the end of the exercise that the one element that was not essential to their description of a learning community was teachers! As they reviewed their list, they acknowledged (somewhat sheepishly) that while their view of a learning community required parents, the administration, the board, and students to play important roles, not a single item referred to anything that teachers could do.

There is a universal human tendency to point out what others must do to bring about desired change, but this tendency must be avoided—in school improvement in general, but particularly in developing value statements. The focus outward, looking for the difficulty in others, is always counterproductive. Each group must look to the one group over which it has the greatest influence—itself. Rather than insisting that others should change, individuals must demand it of themselves.

Furthermore, educators must accept some responsibility for the existing problems in their schools. They must recognize that they are part of the problem rather than helpless victims of circumstances over which they have no control. The traditional structures and cultures of schools are not the result of divine intervention. We educators have created them! It is important that we acknowledge that transforming schools will challenge us to change ourselves.

The Need to Identify Shared Values

Several significant benefits will accrue to the school that engages its members in the identification and promotion of shared values. Clarity on organizational values fosters strong feelings of personal effectiveness, promotes high levels of loyalty, facilitates consensus about key organizational goals, encourages professional behavior, promotes strong norms about working hard and caring, and reduces job tension and stress (Kouzes & Posner, 1987).

Most importantly, shared values provide the direction that enables individuals to act autonomously. If the members of a school know what they are trying to create and are using the values as guiding principles for their actions and decisions, there is little need for the ubiquitous rule book that is meant to cover all possible situations in a school setting.

In our work with schools across the country, we have found that the process of articulating shared values is largely ignored in school improvement initiatives. Almost all schools have written mission statements, and most have developed some form of a vision statement. But precious few have taken the next important step of asking what commitments the members of the school are prepared to make in order to fulfill their mission more effectively and to advance their vision. This inattention to articulating shared values is a critical flaw in most school improvement initiatives. When educators discuss mission, they can wax philosophic. When they consider vision, they have a future orientation—"Wouldn't it be nice if someday we could look like this?" But when people clarify values, they must make commitments about what they are prepared to do **now!** Perhaps it is this sense of immediacy that puts people off. Still, it is at this point that significant school improvement begins. While all of the building blocks of school improvement are significant, implementing values represents the critical cornerstone of the process.

The term "values" is certainly an emotion-laden word in the current political climate. In some communities, it is bound to cause an adverse response among those who contend that schools should focus on teaching academic content and leave the job of teaching values to parents. Yet it should be evident that in the context of school improvement, clarifying shared values is an apolitical process. It does not represent an attempt to project one's views upon another. Rather, the process calls for groups to identify the commitments that will help them achieve mutual goals.

Each school should, of course, assess the climate of its own community. If the term "values" is likely to be problematic, the group can use a different term such as "guiding principles" or "collective commitments." Regardless of the terminology, the identification of the attitudes, behaviors, and commitments that will advance the vision of a school is crucial to the process of building a professional learning community.

The Fourth Building Block: Goals

Which steps will we take first, and **when?** The fourth building block in creating a professional learning community calls for establishing priorities. This task determines what must be accomplished first, the specific steps that must be taken to achieve the objectives, and the timeline for the process. Goals represent measurable milestones that can be used to assess progress in advancing toward a vision; thus, they make visions more substantive. It has often been said that an improvement process represents a journey rather than a destination, but even a journey needs ports of call along the way. Goals provide these ports of call and serve as landmarks in an improvement process. Visions may inspire, but goals foster ongoing accountability.

Unlike most industrialized countries, the United States has never had either a formal set of expectations for its public schools or a national system of assessment to provide benchmarks for the progress of individual students. Left to their own devices, schools have typically been unable to articulate clear, limited, well-defined goals. Schmoker (1996) describes this gap between the need to improve schools and the absence of clear, concrete, academic goals as "the most striking, contradictory, self-defeating characteristic of schooling and our efforts to improve it" (p. 18). It is the identification and pursuit of explicit goals that foster the experimentation, results orientation, and commitment to continuous improvement that characterize the professional learning community.

Goals also serve another important purpose in the change process. Implementing meaningful change is a long, arduous challenge. Day-to-day demands, competing responsibilities, and the slow pace at which gains are made can drain the initial enthusiasm for any improvement initiative. People need to see some results if they are to sustain the effort needed to transform a school into a professional learning community. An initiative will lose critical momentum if there are no short-term wins to celebrate. Goals create the opportunity for the short-term wins that fuel the change process.

A school improvement plan must be attentive to *creating* some clear, discernible victories, not just hoping for them. Kotter (1996) advises that at least some of the initial improvement goals should be specifically designed to create short-term wins that are:

1. *Visible*—large numbers of people can see for themselves whether the result is real or just hype.

2. *Unambiguous*—there can be little argument over the results.

3. *Clearly related to the change effort.* (pp. 121–122)

Schools that address the issue of goal setting should be alert to two common mistakes. Often, in the euphoria that follows the drafting of a vision statement, schools may take on too many initiatives at once. Some schools have created as many as 10 different task forces, all working simultaneously. While this flurry of activity ensures staff involvement, it may also prevent the focus that is essential to a concentrated school improvement effort. It has been said that to have more than one goal at a time is to have none at all. Perhaps no school has the luxury of establishing just *one* goal, but schools must limit and control the number of their initiatives if they are to make substantive progress.

A second common mistake in establishing school improvement goals is identifying goals that are too general, merely giving the illusion that the school is clear about what it is trying to accomplish. Goals should be specific and measurable if they are to be meaningful. Effective goals will specify:

- Exactly what is to be accomplished.

- The specific steps that will be taken to achieve the goal.

- The individual or group responsible for initiating and/or sustaining each step toward achieving the goal.

- The timeline for each phase of the activity.

- The criteria to be used in evaluating progress toward the goal.

In short, the school that is trying to change so that it can function as a professional learning community should establish written goals that are:

- Clearly linked to the vision.

- Limited in number (five or fewer) to ensure focus.

- Focused on the desired outcome rather than on the means to achieve the outcome.

- Translated into clear, measurable performance standards.

- Monitored continuously.

- Designed to produce some short-term wins.

- Understood and accepted as significant by all parties.

Summary

Educators who hope to transform their schools into professional learning communities must be attentive to developing the building blocks of any improving organization—mission, vision, values, and goals. Placing each of these four building blocks requires a school to answer a number of difficult questions:

- Why do we exist?

- What kind of school are we trying to create?

- What attitudes, behaviors, and commitments must we demonstrate in order to create such a school?

- Which steps should we take first?

- What is our timeline?

- What evidence will we present to demonstrate our progress?

When the personnel of a school have seriously discussed these questions and arrived at a consensus on answers to each question, the school will then have a solid foundation for future improvement efforts. School members will also feel the camaraderie that accompanies a shared commitment to change and should begin to see evidence of positive results. At this point, schools will be tempted to assume that the hard work of change is over. In fact, it is just beginning. Chapter 6 discusses the difficult task of sustaining the change process.

Chapter 6

Sustaining the School Improvement Process

Communication seems to work best when it is so direct and so simple that it has a sort of elegance.

—John Kotter (1996, p. 89)

You cannot have students as continuous learners and effective collaborators, without teachers having the same characteristics.

—Michael Fullan (1993, p. 46)

Educators who have laid the foundation of an improving organization by articulating their school's mission, vision, values, and goals can and should celebrate their accomplishments. But they must also recognize that they have merely taken the first few steps on the long journey to transforming their schools into professional learning communities. Schools have demonstrated time and again that it is much easier to initiate change than to sustain it to fruition. Until changes become so entrenched that they represent part of "the way we do things around here," they are extremely fragile and subject to regression.

Although charismatic leaders or influential committees can help generate initial enthusiasm for change, neither can sustain the change process over time. A school will experience a fundamental shift only when its members can generate a sufficient number of supporters for new ideas and practices. The challenge of sustaining the change effort to transform schools into professional learning communities is the challenge of developing a critical mass of teachers who are prepared to function as change agents (Fullan, 1993). The keys to developing this "critical mass" of educators within a school are found in the three Cs of sustaining an improvement initiative—communication, collaboration, and culture. This chapter examines communication and collaboration. Culture is addressed in Chapter 7.

Sustaining the Change Initiative through Communication

Effective communication is an essential component of the change process. The importance of communication has been cited as "the one major lesson that has emerged from the extensive research studies on innovation," and the pathways for communication within an organization have been described as "the veins and arteries of new ideas" (Kouzes & Posner, 1987, p. 56). Conversely, insufficient attention to communication has been cited as one of the most common causes of the failure of change initiatives (Kotter, 1996). Mission, vision, values, and goals will become irrelevant, and the change process will stall unless the significance of these building blocks is communicated on a daily basis throughout the school. Volumes of philosophy statements, strategic plans, and long-range goals have been written by school districts, only to end up gathering dust in file cabinets as educators continue with business as usual. The same fate awaits those who attempt to create professional learning communities unless they appreciate the need for clear, constant communication in support of their objective.

Furthermore, effective communication is not a product of eloquence or slick materials. Like any organization, schools communicate what is important to them and what is valued by what they focus on. In fact, Peters and Austin (1985) contend that "paying attention" is the only strategy available to any organization that hopes to communicate new commitments and priorities. Educators who are attempting to create a learning community can use the following eight-element communication audit to assess the focus of their attention and, thus, the effectiveness of their communication.

1. What do we plan for? When a school develops and articulates specific plans to advance its vision and values and achieve its goals, it sends the message that these areas are priorities. The preparation and public presentation of a plan signals that this issue is so significant that the school intends to be purposeful in pursuing it.

2. What do we monitor? In most organizations, what gets monitored gets done. When a school devotes considerable time and effort to the continual assessment of a particular condition or outcome, it notifies all members that the condition or outcome is considered important. Conversely, inattention to monitoring a particular factor in a school indicates that it is less than essential, regardless of how often its importance is verbalized.

Educators must not only establish procedures for monitoring, but they must also monitor the significant factors that are fundamental to a professional learning community. Virtually all schools have some systems for monitoring that are already in place. For example, schools typically devote considerable efforts to monitoring whether students are on time and in their seats. Unfortunately, they often are much less attentive to assessing whether the students' physical presence has resulted in the acquisition of intended knowledge and skills.

Teachers also learn what is important in their schools by observing what is monitored. The naive principal of one school focused on the number of students who raised their hands following a teacher's question. One enterprising teacher in this school worked out an arrangement with his students. Whenever the principal was visiting the class, if students knew the answer to a question, they were to raise their right hands; if they did not know the answer, they were to raise their left hands, but everyone was to raise a hand for every question. The principal consistently lauded the teacher as exemplary, despite the fact that he had no idea whether or not students were mastering the intended outcomes.

Similarly, some schools are vigilant in their efforts to monitor their teachers' use of the copier, the attractiveness of bulletin boards, or the adherence to dress codes. There is little to suggest that this kind of vigilance will enhance the effectiveness of those schools. *What* a school is monitoring is more important than *if* a school is monitoring. A professional learning community will focus on substantive issues and communicate the importance of those issues by:

1. Identifying the criteria with which it will monitor the advancement toward its vision, the presence of its values, and the accomplishment of its goals.

2. Systematically gathering information on those criteria.

3. Sharing data with the entire staff.

4. Engaging the entire staff in collective analysis of the information that is gathered.

5. Developing new strategies for achieving its objectives more effectively.

6. Carefully monitoring the results of implementing those strategies.

3. What questions do we ask? The questions that an organization poses and pursues communicate priorities and point its people in a particular direction. Many school improvement initiatives are driven by such questions as "How can we get students to behave better?" "How can we persuade parents to assume greater responsibility for their children's learning?" or "What can we do to improve faculty morale?" While these are legitimate inquiries, they will not achieve the goal of advancing a school's capacity to function as a professional learning community. The questions posed by the building blocks of mission, vision, values, and goals advance this objective, but they, too, are insufficient.

All learning organizations are driven by the persistent questioning of the status quo and by a constant search for a better way to fulfill the organization's purpose more effectively. For schools, the focus of the driving questions must be enhanced student achievement. Schools that are in the habit of asking themselves tough questions that focus on the achievement of their students are cited by researchers as "the schools most likely to see significant gains as a result of their change efforts" (Wasley, Hampel, & Clark, 1995, p. 351).

Once a school has answered the questions that are posed when developing its mission, vision, values, and goals, it can help sustain its initiative to create a professional learning community by asking tough questions such as the following:

- Are we acting in accordance with our fundamental mission?

- Have we clarified what we want all students to know and be able to do?

- What is the most effective response for students who are not succeeding?

- What are the discrepancies between actual conditions in our school and the school we hope to become?

- What are our specific plans to reduce these discrepancies?

- Are the proposals under consideration consistent with our vision and values?

- What steps are we taking to advance vision and values in the day-to-day operation of the school?

- What results do we seek, and what evidence are we gathering to assess our effectiveness?

- Have we established systematic collaboration as the norm in our school?

- Are there more effective ways to fulfill our mission, vision, and values?

4. What do we model? One of the best strategies for communicating what is important within an organization is modeling. It is said that people communicate most eloquently through their actions, not through their words. To paraphrase Ralph Waldo Emerson, "What you do thunders above you so loudly all the while, I cannot hear what you say." If teachers encourage students to become lifelong learners but provide no evidence of their own intellectual curiosity, if principals extol the virtues of collaboration but use autocratic leadership styles, if superintendents advocate innovation and risk-taking but punish those whose experiments fail to produce the desired results, then the incongruity between words and actions will inevitably result in cynicism. Students are more likely to function as continuous learners and effective collaborators if their teachers demonstrate those characteristics. Teachers are more likely to work collaboratively if their principals engage them in collaborative decision making. Principals are more likely to experiment if their superintendents take risks and regard failed initiatives as opportunities to begin again more intelligently.

Modeling is particularly critical for those who lead a change effort. In describing the conditions necessary to build a learning organization in the private sector, Thompson (1995) argues that the modeling of leaders is "the single most powerful mechanism for creating a learning environment" (p. 96). Chapter 9 will elaborate on the importance of modeling by the principal.

5. How do we allocate our time? The allocation of time is one of the truest tests of what is really important in any organization. The time devoted to an issue on both the annual calendar and within the daily schedule of an organization tells its people what is really valued.

Providing school personnel with adequate time to work through the problems associated with change is a crucial factor in successful reform (Klein et al., 1996). When teachers are expected to implement substantive changes at the same time that they manage everything else in their already overburdened schedules, there is little chance that the initiatives will be sustained. Nevertheless, the time essential for reform is often not made readily available for school personnel (Adelman & Panton Walking Eagle, 1997).

Some school administrators tend to say, in effect, that "the implementation of our new vision is critical, so do everything else you have always done and then figure out on your own how to address the vision, too." Or, "Collaboration is valued in our school, so see if you can find some time to collaborate." The real message conveyed in these situations is unmistakable. Teachers and principals will know a district is serious about transforming schools into professional learning communities only when they are given the time they need to handle the complexity of that task.

6. What do we celebrate? Regardless of the eloquence of vision and values statements, those statements will not have an impact on people in a school unless progress toward the vision is apparent and unless the implementation of the values is recognized and celebrated on a consistent basis. When reaching a milestone in the journey toward the vision is noted and celebrated, and when examples of the commitment to values are publicly acknowledged and rewarded, everyone in the school is reminded that vision and values are important.

Schools can develop ceremonies and rituals to provide faculty with evidence that their efforts are making a difference. Such public recognition offers real-life examples by which members of the staff can assess their own commitment to vision and values. Celebration represents a powerful instrument for shaping the culture of a professional learning community. This topic will be addressed in greater detail in Chapter 7.

7. What are we willing to confront? If the vision and values of the school are to be communicated in a clear and unequivocal manner, those who violate the vision and values must be confronted. In an ideal world, every member of the staff would be willing to challenge a colleague who was acting in a way that was contrary to collective commitments. In the real world of schools, this task will most likely fall to principals.

It is critical that principals fulfill this leadership responsibility if vision and values are to be reinforced. If a school claims to value an orderly atmosphere conducive to learning, the principal must be prepared to confront the unruly student, the teacher who ignores such behavior, or the parent who seeks to justify it. If teachers have agreed, for example, that working in collaborative teams is essential to becoming a professional learning community, the principal must be willing to insist that a teacher who works in isolation change his or her behavior.

Principals who are unwilling to defend and protect the vision and values of their schools put improvement initiatives at risk. The school suffers when individuals are free to act in a manner that the staff as a whole has agreed is contrary to the school's best interest. The principal suffers because his or her credibility as a leader is diminished by an unwillingness to address an obvious problem. The individual who is acting inappropriately suffers because he or she has been deprived of an opportunity for learning and growth. Most important, the improvement initiative suffers because the staff will soon come to recognize that the principal assigns a higher priority to avoiding conflict than to advancing vision and values.

This notion of confrontation may seem antithetical to a proposal for schools built upon shared visions and collaborative relationships, but we believe it is consistent with the idea that if schools are to improve, individuals must fulfill their respective responsibilities and commitments. The message from both research and practice is clear: Change efforts stall when leaders do not address violations of vision and values (Burns, 1978; Kotter, 1996; Maxwell, 1995; Peters & Austin, 1985).

It is understandable that principals feel the basic human desire to secure the approval of their co-workers; however, they must care more about advancing shared vision and values than they do about constant approval. What James McGregor Burns (1978) said about leaders in general applies specifically to principals: they "must settle for far less than universal affection. . . . They must accept conflict. They must be willing and able to be unloved" (p. 34).

Confrontation is not, however, synonymous with personal attack. Maxwell (1995) offers the following guidelines for confrontation:

1. Conduct the discussion as soon as possible.

2. Focus on the behavior or action, not the person.

3. Be specific.

4. Give the person an opportunity to respond and grant the benefit of the doubt.

5. Avoid sarcasm and words such as "always" and "never."

6. Attempt to develop a mutual plan to address the problem.

7. Affirm the person. (pp. 126–127)

It is almost always preferable for a principal to hold a face-to-face meeting for this purpose rather than to write a memorandum. The managerial maxim, "reprimand in person but praise in writing," has considerable merit. A meeting provides an opportunity not only for honest dialogue but also for a better understanding of perspectives. It gives the principal the opportunity to say, "Here is what we agreed to do as a faculty. This is what I see you doing that is contrary to that agreement. We need this change from you in order for you to help us achieve our collective goals. What can I do to help you make the necessary change?"

8. Keep it simple. One of the most effective strategies for clear communication is the KISS principle (keep it simple, stupid). Educators should not be expected to memorize their school's mission, vision, values, and goal statements. The message of change must be simplified and amplified. Metaphors, analogies, logos, and examples can present verbal pictures of a change initiative more effectively than pages of text.

In fact, Bennis and Nanus (1985) advise those seeking to assess the effectiveness of their communication to ask, "How clear is the metaphor?" A high school faculty that developed a vision statement based on the belief that the school had an obligation to meet the needs of each student expressed their commitment in a new school slogan, "Success for Every Student." That simple slogan gave voice to a new guiding principle and served as a benchmark for improvement initiatives. Elementary school teachers who emphasized providing students with a nurturing environment referred to their school as "The Little School with the Big Heart" and created a ubiquitous logo of a schoolhouse encasing a huge heart. Another elementary school created a logo with pictures in each quadrant that represented key aspects of the school's vision statement—joining hands, opening minds, touching hearts, and creating the future for our children.

An initiative to transform a school into a learning community is certain to sputter and stall unless its importance is communicated throughout the school on a daily basis. Effective communication can help sustain the effort, but effective communication requires constant repetition. Mission, vision, values, and goals must be continually referenced in the day-to-day workings of the school. Redundancy is not only permissible—it is desirable.

Sustaining the Change Initiative through Collaboration

Despite the unceasing waves of reforms that have washed up on the public schools, the fundamental facts of teaching seem to have changed very little. The task of teaching continues to fall to a single individual who stands alone before a group of students and works in isolation. Teaching has been described as the second most private act in which adults engage. In fact, schools have been characterized by some critics of public education as little more than independent kingdoms (classrooms) ruled by autonomous feudal lords (teachers) who are united only by a common parking lot.

The fact that there is considerable truth in this metaphorical picture should be cause for alarm. Donahoe (1993) describes schools as "convenient places for a bunch of individual teachers, like independent contractors, to come to teach discrete groups of children" (p. 299). Sarason (1996) contends that schools foster a culture of individuals rather than the culture of a group. He concludes that teachers are apt to focus on their personal concerns because there are absolutely no forums or traditions that present them with opportunities to come together to discuss the practical problems and issues of the classroom and the school. Linda Darling-Hammond (1995) presents a similar conclusion when she writes, "Separated by their classrooms and packed teaching schedules, teachers rarely work or talk together about teaching practices" (p. 172). Many teachers feel this sense of isolation and report that one of their greatest sources of dissatisfaction is their perception that they scarcely know their colleagues and have little time to discuss issues related to curriculum and instruction (Poplin & Weeres, 1992).

The way a former high school English teacher describes his experience rings true for many teachers:

> The crush of . . . our myriad daily events and duties kept us from collaborating on such obvious and challenging concerns as how to teach composition more effectively, how to conduct discussions about literature more effectively, and how to make literature more exciting. We did not know if or how anyone was teaching composition—or even what that meant. So we worked, consciously or unconsciously, toward our own goals, within the limitations of what each of us knew or did not know. Day-to-day concerns kept us from reflecting on what our most important goals should be. (Schmoker, 1996, pp. 10–11)

This isolation of teachers presents one of the most formidable roadblocks to creating a professional learning community. Although a lone teacher can impart the causes of the Civil War, the rules of grammar, or multiplication tables, transforming a school into a professional learning community is a collective endeavor. Collaborative structures support that endeavor because they:

- Enable teachers to test their ideas about teaching and expand their level of expertise by allowing them to hear the ideas of others (Wildman & Niles, 1987).

- Foster better decisions and increase the likelihood of ownership in the decisions (Dillon-Peterson, 1986).

- Help to reduce the fear of risk-taking by providing encouragement and moral support (Fielding & Schalock, 1985).

- Can be linked to gains in achievement; higher quality solutions to problems; increased confidence among all members of the school community; more systematic assistance to beginning teachers; and an increased pool of ideas, materials, and methods (Little, 1990).

- Reinforce changes in school culture and commitment to improvement initiatives (Klein et al., 1996).

Creating a collaborative environment has been described as "the single most important factor" for successful school improvement initiatives and "the first order of business" for those seeking to enhance the effectiveness of their school (Eastwood & Louis, 1992, p. 215). Virtually all contemporary school reformers call for increased opportunities for teacher collaboration.

It is clear that the effort to transform a school into a professional learning community is more likely to be sustained when teachers participate in reflective dialogue; observe and react to one another's teaching; jointly develop curriculum and assessment practices; work together to implement new programs and strategies; share lesson plans and materials; and collectively engage in problem solving, action research, and continuous improvement practices. Unfortunately, the tradition of teacher isolation is still so entrenched in schools that fostering meaningful collaboration is a significant challenge.

Collaboration by Invitation Does Not Work

Here is a true story. In his first presentation to the faculty, a newly appointed high school principal expressed his desire to foster collaboration among staff. He then made an extraordinary commitment: whenever two or more teachers wanted time to collaborate on matters related to teaching and learning, he would provide them with time during the school day to do so. He promised that he would arrange for substitute teachers for a morning, for a day, or even for several days to allow teams of teachers or entire departments to work together. The offer received a warm response from the faculty, and the principal received a great deal of positive feedback from teachers who expressed appreciation for the fact that the school finally had a leader who recognized the importance of teachers working together. The principal basked in the knowledge that he had acted as an enlightened education leader. But at the year's end, he was confronted with a grim reality: not a single teacher from a faculty of over 100 teachers had taken advantage of the offer of released time for collaborating with colleagues!

This story contains an important lesson: the isolation of teachers is so ingrained in the traditional culture of schools that invitations to collaborate are insufficient. To build professional learning communities, meaningful collaboration must be systematically embedded into the daily life of the school.

Collaborative Teams

The best structure for fostering collaboration is the team— "the basic building block of the intelligent organization" (Pinchot

& Pinchot 1993, p. 66) and the "essence of a learning organization" (Dilworth, 1995, p. 252). Senge et al. (1994) contend that "history has brought us to a moment where teams are recognized as a critical component of every enterprise—the predominant unit for decision making and getting things done" (p. 354). Arranging personnel into teams has also been identified as an important factor linked to the process of improving schools (Darling-Hammond, 1996; Newmann, 1996). Building collaborative cultures requires that schools create structures to ensure that every staff member is assigned to a team that works together on substantive issues.

There are a number of ways that the team concept can be implemented in schools to promote collaboration. Here are some examples:

Implement team concept by grade level or subject. All teachers who share the same teaching assignment in a building (for example, all the third-grade teachers in an elementary school or all the biology teachers in a high school) can be grouped into a team that is responsible for identifying curriculum outcomes, assessing student achievement, selecting instructional materials, planning and presenting staff development programs, participating in peer observation and coaching, developing schedules, hiring new staff, or serving as mentors for new colleagues. In very small schools with only a single teacher for a grade level or subject, the teams can be formed according to several grade levels (kindergarten through third grade) or according to discipline (science teachers).

Implement team concept on the basis of shared students. Interdisciplinary teams can be created on the basis of shared students. These teams could focus not only on curriculum content, but also on the needs of a common group of students.

Implement team concept in schoolwide task forces. Teams of staff members can be created periodically to consider a particular problem, develop recommendations for resolving it, and share their findings with the rest of the faculty.

Implement team concept by area of professional development. Teachers can be formed into teams to pursue training in a given area of professional development. For example, teachers interested in applying cooperative learning techniques in their classrooms could meet as a team to react to presentations on the topic, develop strategies for using the technique in the classroom, share related articles, plan peer observation and feedback sessions, or serve as a support group that discusses and analyzes successes and setbacks in its attempt to use the new technique.

But it is important to remember that creating configurations for teams does not ensure an effectively functioning team. Giving an English teacher, a mathematics teacher, a science teacher, and a social studies teacher responsibility for the same group of students does not necessarily establish an interdisciplinary team; it merely creates a group comprised of four teachers from different disciplines! Certain conditions must be present if this group is to operate as a capable, collaborative team. After working with more than 150 teams over an eight-year period, Dukewits and Gowin (1996) concluded that effective teams are characterized by:

1. Shared beliefs and attitudes.

2. High levels of trust that in turn result in open communication, mutual respect for people and opinions, and a willingness to participate.

3. The belief that they had the authority to make important decisions and a willingness to assume responsibility for the decisions they made.

4. Effectively managed meetings with clear operational norms or ground rules, agendas developed with input from all, defined roles for members, and minutes to provide continuity.

5. Ongoing assessment of and discussions regarding the functioning of the team.

To create effective collaborative teams, educators must address at least four prerequisites:

1. Time for collaboration must be built into the school day and year. The way in which a school structures its time can have a tremendous impact upon commitment to a change process. This fact is often overlooked in school improvement initiatives. Typically, if teachers are given any time to collaborate on improvement projects, the time is offered as an add-on (after school or on Saturdays) rather than incorporated as an integral part of the school day.

The lack of time for collaboration is a product of the factory model upon which schools were organized. The American vision of teaching has traditionally called for teachers to instruct large groups of students for virtually the entire school day. Thus, the other tasks of teaching—preparation, planning, curriculum development, collaborating with colleagues, etc.—are often deemed to be so unimportant that little or no time is provided for them (Darling-Hammond, 1995). Time for reflection and discussion has traditionally been viewed as unproductive in the educational arena. Therefore, teachers are not usually given time to collaborate because it would give them less time with their students. And so most educators continue to work in isolation—a situation that reduces their effectiveness. But because the traditional view assumes that productivity is a function of activity, or contact hours, the traditional response to unsatisfactory results calls upon teachers to teach more hours in the day or more days in the year. Clearly, this logic is flawed, even when considered from the perspective of the factory model. If an assembly line were producing defective products, an appropriate response would be to examine the process and improve it, not run the line an extra hour each day or an extra month each year.

The distinction that is frequently drawn between thinking and doing in education does not seem to prevail in other professions. Attorneys recognize that their effectiveness in the courtroom will depend, to a large degree, upon the thoroughness of their preparation. Physicians routinely consult with other doctors in deciding the most appropriate treatment for a patient. The quality initiative in the private sector has demonstrated the benefit of providing employees with time to discuss how to do things better. Even so, Americans tend to regard any time that a teacher is not standing in front of a class as "down time."

Ironically, American teachers already spend more time in the classroom per week than teachers in Europe and Asia (Consortium on Productivity in the Schools, 1995; Darling-Hammond, 1995; Perkins, 1992). Teachers in Japan, China, France, Switzerland, England, and Germany teach students only 15 to 20 hours out of a 40- to 45-hour work week. The rest of the time is available for them to think about and discuss the lessons they teach; to share plans, materials, and ideas; to tutor students; or to consult with parents.

The schools that are successful in implementing significant change regard collaborative time for teachers as a critical resource—an essential tool that enables teachers to enhance their individual and collective effectiveness (Louis, Kruse, & Marks, 1996). One of the key recommendations from the National Commission on Teaching and America's Future (1996) calls for providing teachers with regularly scheduled time for collegial work and planning. The school that hopes to become a professional learning community must provide teachers with time to reflect, to engage in collective inquiry, to collaborate, and to participate in continuous improvement processes. It will regard these activities as productive and will provide time for them in a systematic way. By providing this time, the school will help sustain the improvement initiative.

2. The purpose of collaboration must be made explicit. Forming teams is a means to an end, not the end itself. A team is a group of people who need each other to accomplish an objective. Four individuals who are on an elevator do not represent a team. If the elevator breaks down between floors and the passengers must plan and work together to escape, they begin to function not as a group, but as a team. Teams are most effective when they are clear about the results they are to achieve. This clarity of purpose is enhanced when teams are provided with clearly stated performance goals that indicate what the team is to produce or accomplish. For example, teams might be given the following tasks to complete over the course of two or three years:

A. Review the curriculum guidelines of our state and the recommendations of the national professional association in your subject area. Compare our curriculum to the state and national recommendations. Are there gaps between what is recommended and what is taught in our school? If so, what are they and how should we respond? Use the following format to present your findings.

B. Develop a common course description to be presented to all students enrolled in your course in order to help them understand its major purpose, the intended outcomes, and the criteria for assessment. (Note that elementary school teams should focus on grade-level goals and outcomes for each subject and will write their descriptions for parents rather than for students.)

Report on Curriculum Analysis

Briefly summarize the state or national curricular goals for your grade level or course that are not addressed adequately in our local curriculum.

Briefly summarize areas taught in our local curriculum that are not called for in the state or national recommendations.

What is your team's recommendation? Should we take steps to address any of the discrepancies?

Please explain the rationale for your recommendation.

If you are recommending additional objectives for our curriculum, you should identify existing areas that might be eliminated or given less emphasis in order to provide your team with enough time to address the additional content.

C. Develop and present a common comprehensive assessment for your students. Include a brief explanation of the proficiency levels that you anticipate students will achieve for each major outcome.

D. Analyze the results of your common assessment of students. Where did students fail to meet the proficiency levels that you had anticipated? Identify your strategies to address any discrepancy.

E. Review the attached samples of student work. Working individually, assign a grade for each sample. Then, as a team, compare the grades you have assigned and discuss the criteria that you used in determining your grades. Develop and present a rubric that the team will apply to student work.

F. Review the attached article on effective teaching. Discuss your reactions. Do you concur with the premise of the article? Why or why not?

It is important to remember that collaboration is not a natural act in the traditional culture of American education in which teachers work in isolation. Thus, providing a team of teachers with explicit questions to consider and tasks to accomplish will give team members the sense of direction and the confidence they need as they begin to work together.

3. School personnel need training and support to be effective collaborators. In their effort to foster a collaborative culture, educators must not lose sight of the fact that collaboration is a morally neutral activity. Providing teachers with time for collaboration does not ensure that they will engage in deep discourse about how they can achieve the goals of the school more effectively. In fact, without the proper training, much of what occurs in schools in the name of collaboration can be counterproductive (Little, 1990). In the wrong school culture, the time set aside for educators to work together will simply reinforce the negative aspects of that culture.

First and foremost, the potential benefits of collaboration will never be realized unless educators work together in matters directly related to teaching and learning. The focus of their efforts and inquiry must be instruction, curriculum, assessment practices, and strategies for improving the effectiveness of the school. Structuring the process so that teachers work together to answer an engaging question or to present a product can help provide the clear focus and goal orientation essential to the process. But even with clear goals and the best of intentions, teachers may struggle initially as a school moves toward embracing a more collaborative environment.

A professional learning community requires a great deal of its members. It requires them to change their traditional be-havior! Anyone who has ever tried to stop smoking or to adhere to a new diet knows very well that changing behavior is difficult. Simply exhorting teachers to collaborate is insufficient. Educators are likely to require considerable training in group processes and continued reinforcement in order to develop skills as collaborators.

Asking teams to reach consensus on the following questions can help team members address potential problems and increase the likelihood of teams developing the necessary clarity and skills to work well together:

- What are our expectations for how our team will operate?

- What are our two or three most important goals this year?

- What indicators will we use to assess the effectiveness of our team?

- What process will we use to resolve conflict?

Teams should establish norms for their operation. Members might discuss the following suggested commitments:

- We will articulate our specific commitments to the team and will fulfill those commitments.

- We will work toward consensus.

- We will solicit, consider, and value the input of each team member. No individual will be allowed to dominate the discussion, nor will one individual be expected to carry the workload of the team.

- We will be candid and will seek to understand one another by articulating and investigating the reasoning behind our respective positions. We will assume our colleagues have good intentions even if we disagree with them.

- We will attend all meetings.
- We will support a decision once it is clear that there is a consensus for it.

Once team members have been working together for a while, they should be asked to reflect on how the team is functioning. This reflection can be prompted by asking each member to consider the following:

- A team committed to serious inquiry requires open communication. An environment must be created in which each member feels that his or her suggestions will be given serious consideration by the group. How would you describe the status of open communication on your team?

- Review the expectations and goals for your team that you developed when the team was formed. Rate your team's effectiveness on a scale of 1 (low) to 10 (high) for each statement of expectations and goals.

- Identify an example of your team's exceeding an expectation or goal this year.

- Identify an example of your team's failing to meet an expectation or achieve a goal this year. Should this area be addressed next year? If so, how?

- What is the most positive aspect of being a member of this team?

- What is the most frustrating aspect of being a member of this team?

- What are your ideas for improving the team's effectiveness in the future?

Sometimes teams are assessed on the basis of congeniality alone—whether team members get along and how cordial they are to one another. While civility can lubricate the workings of a team, it most definitely does not ensure a team's effectiveness. Conversely, serious debates and arguments within a team do not suggest that it is malfunctioning. Collaborators can disagree without being disagreeable, and individuals often require different perspectives before they gain new insight.

Sustaining an improvement initiative, therefore, requires much more than congeniality. It requires the common goals, collective efforts, and shared insights of people deeply engaged in the analysis of their current practice and behavior. But even with those elements in place, the process of learning as a team will be an unfamiliar one that is likely to be stressful for participants. It is important to keep in mind that team members are, first and foremost, human beings. One of the first skills members should learn is "the art of forgiveness" (Senge et al., 1994, p. 356).

4. Educators must accept their responsibility to work together as true professional colleagues. Even if teachers have the time, structure, and training to engage in collaboration, one prerequisite remains—they must acknowledge their responsibility to do so. Educators often bemoan their lack of opportunity to work together, but little will change unless they also acknowledge that they have contributed to the problem. As Barth (1991) writes:

> God didn't create self-contained classrooms, fifty minute periods, and subjects taught in isolation. We did—because we find working alone safer than and preferable to working together. (p. 128)

In his study of the characteristics that contribute to successful individuals, Sternberg (1996) concludes that successful people accept responsibility for their lives. They are self-motivated;

above all else, they have a sense of self-efficacy and an internal locus of control. They believe that they can achieve their goals and improve their situations through their own efforts. Even when presented with obstacles or personal difficulties, they do not resort to self-pity or use their problems as an excuse for failure to act. Instead, they persist in their efforts. What is true of individuals is also true of organizations. No factor is more significant in a school's change process than the faculty's sense of self-efficacy (Sagor, 1997). The schools most likely to create a collaborative learning community are those with educators who are willing to accept responsibility for doing so.

Summary

The challenge of sustaining the change process is the challenge of creating a critical mass of educators within the school who are willing and able to function as change agents. Creating this critical mass requires attention to the three Cs of sustaining a change initiative—communication, collaboration, and culture.

The importance of communication has emerged from research on innovation. Inattention to communication is a leading cause of the failure of change efforts. The most effective strategy of communication is attention. Paying attention to the core values of the school is the most important way for leaders to communicate effectively. Often leaders verbally express one set of values, but then pay attention to other things as they routinely do their jobs. Schools that hope to become professional learning communities must examine what they are being attentive to: what do they plan for, what do they monitor, what questions do they ask and investigate, what do they model, what do they celebrate, what are they willing to confront, and how do they allocate their time? Furthermore, schools should simplify their message and encourage people to rally around a few key ideas through the use of metaphors, slogans, logos, and stories. Finally, they must continue to communicate the significance of the school's mission, vision, values, and goals on a daily basis, forever.

Creating a collaborative environment has been called the single most important factor in sustaining the effort to create a learning community. Collaboration by invitation is ineffective: meaningful collaboration must be embedded into the daily life of the school. Creating teams is one of the most effective ways to promote such collaboration, but for teams to become part of a school's culture, four prerequisites must be met. First, time for collaboration must be built into the school day and year. Second, the purpose of collaboration must be made explicit, and structures must be provided to facilitate it. Third, educators must be trained and supported in their efforts to become effective collaborators. Fourth, educators must accept their individual and collective responsibilities for working together as true professional colleagues.

Chapter 7

Embedding Change in the Culture of a School

To put it as succinctly as possible, if you want to change and improve the climate and outcomes of schooling both for students and teachers, there are features of the school culture that have to be changed, and if they are not changed, your well-intentioned efforts will be defeated.

—Seymour Sarason (1996, p. 340)

The structure of an organization is founded upon its policies, procedures, rules, and relationships. The culture of an organization is founded upon the assumptions, beliefs, values, and habits that constitute the norms for that organization—norms that shape how its people think, feel, and act. As its name implies, the Restructuring Movement of the 1990s tended to focus on structural issues such as shifting authority for some decisions to the school site, revising procedures for grouping students, and altering schedules. This emphasis on structure and its inattention to culture is repeatedly cited as the major flaw in the movement's effort to reform schools. Consider the following:

The restructuring movement is trying to design organizational structures without sufficient regard for the culture the schools need in order to clarify purposes, reach consensus, and ratchet student learning to a higher level.

—Tom Donahoe (1993, p. 301)

The reform movement focuses on structural and curricular changes as the main ingredients of effective schools, but pays less attention to the day-to-day work of teachers. . . . By emphasizing needed changes in the culture of the schools and the daily practice of professionals, the reform movement can concentrate on the heart of the school—the teaching and learning process.

—Louis, Kruse, and Raywid (1996, p. 9)

Structural change that is not supported by cultural change will eventually be overwhelmed by the culture, for it is in the culture that any organization finds meaning and stability.

—Phil Schlechty (1997, p. 136)

Structural innovation cannot be understood, and should not be undertaken, without considering school culture.

—Newmann et al. (1996, p. 14)

If you intend to introduce a change that is incompatible with the organization's culture, you have only three choices: modify the change to be more in line with the existing culture, alter the culture to be more in line with the proposed change, or prepare to fail.

—David Salisbury and Daryl Conner (1994, p. 17)

The tendency for schools to focus on structure rather than culture is understandable. Changes in structure are tangible and can be announced with a flourish. This example might sound familiar: "In our never-ending quest to improve our school, we are moving to block scheduling next year." Such claims simply offer the appearance of substantive change. Cultural changes are less visible, more amorphous, and much more difficult to make. While organizations can pronounce a change in policy or procedures, they cannot proclaim a change in attitudes, beliefs, or behaviors. Furthermore, people are often unaware of the uniqueness of their organization's culture. In fact, culture has been described as "the way we do things around here" and "the assumptions we don't see" (Schein, 1992, p. 21). Schools can, of course, have distinctly different cultures. They may foster isolation or collaboration, promote self-efficacy or fatalism, be student-centered or teacher-centered, regard teaching as a craft that can be developed or as an innate art, assign primary responsibility for learning to students or teachers, view administrators and teachers as colleagues or adversaries, en-courage continuous improvement or defense of the status quo, and so on.

The concept of changing culture may seem simple enough, but changing culture is not like changing the decor. Altering beliefs, expectations, and habits that have gone largely unexamined for many years is a complex, messy, and challenging task. Furthermore, any existing culture is a powerful representative of the status quo and will typically resist attempts to change it. Yet those who hope to develop their school's capacity to function as a professional learning community must face the challenge of shaping culture. And if a change initiative is to be sustained, the elements of that change must be embedded within the culture of the school. Unless collective inquiry, collaborative teams, an orientation toward action, and a focus on results become part of "the way we do things around here," the effort to create a professional learning community is likely to fail. Thus, the critical question is, "How can educational personnel shape the culture of their schools?"

Shared Values Shape Culture

The most effective strategy for influencing and changing an organization's culture is simply to identify, articulate, model, promote, and protect shared values. When school personnel make a commitment to demonstrating certain attitudes and behaviors in order to advance the collective vision of what their schools might become, they are, in effect, describing what they hope will be the visible manifestations of their schools' cultures. Furthermore, shared values provide personnel with guidelines for monitoring their day-to-day decisions and actions. The process for developing this explicit commitment to specific attitudes and behaviors, or shared values, has been described in detail in Chapter 5.

Reflective Dialogue

Another strategy for shaping culture is to bring teachers together on a regular basis to engage in reflective discussions on the practices in their schools and classrooms and to evaluate new concepts and ideas that bear upon those practices. When educators engage in this dialogue, they examine their school's operation and their individual practices with a critical eye, looking for discrepancies between the values they have endorsed and the day-to-day workings of their school. They articulate their assumptions, attempt to identify the origins of those assumptions, and then explore them from new angles. They recognize their obligation to explore collectively "a world of ideas, theory, research and practice . . . if they are not to wither on the vine, if they, like their students, are to avoid passive resignation to routine" (Sarason, 1996, p. 369).

Reflective dialogue is critical to a change effort for several reasons. First, without it most teachers will find it difficult to sustain the energy necessary to improve their teaching practice (Louis, Kruse, & Marks, 1996). Second, in the absence of systematic forums to ensure reflective dialogue, educators will be unable to sustain meaningful change efforts (Sarason, 1996). Finally, reflective dialogue is an important strategy for changing a school's culture. It represents a purposeful attempt to make conscious that which is unconscious. When teachers become more aware of their school's culture, they will be better able to shape that culture.

The Stories We Tell Ourselves

Jennifer James (1996) describes culture as "the stories we tell ourselves." These stories clarify what a group values, explains the group's view of the world, reinforces its interpretation of events, instructs group members in appropriate conduct, and identifies both heroes to emulate and villains to disdain. Our work in schools around the country has enabled us to witness firsthand some of the stories that prevail in different schools. Here are some examples:

We're OK, but they're not OK. "We have a wonderful faculty, but we cannot be expected to get results because the people in this community do not value education."

We care too much to worry about learning. "The kids here are so needy that we must focus on their emotional needs. For our kids, academic concerns are a secondary consideration."

If it ain't broke, don't fix it. "Our tests results are good, and the community seems satisfied. We are doing a good job so it would be foolish to rock the boat. We just need to maintain what is working."

Nobody knows the troubles we've seen. "No one outside of education can appreciate just how impossible it is to teach today. How can we be expected to teach in light of the deterioration of traditional values and the overwhelming problems of society?"

Solidarity. "We must wage a perpetual battle with our adversaries—the mindless bureaucrats and bumbling administrators who are trying to cut costs while foisting more responsibility on us. The only improvement initiative worthy of our efforts is the struggle for higher salaries and better working conditions."

They don't make 'em like they used to. "Kids today just are not as well behaved or as willing to work as the kids of the past. How do they expect us to keep the attention of the Nintendo generation?"

John Donne was wrong: I can be an island. "There is no need to concern ourselves with issues outside of our classrooms. When the bell rings, each of us can close our classroom doors and serve as the rulers of our respective kingdoms."

The solution is out there. "School improvement depends on increased state or federal support for education (or decreased state and federal involvement in education). We must wait for others to take the action that will improve our school."

Been there, done that. "School reform efforts run in a predictable cycle and merely represent the fad *du jour*. There is nothing new under the sun. This too shall pass."

Social Darwinism. "Kids are limited by their innate ability and the environments in which they are raised. These are the factors that determine student achievement, and these factors are beyond our control."

These stories represent classical examples of the art of rationalization. But stories can also be used to shape a new culture. In fact, Senge et al. (1994) argue that the effort to create any learning organization requires a never-ending process of articulating common stories that embody the organization's purpose and shared values. If schools are to function as professional learning communities, educators must engage in a deliberate and sustained attempt to communicate new stories that express, amplify, and validate the principles of a learning community.

One strategy for using stories to influence culture is to include several examples of the school's commitment to being a learning community at every faculty gathering. For over a decade, a portion of every faculty meeting at Adlai Stevenson High School in Lincolnshire, Illinois, has been devoted to sharing accounts of individual and team efforts that illustrate the principles of a learning community. Here are just a few examples:

> We have made a commitment to looking continuously for new ways to help students achieve at higher levels. Today, I want to tell you about a colleague who has taken that commitment to heart. Conventional wisdom had always held that the rigors of the advanced placement (AP) examinations were beyond the abilities of high school sophomores. This teacher was willing to challenge that thinking. At his request, we opened the advanced placement course in European history to sophomores and created two sections of virtually all sophomore students. He challenged his students to rise to the task. He devoted extra time in the evenings and on Saturdays for study sessions, and he had such success in motivating his students that virtually all of them attended these voluntary sessions. The College Board has advised us that 96% of his students earned honor grades on the exam, and now other departments are considering ways to give sophomores greater access to AP classes. Please join me in expressing our appreciation to a colleague who illustrates

Stevenson's commitment to searching for new ways to help students achieve at high levels: Mr. Paul Fitzgerald.

Our traditional approach to students whose test scores indicated a lack of the prerequisite knowledge and skills to be successful in our regular program was to assign those students to remedial courses that were less rigorous. The freshman English team was not satisfied with the results of that approach, and they decided to try something new. Last year they assigned students who had been in the remedial program into regular courses. They also established a tutorial center to assist students whenever their grades fell below a C. The results were fantastic. Not only did every student earn at least a C in the course, but a survey of those students also demonstrated the tremendous satisfaction they had in their accomplishment. Congratulations to the members of the freshman English team.

One of our departments decided students would be more engaged and their work would be more authentic if they were organized into teams of four as the standard structure in their classrooms. For the past three years, students have worked together throughout the period in the teams-of-four format—collaborating on problems and helping each other master the material. For five consecutive semesters, students have established new school records in every academic standard monitored by the department. Congratulations to the math department for demonstrating the power of student collaboration in the classroom.

Three years ago, four teachers from the math, English, science, and social studies departments developed and presented an integrated curriculum to a randomly selected group of students. This team of teachers remained with those students for three consecutive years. Although these students express significantly higher levels of satisfaction with their school experience and score higher in the area of problem solving than their peers, their achievement in mathematics has lagged behind other students. The team's analysis of their longitudinal data has led team members to hypothesize that it is more difficult to incorporate the highly sequential content of mathematics into a project-based, integrated curriculum. Thanks to their efforts, we have a better understanding of the benefits and challenges of an integrated curriculum as we continue to explore this area. Congratulations and thanks to the team that leads our Academy of Integrated Learning.

In 1985 only 88 of our students attempted to complete the rigorous examinations of the Advanced Placement Program. We did not rank among the top 50 schools in the Midwest in terms of student participation in that program. Our teachers decided to reexamine prerequisites for admission to courses that would qualify students for the advanced placement challenge and to adopt a posture of encouraging rather than discouraging student participation. The results have been phenomenal. The participation of our students has increased more than 1,000% over 1985 levels. We now rank first in the 13-state Midwest region and ninth in the world in terms of the number of exams written. Furthermore, the percentage of honor grades earned by our students has also increased. This year they established a new school record in terms of honor grades. Thousands of students have benefited from this initiative over the past decade. Today we celebrate the collective achievement of teachers in every department who were willing to reexamine assumptions, change policies, and work together to achieve dramatically improved results.

Literally hundreds of these stories have been shared with the Stevenson faculty in the past 10 years. They have helped to shape a culture of high expectations and continuous improvement that has enabled the school to win five national awards as one of America's best high schools.

Another strategy that schools have used to spread stories that strengthen the culture of a learning community is to take the time to listen to the testimonials of colleagues. For example, one school begins faculty meetings by placing a vase of roses at the front of the room to help create an atmosphere of appreciation. Staff members are then invited to share anecdotes about colleagues who have contributed to their professional understanding, helped them, or inspired them. These heartfelt, spontaneous tributes represent a powerful way of celebrating the contributions of the members of a professional learning community.

Students, too, represent an excellent source for stories. Schools can ask each student in a graduating class to write an essay describing the teacher or teachers who had the biggest impact on his or her life. These essays can then be collected by the school, and excerpts can be distributed to the entire staff on a regular basis in a "kudos" memorandum. Parents can also be encouraged to advise the school administration whenever a teacher has gone above and beyond the call of duty, and these testimonials can be shared with the entire faculty. All of these efforts serve to remind the staff not only that their efforts are noted and appreciated by others, but also that those efforts have a direct impact on the effectiveness of their school. Inundating staff with stories that illustrate the culture of a professional learning community at work is one of the best strategies for promoting that culture.

Celebration

One of the most important and effective strategies for shaping the culture of any organization is celebration. The celebrations, ceremonies, and rituals of an organization reveal a great deal about its culture—how its people link their past with their present, what behaviors are reinforced, what assumptions are at work, and what is valued. In fact, while articulating shared values can be a powerful force for shaping the culture of a school, those carefully articulated values will have little impact in the absence of ceremony and ritual that support them (Deal & Kennedy, 1982). Lee Bolman and Terry Deal (1995) describe the importance of celebration this way:

Ritual and ceremony help us experience the unseen webs of significance that tie a community together. There may be grand ceremonies for special occasions, but organizations also need simple rituals that infuse meaning and purpose into daily routine. Without ritual and ceremony, transitions become incomplete, a clutter of comings and goings. Life becomes an endless set of Wednesdays. (pp. 110–111)

The importance of attention to celebrating individual and collective accomplishments has been cited as a major factor in influencing organizational culture (Peterson, 1988), an essential strategy for enhancing organizational effectiveness (Kouzes & Posner, 1987), and a necessary condition for creating a learning community (Thompson, 1995). It is an area that must not be overlooked in the change process.

But the challenge of making celebration an integral part of a school improvement effort is formidable. Recognition of individuals or groups is contrary to the existing culture of most schools. Faculties often adopt an "all-for-one and one-for-all" approach that discourages calling attention to an individual teacher and responds with suspicion if such attention is given. School administrators soon learn that publicly commending a teacher or team of teachers for a job well done is likely to result in jealousy or adverse responses from others on the staff: "We do a good job, too. Don't they appreciate us? Is that teacher the 'pet' of the administration? Does this represent the first step in an attempt to introduce merit pay?"

In many schools, if recognition is given to individuals at all, it is a surreptitious acknowledgement. A principal may call a teacher to the office where, behind closed doors, he will express appreciation for a job well done. Or, if an administrator is wildly enthusiastic about a teacher's contribution to the school, a letter of commendation may be placed in the teacher's private, confidential personnel file. But this kind of recognition is ineffective in shaping culture. It will be difficult to sustain the change process if school personnel are more interested in avoiding the appearance of favoritism than they are in shaping culture, if they are more concerned about the feelings of colleagues who may feel slighted than they are in celebrating examples of a learning community at work.

Why Celebrate?

There are several important benefits that result from using celebration, ceremonies, rituals, and stories to help foster the culture of a learning community.

The recipients of the recognition feel noted and appreciated. Public recognition of individuals is likely to have a positive effect on those who receive it. The research on what motivates people has offered a consistent finding: individuals are more likely to believe their work is significant, to feel a sense of achievement, and to be motivated to give their best efforts to the tasks before them when they feel that those efforts will be noted and appreciated.

It reinforces shared values and signals what is important. The celebration of behaviors consistent with the values of a school serves as a reminder of the importance of those values. As Peters and Austin (1985) observe, "well constructed recognition settings provide the single most important opportunity to parade and reinforce the specific kinds of behavior one hopes others will emulate" (p. 370).

It provides living examples of the values of the school at work and encourages others to act in accordance with those values. People tend to assess their own performance not on the basis of some arbitrary standard, but in relationship to the performance of others. As Deal and Kennedy (1982) conclude:

> *People can't aspire to be "good" or "successful" or "smart" or "productive" no matter how much management encourages them in that direction. They can, however, aspire to be like someone: "He's just an ordinary person but look how successful he is. I can be successful like that too."* (p. 38)

Recognition of individuals and teams provides the remaining staff members with examples and models that motivate them to engage in similar behavior. As Peter Drucker writes (1992), "Changing behavior requires changing recognitions and rewards. . . . For over a century we have known that people in organizations tend to act in response to being recognized and rewarded" (p. 195).

It fuels momentum. Calling attention to the presence of behaviors that are consistent with the values of the school and highlighting the positive results that are produced by those behaviors reinforces the improvement initiative. Acknowledging, honoring, and thanking everyone who contributes to the building of a learning community increases the likelihood that the effort will be sustained. Furthermore, ceremonies and stories can provide evidence of the short-term wins that are critical to sustaining change (Kotter, 1996).

It is fun. Celebrations can be fun, and even the most serious commitment to school improvement should include time for play. As Senge et al. (1994) ask, "What's the point of building [a learning] community if we can't have fun?" (p. 527)

Tips for Incorporating Celebration into the Culture of a School

Explicitly state the purpose for attending to the need for celebration. Since public recognition of individuals and groups is so contrary to traditional practice in most schools, the rationale for incorporating celebration should be carefully explained not only at the beginning of the initiative but periodically thereafter. Staff members should be reminded that the celebrations represent an important strategy both for reinforcing the importance of the vision and values they have endorsed and for helping the school sustain its improvement initiative.

Make celebration everyone's responsibility. Every member of the staff should be asked to help identify individuals and groups whose behaviors and commitments warrant recognition. Promoting shared values is everyone's business in a professional learning community. All staff members, for example, should have the opportunity to nominate someone for special recognition. Furthermore, recipients should not be determined exclusively by the administration. Establishing a committee for selecting staff to be honored at each meeting is usually preferable to having the principal act as the sole arbiter of who will be recognized.

Establish a clear link between public recognition and the advancement of vision and values. It is important that educators view public commendation as a means to an end rather than the end itself. The ultimate goal is the creation of a professional learning community that continuously improves its effectiveness. When recognition is explicitly linked to efforts that advance the vision or demonstrate the values of a learning community, it can make a significant contribution to that objective. But the recognition will have little impact if a staff believes that recognition is presented randomly, that each person deserves to be honored regardless of his or her contribution to the improvement effort, or that rewards are given for factors unrelated to the goal of creating a learning community. Therefore, any public commendation should always be accompanied by a story that specifically explains how the recipients have contributed to the collective effort to improve the school.

Create opportunities for lots of winners. Celebration is most effective in promoting the values of a learning community when it is structured so that all staff members feel that they have the opportunity to be publicly recognized and applauded for their individual efforts and contributions. A school that bases its recognition effort on a teacher-of-the-year program may have the best of intentions, but it will be pursuing a strategy that ensures only one teacher will be recognized as a winner. Every other member of the faculty will be a loser! Establishing such artificial "caps" as "we will present no more than five commendations per meeting," "no more than 10% of the faculty can be acknowledged in a given year," or "only teachers with 10 years of experience can receive an award" also limits the impact that a commendation program will have on a school. The most effective programs will provide for a wide distribution of awards. Developing a learning community requires creating systems specifically designed not only to provide celebrations, but also to ensure that there are lots of winners.

An achievement or contribution need not be monumental to warrant recognition. Educators should aggressively seek out simple examples of their values at work and evidence of incremental improvement—and then simply celebrate their findings!

The issue that will inevitably arise in this effort to ensure a multiplicity of winners relates to the law of diminishing returns. Conventional wisdom suggests that if awards are too frequent, they lose their impact. Even a school that is committed to celebration must question at what point the effort to recognize staff may become too much of a good thing. Still, there is only one criterion that should be used in addressing this question—the sincerity with which the recognition is given. A commendation should represent genuine appreciation and admiration. If that sincerity is lacking, celebration can be counterproductive.

Recognition as Its Own Reward

Boards of education are often criticized for a failure to provide financial rewards for high-performing schools and individuals (Consortium on Productivity in the Schools, 1995; Fiske, 1992; Gerstner et al., 1994). Yet periodic attempts to establish merit pay systems in schools have usually proven to be ineffective. The recognition advocated in this chapter is not a call for significant financial incentives or bonuses. Practitioners are typically not in a position to implement significant changes in the traditional compensation systems of public education, and this book is intended to focus on issues that are within the sphere of influence of practitioners.

Educators can, however, develop and implement creative systems of informal rewards, recognition, and ceremonies that both express appreciation and signal what is valued. These kinds of symbolic awards appeal to intrinsic motivation and can be more effective than bonuses or compensation, which have a tendency to be resented by those who are not rewarded (Dilworth, 1995). Public acknowledgment for a job well done and symbolic awards such as certificates, pins, or plaques can be more important tools in building a professional learning community than monetary rewards.

Final Cautions about Culture

Focusing on culture does not mean ignoring structure. The significance of culture in the change process should not be interpreted to mean that a school's structure—its policies, procedures, rules, and relationships—does not deserve attention as well. Although it is certain that changes in structure do not automatically result in changes in the attitudes, beliefs, assumptions, and habits of personnel, it is equally certain that structure can affect a school's culture. For example, policies and procedures that result in teachers working in isolation will make efforts to create a professional norm of collaboration more difficult. Furthermore, changes in the culture of a school can lead to a reexamination of the policies, procedures, rules, and relationships that are in place. Michael Fullan (1993) describes the relationship this way:

> *Reculturing leads to restructuring more effectively than the reverse. In most restructuring reforms new structures are expected to result in new behaviors and cultures, but mostly fail to do so. There is no doubt a reciprocal relationship between structural and cultural change, but it is much more powerful when teachers and administrators begin working in new ways only to discover that school structures are ill-fitted to the orientation and must be altered.* (p. 68)

A professional learning community will be attentive both to structure and to culture in its effort to create the best climate for improvement.

Culture needs constant attention. Developing a new culture is akin to gardening (Kofman & Senge, 1995). Just as weeds can take over a garden if it is left unattended, so bad culture will inevitably drive out the good unless the desired culture is tended. Good cultures require hard work to establish and maintain; bad cultures do not. Good cultures require constant cultivation; bad cultures are "low maintenance." As Champy (1995) advises, "Only a very strong, constantly cultivated culture can prevent the weeds of mistrust, disrespect, and uncooperativeness from taking over the garden" (p. 84). Shaping culture is not a task to complete; rather, it is an ongoing commitment.

Summary

Schools have tended to focus their improvement efforts on their structures—policies, procedures, and rules. It has become clear, however, that sustaining an improvement initiative requires attention to anchoring changes in the school's culture—the assumptions, beliefs, values, and habits that constitute the norm for the people in a school. Effective strategies for shaping culture include:

1. Articulating, modeling, promoting, and protecting the shared values that have been identified.

2. Systematically engaging staff in reflective dialogue that asks them to search for discrepancies between the values they have endorsed and the day-to-day operation of the school.

3. Inundating staff with stories that reflect the culture at work.

4. Celebrating examples of shared values and progress in the improvement process with ceremonies and rituals. The link between the celebration and the value that is being promoted should be clear and explicit, and it should be everyone's job to identify individuals and teams that warrant this special recognition; most important, the strategies for celebration should ensure lots of winners, so that everyone in the school feels that he or she can be recognized for contributing to the improvement process.

The importance of embedding change initiatives in the culture of the school does not mean that structure is insignificant in that process. Although structure and culture interact, it is more effective to focus on how changes in culture can stimulate a reexamination of structure rather than vice versa. Finally, shaping culture is a never-ending task. Like a garden, a healthy culture requires constant cultivation.

Chapter 8

Planning for Learning: Curricular Focus in a Learning Community

A crucial element has been missing from our debate about curriculum. No one has been interested in discussing the interrelationships of what I call the four C's: the process of change, the culture of schools, the context of classrooms, and the content of the curriculum.

—Anne Lieberman (1990, p. 531)

The first question in increasing productivity in knowledge work has to be: what is the task? What do we try to accomplish? Why do it at all? The easiest and the greatest increases in productivity in knowledge work come from redefining the task and especially from eliminating what needs not be done.

—Peter Drucker (1992, p. 98)

Until a school has clarified what students should know and be able to do and the dispositions they should acquire as a result of schooling, its staff cannot function as a professional learning community. Attentiveness to student learning represents a core characteristic of schools where there is a strong professional community (Louis, Kruse, & Marks, 1996). These schools move beyond discussions about changing the criteria for student council membership, revising the schedule, or establishing new governance structures. Instead, they focus on the areas that can result in significant school improvement—curriculum, instruction, assessment, and culture (Wasley et al., 1995). Teachers increase the effectiveness of their schools when they collectively identify and work toward the results they desire, develop collaborative strategies to achieve their goals, and create systems to assess student learning. A professional learning community strives to provide its students with a curriculum that has been developed by the faculty through a collaborative process and enables the school to foster a results orientation in its most critical area—student learning.

The link between collaborative processes to resolve key instructional questions and a commitment to results cannot be overstated. Too often, educators are detached from the results of their teaching because they have had so little voice in the key decisions leading to those results. They teach a curriculum that has been developed by someone else (the state, a textbook publisher, or the district curriculum committee); use textbooks and materials selected by someone else; adhere to a pace and sequence determined by someone else; and use assessment instruments chosen by someone else. Then, when student achievement falls short of expectations, teachers cite unrealistic curricular outcomes, poor instructional materials, inappropriate pacing, or misaligned assessments as reasons that they could not be more effective. It is very difficult to establish an orientation toward results in such an environment; nevertheless, some states and districts continue to operate on the premise that they can improve the effectiveness of their schools by simply mandating what teachers are to teach and what students are to learn.

Teachers recognize the inherent unfairness of a system that asks them to be accountable for results, but provides them with little or no opportunity to make the decisions that affect those results. Effective organizations link responsibility and authority, but this link is typically not present in schools. As the Consortium on Productivity in the Schools (1995) concludes:

> *The management pattern that prevails in American education separates responsibility for learning from the authority to make the decisions needed to meet this responsibility. Teaching and learning occur at the school level, and teachers and schools are held accountable for the results. However, individual schools have little control over their own resources and enjoy little autonomy.* (pp. 45–46)

Many times board members and administrators object to giving teachers the authority to make key instructional decisions. They point to the hierarchy of the organizational chart and insist that they must make the decisions because they are responsible for the consequences. "After all, who is in charge?" they ask. That question is appropriate for the hierarchical model of the past. However, the relevant question for the learning community is not, "Who is in charge?" but rather, "How can we best get results?" The answer to that question lies in empowering teachers through collaborative processes that provide them with authority that is commensurate to their responsibility. Schools that simply adopt canned curriculum programs or allow textbooks to dictate the curriculum make a fundamental mistake. Without collaborative processes that foster ownership in decisions, schools will not generate the shared commitments and results orientation of a learning community. Thus, the *process* of curriculum development is at least as important as the final product.

The fact that teachers should play a major role in curriculum development does not mean that each teacher should be free to determine what should be taught in his or her classroom. Both research and practice have demonstrated that curriculum content and the amount of time devoted to critical content is more a function of independent and idiosyncratic decisions on the part of individual teachers than purposeful consensus on essential learning (Berliner, 1984; Doyle, 1992). Once again, the important determination of what students should know and be able to do as a result of their education should be a collective, rather than an individual, decision.

Some administrators contend that they simply hire good people and then trust them to perform their jobs according to their best professional judgment. This argument might be more persuasive if the approach were somehow distinguishable from the laissez faire approach of administrators who lack the commitment and/or energy to monitor student learning. As Kanter (1983) observes, "Freedom does not mean the absence of structure—letting employees go off and do whatever they want—but rather a clear structure that enables people to work within established boundaries in creative and autonomous ways" (p. 248). The members of a learning community give up a measure of individual autonomy in exchange for significantly enhanced collective empowerment.

Nor is the contention that teachers should have a voice in curriculum development tantamount to saying that national, state, or district curriculum frameworks should be ignored. These frameworks can serve as excellent resources in the investigation of curriculum by teachers. In fact, teachers are likely to find that there is little with which they disagree when they take the time to analyze national, district, or state frameworks. An external source of recommended curriculum can serve as a powerful stimulus in the process if teachers are asked to reflect upon and critique the curriculum rather than to passively implement the work of others.

Assumptions Regarding Curriculum Development

How should a school develop a curriculum that is a product of collaboration among the faculty and has an orientation toward results? While there may be no single "right" way, there are five important assumptions that can help guide a curriculum development process:

1. Teachers should work collaboratively to design a research-based curriculum that reflects the best thinking in each subject area.

2. The curriculum should help teachers, students, and parents clarify the specific knowledge, skills, and dispositions that students should acquire as a result of their schooling.

3. The results-oriented curriculum should reduce content and enable all parties to focus on essential and significant learning.

4. The curriculum process should enable an individual teacher, a teaching team, and the school to monitor student achievement at the classroom level.

5. Curriculum and assessment processes should foster commitment to continuous improvement.

A curriculum and assessment process that is built around these assumptions can help schools operate as professional learning communities and focus on the student learning that is central to such communities. The assumptions warrant elaboration and are discussed in detail below.

Assumption One: Teachers should work collaboratively to design a research-based curriculum that reflects the best thinking in each subject area. The curriculum development process should begin with in-depth discussions regarding the most current thinking about what schools should teach our children. If the curriculum of a school seems to suggest, "Pay attention to everything—everything is important," it cannot have the necessary focus on results.

Because we want and expect so much from our schools, and because the issue of what we should teach our children is so important, many significant curriculum initiatives have been proposed and developed. The members of a learning community should not only be familiar with the literature on these initiatives, they should also study, analyze, and evaluate it as they search for the right combination of theory and practice for their students and their schools at a particular time. Pooling uninformed opinions simply results in making uninformed decisions. Therefore, a learning community should begin its investigation with an examination of what is known about best practice and should use its findings to guide its decisions and help identify benchmarks.

The link between curriculum development and staff development is essential. Helping teachers learn about the ideas, trends, innovations, and best thinking in their disciplines is a prerequisite for successful curriculum development. Appendix B presents a synthesis of different research findings and models as an example of some of the ideas and concepts that could be explored by faculty members as part of their curriculum development process.

Assumption Two: The curriculum should help teachers, students, and parents clarify the specific knowledge, skills, and dispositions that students should acquire as a result of their schooling. School leaders must take steps to involve key groups within the school community in the curriculum development process. Parents, business representatives, and community members should participate with teachers and administrators in the earliest, most general discussions of the curriculum and should be invited to respond to early drafts of the goals and standards of the curriculum. However, as the focus of the discussion shifts to the particular content in individual classrooms, participation in the process should become more narrow, with teachers assuming the major role. The challenge for school leaders is to maintain an effective balance of and timetable for community participation.

The steering committee that guides the curriculum development process should include members of the community, and should make a conscious effort to involve community members in initial discussions about the basic beliefs and assumptions that represent the philosophical underpinnings of the curriculum. While many people consider educational philosophy to be esoteric and irrelevant, almost anyone with an interest in education welcomes the opportunity to discuss such topics as the characteristics and needs of children, the expectations of the community for the school, societal factors that should influence education, the relative importance of particular content or knowledge, and so on. Thus, the process of developing curriculum should begin by engaging people in a discussion of some fundamental questions:

- **What do we believe about students who will be attending our schools?** Discussions about the nature of students should be both general and specific. In initial discussions, participants should have the benefit of articles, pamphlets, speakers, films, or videos that can help them identify the general physical, intellectual, and emotional characteristics of the age group under consideration. Once members understand this common background information, they can discuss their beliefs about the students who attend their particular school. The group should understand the student body in terms of its socioeconomic levels, the percentage of students who are working below grade level, the percentage who will pursue postsecondary education, the percentage who are enrolled in particular special education programs, and so on. The fundamental objective of these discussions is to develop a genuine and accurate understanding of the students who will be served by the curriculum the group will design.

- **What are the expectations of the community for our school?** Schools do not operate in a vacuum—they must serve the public. If a curriculum is to serve the entire community, the curriculum development process should try to ascertain the desires and expectations of the community. There are many ways to gather community input about what the school should be doing and what curricular programs should be emphasized. Some schools hold community meetings where the school program is discussed and community decisions are made. For example, one school district in the state of Washington hosts a goal-setting dinner each year that is open to the public. At this dinner, attendees are presented with an evaluation of the previous year's goals and then discuss, clarify, and rank priorities for the coming year. Surveys, interviews, and focus groups are other strategies for adding the community perspective to a discussion of curriculum goals. Whatever strategies are used, however, the point to remember is that community acceptance and support are often critical to the success of a school program. If community desires and expectations are ignored or are misunderstood, serious problems may develop in the day-to-day operation of the school.

- **What are the social influences on the curriculum?** Although it is important to consider what the local community expects of the school, ultimately students must function in a larger society. If the process of identifying curricular goals fails to look beyond the local community, schools run the risk of developing a narrow and provincial curriculum. Inattention to societal trends increases the likelihood that schools will prepare students to operate in a world that no longer exists. Study and discussion of contemporary life and of the larger society outside the school should be an important part of the goal-setting process. The Ecology Futures and Global Studies Curriculum Collaborative established by futurist Joel Barker is a helpful source for identifying the societal issues that should be considered when a school develops a curriculum to prepare its students for the future. The EFGS Curriculum Collaborative can be contacted at Box 5476, Irvine, CA 92716, (714) 854-4454, FAX (714) 854-0074.

Specifying Curriculum Goals and Standards

Discussions about the best thinking in curriculum, the nature of students to be served, community expectations for the school, and trends and contemporary society outside the school should result in written goal statements and standards that are specific enough to give direction to the school program. This writing task should be undertaken by subject area specialists rather than the community at large (Kendall & Marzano, 1996). Community members should, however, have several opportunities to review and comment on drafts of curriculum goals and standards before their final adoption.

Goal statements should be written in short, declarative sentences that provide direction to the school's daily program. Normally these statements will be fairly broad and will encompass intellectual, social, personal, and physical development. The statement of curriculum goals developed by a nationally recognized school district after extensive community input is presented below as an example.

Each student will be expected to:

1. *Learn independently and appreciate learning.*

2. *Solve problems; know where and how to get relevant information for solving problems; and use technology as one problem-solving tool.*

3. *Analyze and synthesize knowledge.*

4. *Be a creative, imaginative thinker.*

5. *Be an independent, responsible citizen.*

6. *Have good collaborative skills.*

7. *Have a sense of history.*

8. *Have a strong foundation in traditional course areas.*

9. *Possess good speaking, writing, reading, and listening skills.*

10. *Develop an aesthetic appreciation.*

11. *Recognize values and underlying biases.*

12. *Engage in disciplined work habits.*

13. *Respect honest differences of opinion; and tolerate diversity.*

14. *Understand and practice good health habits.*

15. *Develop a postsecondary educational plan.*

Making Goal Statements Public

Too often, groups work diligently to develop curricular goal statements only to see them be filed away, never to be used again except for accreditation purposes. Curriculum goals must be communicated and monitored if they are to influence what happens in a school. A small, attractive brochure outlining the school curriculum can be produced inexpensively. The brochure should be made available to anyone, but especially to parents who will be sending their children to the school for the first time. The brochure should contain such information as the makeup and size of the student body, data on the faculty, the philosophy and goals of the school program, a brief description of the curriculum, and other more mundane facts such as hours of school operation, telephone numbers, and what to do in case of an emergency.

Many schools display a framed copy of their curriculum goals in the lobby or near the entrance of the school. Such displays serve as a constant reminder of what the school is trying to accomplish.

Finally, the best way to make curriculum philosophy and goal statements public is simply to use them. Throughout the year, groups and committees must be encouraged to make their decisions in light of the school's goals. If educators actually use goal statements, parents, students, and community members will have a better understanding of what the school stands for and the knowledge and skills students are to acquire as the result of their schooling.

Assumption Three: The results-oriented curriculum should reduce content and enable all parties to focus on essential and significant learning. There is a saying among those who sell real estate that the three most important factors to consider when buying property are location, location, and location. The appropriate analogy for curriculum development is that the three most important factors are focus, focus, and focus! Schools cannot develop a results orientation or a commitment to continuous improvement until they can focus on what students are to accomplish as a result of their education.

General curriculum goals offer a broad statement of the knowledge or skills to be achieved in a learning area, but typically lack the specificity to provide focus. Therefore, curriculum goals must first be translated into the more specific standards of learning that all students should achieve and then be used to establish benchmarks for monitoring student learning at different grade levels. Standards offer a more specific statement of knowledge and/or skill within the goal. Benchmarks are progress indicators for measuring a student's achievement of a standard. Consider the following example:

> **General Goal:** As a result of their schooling, students will be able to understand, analyze, and compare political systems, with an emphasis on the United States.
>
> **Standard:** Students will be able to compare and analyze the structures and functions of the political systems of the state and nation.
>
> **Benchmarks:** Students will be able to do the following in each level of education:
>
> • Early elementary: identify local, state, and national political systems and structures.

- Late elementary: give examples of government responsibilities at the local, state, and national levels and distinguish among them.

- Middle/junior high school: compare and contrast the political systems of the individual state and the United States.

- Early high school: compare and contrast the political systems of the United States with other nations.

- Late high school: analyze the workings of different political systems through examination of significant contemporary events.

One of the most consistent messages of educational research is that effective teachers and schools clearly identify what they are trying to accomplish. Without that clarity, a school and its teachers will not be able to establish or verify when either learning or improvement has occurred. A learning community will first identify academic goals, specific standards, and clear benchmarks, and then it will focus, focus, focus on achieving the articulated results.

Organized Abandonment: Deciding What Not to Teach

Having a clear curriculum focus means that teachers in a learning community not only decide together what students should be able to do, they also decide what not to teach. Curriculum design has increasingly become an issue of identifying what content to exclude. Because we cannot teach everything in this age of information, a key to establishing a curricular focus is to make sure the curriculum focuses on significant learner outcomes.

One of the major barriers to improving public schools is the fact that their curricula are packed with trivia. As one major study of school improvement concluded, "Meaningless school work is a consequence of a number of factors but especially curriculum that emphasizes superficial exposure to hundreds of isolated pieces of information" (Wehlage, Newmann, & Secada, 1996, p. 23). Class time is wasted in the pursuit of insignificant information, and time is a teacher's most precious resource. Increasingly, teachers feel like they have less discretionary time as more and more of their work day is dictated by external forces. They feel a tremendous amount of pressure to "get it all in." As Schlechty (1990) reports:

> Teachers, faculties, and principals have and more importantly feel that they have little control over the way time is allocated in school. The one commodity that teachers and administrators say that they do not have enough of, even more so than money, is time; time to teach, time to converse, time to think, time to plan, time to talk, even time to go to the restroom or have a cup of coffee. . . . [T]ime is indeed precious in school. (p. 73)

One of the basic concepts in economics is the concept of opportunity cost—the idea that everything has a cost. A dollar spent on entertainment is a dollar that is not available for education. The concept of opportunity cost also applies to time. For example, the opportunity cost of a person who decides to go to the library is the thing that person may have done if he or she had not gone to the library. Opportunity cost is a critical concept to apply when focusing a curriculum. Those who are responsible for deciding what students should learn must recognize that when students spend time learning one thing, the price they pay is all of the things they did not learn that may have been more significant. A student who expends effort and energy in search of a definition for the word "isba" (a Russian peasant's hut) has less opportunity to learn the meaning and significance of the word "perestroika." It is imperative that practitioners realize that the time students spend in the study of meaningless facts robs them of the time they should devote to gaining mastery of knowledge and skills that are truly significant.

Like most modern organizations, schools have no procedures for systematically abandoning anything. Typically, there are numerous mechanisms in place at the state, district, and building levels that allow content to be added to the public school curriculum. State legislators, textbook publishers, commercial test developers, curriculum study committees, and special interest groups all serve as instruments for adding to the list of things that students should know. In contrast, school districts typically have no formal procedure for removing content from the curriculum (unless it is too controversial).

It is time to recognize that the major flaw in the *de facto* curriculum of American public schools is not that schools do not do enough, but that they attempt to do too much. Even though American students have fewer school days each year than their Asian and European counterparts, they are expected to learn far more curriculum content. Confronted with a curriculum that is "a mile long and one-half inch deep," teachers have become preoccupied with "coverage." They feel unable to teach for student mastery of knowledge and skills because of the race to cover content. One of the most meaningful steps a school can take to promote significant improvement is to develop a process for identifying significant curriculum content, eliminating nonessential material, and providing teachers with time to teach the significant curriculum.

Teachers can use a number of processes to collaborate on eliminating nonessential content. One school met the challenge by having its teachers agree to collaborate immediately after they finished teaching a unit. For example, after the American history teachers taught a unit, they would come together to consider three questions:

1. What is there in the unit we just taught that every student needs to know?

2. What is there in the unit we just taught that students would benefit from knowing if we have the time to teach it?

3. What is there in this unit that is insignificant enough that we simply should not spend the time to teach it?

Other schools have asked teachers to discuss these questions before teaching a unit. While there is no single way to eliminate nonessential content, it is difficult to overstate the significance of the task. The principle of addition by subtraction applies here. By subtracting content from the curriculum, schools can strengthen their ability to help students master essential knowledge and skills.

Assumption Four: The curriculum process should enable an individual teacher, a teaching team, and the school to monitor student achievement at the classroom level. Once faculty members have worked together to establish curriculum goals, standards, and benchmarks, they should organize at the department or grade level to collaborate on more specific curricular decisions. At the end of the process, every teacher should clearly understand what students should know and be able to do in their course or grade level and how students will demonstrate their mastery. Furthermore, the process should enable the school to monitor each student's performance at the classroom level. The following six steps can provide a framework for this process:

1. Each department or grade-level team uses the district's curriculum goals, standards, and benchmarks to identify

the general goal for the course or grade level they are teaching.

2. The teams of teachers responsible for teaching a particular course or grade level identify the essential student outcomes for each course or grade level.

3. Teaching teams write common course or grade-level descriptions and distribute them to students (or parents of students who are in the elementary grades). These descriptions should include the general goal of the course, the essential outcomes students should achieve, and the means by which student achievement will be assessed.

4. The teams develop common, comprehensive assessment strategies that will produce data on individual and collective student achievement.

5. The teams identify the proficiency levels all students should achieve.

6. The teams review the results of the collective student achievement, identify problem areas in which student performance did not meet anticipated proficiency levels, and develop plans to address those areas.

The listing of outcomes to be included in each course or grade level should provide teachers with considerable flexibility in their daily instruction. Although all students should have access to a common core curriculum, that curriculum should not be so crammed as to require lock-step instruction that robs teachers of their professional autonomy. Teachers must have some room to experiment within the structure of the curriculum, and that is why organized abandonment of nonessential material is so critical.

Determining the sequencing of content is also an important step in this process. For example, to determine the concepts to be taught in a middle school math program, the school's teachers should work with representative math teachers from each feeder school, as well as teachers from the high school, to identify the last few concepts taught in fifth-grade mathematics and the first few concepts taught in the ninth grade. These concepts would then represent the first and last concepts to be taught in the middle school math program. The middle school team would then identify the sequencing of math content from sixth through eighth grade. Although this step is more critical in highly sequential subjects such as mathematics, teachers from any discipline benefit when they have articulated a curricular map that clarifies what has been covered before and what will be covered after their course or grade level (Jacobs, 1997).

Once again, this discussion by teachers should be guided by research and recommended national standards. Textbooks, the national assessment of educational progress, nationally normed tests, professors, and the curricula from model schools might also be referenced in the process. The need to consider the best thinking in a field applies to efforts to develop the specific curriculum of particular courses and grade levels as well as to efforts to develop broad general goals.

Effective Unit Plans

Ultimately, teachers must translate course or grade-level goals into more specific unit plans. The following questions form a useful framework for developing effective, consistent lesson plans, particularly when teachers work together to answer these questions.

What do I want the students to be able to do as a result of this unit? To answer this question, teachers should identify the behaviors that are expected of a student who has successfully completed the unit. Instead of saying that students will "understand" a concept, the teachers should ask what the students will do in order to demonstrate that understanding. Using clear, common-sense terms rather than educational jargon helps make this a meaningful and useful process for teachers.

How will I determine if students are ready for this unit? This question challenges the teachers to determine if there are prerequisite skills or knowledge that students must have in order to succeed in a particular unit, and then to identify how teachers will assess whether students have these skills and knowledge. Preassessment can also provide evidence that students have already mastered the major concept of the unit, in which case further instruction would be an efficient use of time. Preassessment is an important component of planning and ensuring that instruction is presented at the appropriate level of difficulty. It may take many forms: a written test, a review of student homework, an evaluation of test results from a previous unit, teacher observation of students, or question-and-answer sessions. Whatever method is used, it should be designed to help teachers determine if students are ready for a particular unit.

What methods and materials will I use to teach the lesson? Teachers should have a clear idea of the methods and materials they plan to use in each unit of instruction. The constant modification and adjustment of plans based on student performance, which is the essence of good teaching, presupposes the existence of a basic blueprint of how the unit will be taught. One important consideration in preparing the unit plan is providing the opportunity for student practice. Although teachers should be encouraged to include a variety of instructional methods in their unit plans, every unit plan should provide students with an opportunity to practice the behaviors they will be expected to perform as a result of that unit.

How will I know whether the students have achieved the intended outcomes of this unit? There are a number of ways teachers might determine whether students have mastered the intended outcomes of the unit plan. Observation, written tests, questioning, review of homework, student performance, and projects all represent appropriate means for assessing student progress.

Unit plans need not be lengthy. They could be only a page or two. Length is not the issue. Teachers enhance their effectiveness when they work together in developing unit plans and collaborate on the four critical questions discussed above. As one comprehensive study concludes:

> *When teachers collaborate productively, they participate in reflective dialogue; they observe and react to one another's teaching, curriculum, and assessment practices; and they engage in joint planning and curriculum development. All of these forms of collaboration should improve practice.*

> —Newmann et al. (1996, p. 183)

Assumption Five: Curriculum and assessment processes should foster commitment to continuous improvement. The primary purpose of collaborative curriculum development is to help students achieve at higher levels, but a school will never know if that purpose has been achieved unless it is attentive to assessment. A results-oriented school will use a variety of strategies to assess the level of student learning. Assessment provides another important opportunity for teacher collaboration. In fact, collaboration on the criteria to be used in assessing student work can have a positive impact on classroom instruction.

In most organizations, what gets monitored gets done. As Phil Schlechty (1990) explains, "People know what is expected by what is inspected and what is respected . . . evaluation and assessment, properly conceived, are key elements in building . . . a results oriented, self-regulating environment" (p. 111).

It makes little sense to claim that the primary focus of the curriculum is student achievement and then pay scant attention to assessing it. The elements for continuous improvement are in place when teachers have worked together to identify specifically what students should know and be able to do, when they have reached consensus on the criteria with which they will judge student work, and when they collect data that are meaningful and relevant to them in assessing student achievement.

A common reaction to the curriculum development and assessment model described in this chapter sounds something like this: "But if teachers clarify the intended outcomes of their course and agree on how students are to be tested, won't they teach to the test?" The correct response to this query is, of course, "That's the idea!" Teaching to the test is a perfectly appropriate and honorable thing to do, particularly when the test represents a valid assessment of the students' acquisition of meaningful knowledge and skills. Schools may teach more than they test, but they should test only what they teach.

A learning community will not leave curriculum alignment to chance. It will ensure that a teacher's daily instruction is consistent with the essential learning goals identified through the curriculum development process. It will recognize that developing a curriculum is a meaningless exercise if teachers ultimately teach something else. It will insist that students are asked to learn content that has been chosen based on essential outcomes rather than on the idiosyncrasies of an individual teacher. It will establish the expectation that each instructional unit will provide students with the opportunity to practice the kinds of behaviors or skills they will be asked to demonstrate during the assessment phase of the curriculum. Finally, it will ensure that assessments are aligned with curriculum and instruction. Students are much more likely to succeed in school if the teacher teaches to the curriculum developed by consensus, students practice the skills the curriculum emphasizes, and assessment programs are designed to determine the degree to which students have met curricular expectations.

Choosing an Appropriate Assessment Model

Numerous assessment models have been advocated by various writers and researchers. The critical point to remember is that relying on any one model would be a seriously flawed assessment strategy. Assessment of a student's work should provide a rich array of information on his or her progress and achievement. Only multiple assessment procedures can offer such information (Stiggins et al., 1997). The challenge is to match appropriate assessment strategies to curricular goals and instructional methodologies.

Traditional paper-and-pencil tests continue to have a place in comprehensive assessment programs. The Effective Schools Report (Educational Research Service, 1983) lists the following characteristics of an ideal testing program:

1. Tests are developed locally to ensure that students are tested on what they are actually taught.

2. Tests are nationally normed to ensure that the local definition of mastery is generally congruent with student achievement outside of the district.

3. Tests are curriculum-based to emphasize the key concepts of the curriculum to students and teachers.

4. Tests are criterion-referenced to provide an assessment of each student in relation to the objectives established by the school.

5. Some tests are standardized to provide a general assessment of the school as it compares to national norms on the content measure. (p. 3)

But even well-constructed paper-and-pencil tests are not appropriate for monitoring all of the important goals of a school. Much of what schools are trying to teach—the ability to write, speak, reason, create, show tolerance, and make responsible decisions—cannot be measured by a multiple-choice test. Therefore, a professional learning community will work to identify and develop alternative assessment strategies to obtain a better sense of student achievement.

Authentic assessment, one of the most popular forms of alternative assessment, generally requires that students perform a task in a situation that closely matches the challenges of real life. Students are required to demonstrate what they know or can do instead of selecting an answer that someone else has written. Their performance is then assessed by a systematic grading procedure. Authentic assessment is well suited to a learning community's focus on learning and emphasis on results.

Rubrics offer an untapped potential for assessing both individual and collective student progress. A rubric is a written, agreed-upon criteria or guide by which a student product or performance is judged. In addition to providing an excellent way to assess student progress, the development of rubrics provides a framework for collaborative discussions about performance standards for students. Schmoker (1996) lists the following benefits of rubrics:

1. They promote good performance by clearly defining that performance and showing that such work is achievable.

2. They provide better feedback than grades by providing more precision and clarity about the criteria used to evaluate student work.

3. They end the disheartening experience that students often face of handing in an assignment without knowing how the teacher will evaluate it. (pp. 71–72)

Some schools question the ability of a team of teachers to establish inter-rater reliability in the use of rubrics. Yet, the much praised Advanced Placement Program is based on the very premise that unacquainted high school and university teachers from the United States and Canada can collaborate and agree on a rubric of performance on a scale of one to five and can then reliably apply that rubric to exams written by students from throughout the world. Thus, it is ironic that some educators do not believe that the four second-grade teachers in the same school can agree on and apply a rubric for assessing the work of second-grade students in language arts or mathematics. If teachers can establish and articulate rubrics that provide clear performance targets, the concept of success for every student can be viewed as a legitimate, attainable goal instead of as philosophical rhetoric.

Standards for Assessment Programs

Stiggins et al. (1997) offer the following standards as criteria for judging the quality of a school's assessment program.

Standard 1: Quality assessments arise from and accurately reflect clearly specified and appropriate achievement expectations for students. Any assessment process must begin by defining what it means to succeed. To have a quality assessment program, schools must be clear on the knowledge and skills that students are to master.

Standard 2: Sound assessments are specifically designed to serve instructional purposes. Assessments are purposeful when there is a clear understanding as to who will use the results and how. The driving force behind an assessment program should be to provide teachers with the information they need to inform and improve their practices.

Standard 3: Quality assessments accurately reflect the intended target and serve the intended purpose. Assessment should address the concerns and questions of a variety of constituents. Teachers need information on the achievement of each of their students. Students benefit from knowing how their performance compares to achievement benchmarks. Parents need information on their individual children. The community needs data on the collective effectiveness of its schools. A quality program will address the needs of each group.

Standard 4: Quality assessments provide a representative sample of student performance that is sufficient in its scope to permit conclusions about student achievement. A sound assessment system allows for valid inferences because it is based upon sufficient information.

Standard 5: Sound assessments are designed, developed, and used in such a manner as to eliminate sources of bias or distortion that interfere with the accuracy of the results. Many factors can affect the accuracy of an assessment program. Test items can be poorly constructed or may require prior knowledge that is not intended to be tested. Test items may reflect racial, ethnic, or gender biases. The testing environment may be noisy or distracting in other ways. When teachers work together in teams to develop assessment instruments, they can critique the assessment items and strategies proposed by their colleagues and reduce the likelihood of bias or other problems.

The Benefits of Collaborative Curriculum Development

There are several important benefits to be gained from a collaborative curriculum development process that is based on the five assumptions presented earlier in this chapter:

1. The process enables teachers to be more focused in their planning and their teaching. The main difference between effective and ineffective teachers is that effective teachers know what they are trying to accomplish. Thus, they can monitor themselves more or less continuously. The collaborative curriculum development process attempts to provide a systematic method of ensuring that all teachers clearly understand and can focus on the essential outcomes of their course or grade level.

2. The process ensures attention to a common curriculum. If a school truly believes that all students should master certain outcomes, it should take steps to ensure that those outcomes are addressed, regardless of who teaches a particular course. Teachers should play the major role in identifying the outcomes and developing the strategies for assessing student mastery of those outcomes. They should also be given the freedom to decide how the outcomes will be addressed on a day-to-day basis.

    However, teachers should clearly understand that all students should achieve the outcomes by the end of the course. Common final examinations or other strategies of assessment provide teachers with focus and increase the likelihood that all students will have access to the intended curriculum.

3. The process results in the development of better tests. Tests written by a team of teachers are generally superior to those written by individuals because teachers

critique one another's questions for relevance, clarity, and congruence with intended outcomes.

4. The process enables teachers to identify areas of the curriculum in which students are not achieving at the anticipated proficiency levels. If teachers have established benchmarks of student performance and have developed valid and reliable instruments to assess student performance, they will be able to identify an individual student or a group that has not achieved the anticipated level of proficiency.

5. The process provides teachers with useful feedback on their performance. Teachers generally work in a vacuum that separates them from other adults and denies them meaningful, objective, results-oriented feedback on their performance. The teacher who has no idea of how the performance of his or her students compares to that of other students in the next room, the next county, the state, or the nation is unfortunately the norm rather than the exception. People cannot improve their performance when they work in a vacuum. Individuals need feedback and comparative information to help them assess and enhance their effectiveness. This process provides feedback mechanisms that help teachers improve their performance.

6. The process motivates teachers to continually improve. Studies of excellent organizations have concluded that two of the most powerful motivators are the peer pressure that results from working in teams and the ability to compare one's own performance with that of others. This process incorporates both of these motivational strategies. Even the teacher whose students have outperformed the total group on nine of ten subtests will

immediately focus on the one test in which his or her students' performance did not measure up to the rest of the group.

7. The process ensures systematic collaboration. This process calls for teachers to meet periodically to review and discuss these key instructional questions:

    • What should be taught?

    • What is the appropriate sequencing of content?

    • Which instructional materials are aligned most closely with our goals?

    • How will students be assessed?

    • How can we achieve better results?

    In many schools, teachers collaborate on issues that are of little significance to what occurs in the classroom. The process outlined above ensures that the focus of teacher collaboration is where it should be—immersed in issues of teaching and learning.

Summary

The curriculum is a critical component of a school that functions as a professional learning community. The following principles should guide the work of those who are charged with developing school curricula:

• Teachers should work collaboratively to design a research-based curriculum that reflects the best thinking in each subject area.

• The curriculum should help teachers, students, and parents clarify the specific knowledge, skills, and dispositions that students should acquire as a result of their schooling.

- The curriculum should reduce content and enable all parties to focus on essential and significant learning.

- The curriculum process should enable an individual teacher, a teaching team, and the school to monitor results at the classroom level.

- Curriculum and assessment processes should foster commitment to continuous improvement.

In such a school, the various assessment processes would be aligned with the curriculum and would be used primarily to provide information to individual teachers and teams of teachers so that they can plan appropriate improvement initiatives. The curriculum assessment process should provide a framework for teachers that encourages experimentation and flexibility, yet provides a set of standards that will guide day-to-day instructional decision making and create better opportunities for teaching and learning.

Chapter 9

The Role of the Principal in a Professional Learning Community

Without a competent caring individual in the principal's position, the task of school reform is very difficult. Reform can be initiated from outside the school or stimulated from within. But in the end, it is the principal who implements and sustains the changes through the inevitable roller coaster of euphoria and setbacks.

—Louis Gerstner et al. (1994, p. 133)

Schools are trapped by a leadership dilemma: they require skilled, effective principals in order to outgrow their utter dependence on those principals.

—Tom Donahoe (1993, p. 300)

For almost two decades, educational research has reinforced the importance of the principal in creating the conditions for an effective school (Smith & Andrews, 1989). This body of work reinforced the "Principal Principle": the belief that the principal was the key to the success of a school. Lipham (1981) succinctly states the fundamental premise of this research in the title of his book, *Effective Principal, Effective School.* Conversely, John Goodlad (1984) charges that most schools have been unable to solve their problems because principals lack the prerequisite leadership skills. The general agreement in educational research has been that the best hope for school improvement is to be found in the principal's office.

Some observers, however, have suggested that schools have been too dependent on their principals and that school reform cannot proceed on a wide-scale basis until this dependence is lessened (Donahoe, 1993). The Carnegie Foundation Forum on Education and the Economy (1986), for example, urged that principals be replaced with lead teachers and suggested that schools should be run by committees. Michael Fullan (1993) contends that the "inflated importance of the contemporary principalship" is due to the absence of leadership by teachers. He suggests that "if the learning organization really takes hold, the principalship as we know it may disappear" (p. 75).

Is there a place for a strong principal in the professional learning community? Does asking teachers to redefine their tasks to include leadership roles diminish the need for principals who are effective leaders? While there may be some merit to the allegation that school reform has suffered because educators have demanded too much from their principals and too little from themselves, we believe the principalship is as critical as ever in school improvement efforts. Even the commission that has called for greater professionalization of teaching has recognized the importance of the principal in creating schools that are organized for both student and teacher success. Its findings include a recommendation to "select, prepare, and retain principals who understand teaching and learning and who can lead high performing schools" (National Commission on Teaching and America's Future, 1996, p. 100).

The importance of effective leadership in any change process is well established. It is difficult to imagine implementing and sustaining a school change process through all of the inevitable setbacks and frustrations without strong leadership from a competent principal. Furthermore, if someone in a key leadership position is opposed to change, an improvement initiative is almost certainly doomed to fail (Champy, 1995). Therefore, strong principals are crucial to the creation of learning communities, but the image of how a strong principal operates needs to be reconsidered.

Research on effective schools from the 1970s and 1980s placed principals at the head of school improvement efforts. It described effective principals as those who went beyond "running a tight ship." They were certainly expected to ensure that students were well-behaved, that budgets were tightly managed, and that teacher contracts were observed and maintained. But the strong principals described by the research had definite ideas about teaching and a clear understanding of how their schools should operate. Furthermore, they were more than willing to impose their ideas on their schools.

The model principal that emerged from this research was a strong, forceful, assertive individual who was quick to take the initiative. Effective schools were led by "aggressive," "professionally alert," "dynamic" principals determined to create the schools they deemed necessary, no matter what! The research evoked an image of the principal as John Wayne, swaggering into a school and announcing, "Okay, pilgrims, it's my way or the highway."

This autocratic approach may be well suited to the factory model of schooling, with its assumptions that there is one best way to do things and that it is the leader's job to identify the one best way and then make certain everyone adheres to it. But this autocratic approach is incongruent with the assumptions of a professional learning community. Emerging research on effective schools concludes that principals lead from the center rather than the top (Lezotte, 1997). Ann Lieberman (1995) describes the changing image of the principal this way:

> *The 1990s view of leadership calls for principals to act as partners with teachers, involved in a collaborative quest to examine practices and improve schools. Principals are not expected to control teachers but to support them and to create opportunities for them to grow and develop.* (p. 9)

To have the greatest impact, principals must define their job as helping to create a professional learning community in which teachers can continually collaborate and learn how to become more effective. Principals must recognize that this task demands less command and control and more learning and leading, less dictating and more orchestrating.

Principals can play a key role in creating the conditions that enable schools to become professional learning communities (Louis, Kruse, & Raywid, 1996; Newmann & Wehlage, 1995). But what enables them to lead this transformation? How does one lead a learning community? Answers to these questions can be found in the following characteristics of the principal of a professional learning community:

Principals of professional learning communities lead through shared vision and values rather than through rules and procedures. Principals of a learning community engage the faculty in the co-creation of shared vision and values. They facilitate consensus building and conflict resolution and demonstrate their sincere interest in finding common ground. When their staff members have become collectively committed to shared vision and values, principals then focus on these common hopes and commitments as the driving force in school improvement. Rather than relying on regulations and procedures to screen every decision or to control others, they rely on shared vision and values to give people the direction they need in order to act autonomously. In fact, these principals regard identifying, promoting, and protecting shared vision and values as one of their most important responsibilities.

Principals of professional learning communities involve faculty members in the school's decision-making processes and empower individuals to act. People do not want decrees from their leaders; "They want co-design, co-creation, to arrive at solutions jointly, to own what is developed" (Rolls, 1995, p. 106). Involving others in decision-making processes and empowering them to act on their ideas are two of the most significant and effective strategies used by capable leaders (Kouzes & Posner, 1987). Conversely, when improvement initiatives disintegrate, it is often because the leader made the mistake of trying to effect change alone without building a coalition of collaborators (Kanter, 1983; Kotter, 1996).

Principals of professional learning communities make conscious efforts to promote widespread participation in the decision-making processes of their schools. They understand that they cannot do it alone—that the challenge of leading a school is too complex and that information is too widely distributed for a principal to serve as the school's sole problem-solver. Furthermore, they realize that change initiatives are likely to stall unless staff members feel ownership in the decisions that drive them. As Kanter (1995) writes, "Change is always a threat when it is done to people, but it is an opportunity when it is done by people. The ultimate key in creating pleasure in the hard work of change is . . . to give people the tools and autonomy to make their own contribution to change" (p. 83). To be effective agents of change, principals of learning communities disperse power throughout the school to teaching teams and ad hoc committees. They also avoid the mistake of concentrating power in a school council composed of a small group of teachers, because this would suggest to the rest of the faculty that the responsibility for school improvement resides with a committee rather than with each teacher (Klein et al., 1996). Finally, they give authority for decision making to those closest to the task, and they provide collaborative structures that give teachers the responsibility for identifying and solving their own problems.

While the effective principal of the past was portrayed as a person who knew how to dictate solutions, principals of professional learning communities are more likely to ask questions. They delegate authority, develop collaborative decision-making processes, and step back from being the central problem-solver. Instead, they turn to the professional community for critical decisions (Louis, Kruse, & Marks, 1996). Even if staff members persist in turning to them for all of the answers, these principals are likely to respond with questions such as, "What do you recommend?" or "What information do we need to answer this question, and how can we go about getting it?" In short, they work hard at empowering others.

Principals of professional learning communities provide staff with the information, training, and parameters they need to make good decisions. There is no reason to believe that simply involving teachers in the decision-making process and providing high levels of individual autonomy will improve a school. Principals of learning communities certainly do more than delegate, empower, and then hope for the best. They provide staff members with relevant background information and research findings to help them arrive at informed opinions. They ensure that teachers receive the training to master skills that will help them more effectively achieve the school's goals.

They provide time and create structures for staff reflection and discussion. They supply the data, information, and feedback that enable teams to make the necessary course corrections and improvements to achieve their objectives. They recognize that if teachers are to make informed decisions, they themselves must function as staff developers who focus on creating a school culture that enables educators to grow and learn as integral parts of their standard routines.

Even more important, principals of professional learning communities understand that while they must encourage individual and team autonomy, they must also provide their staff members with guiding principles—criteria teachers can use to assess their decisions and actions. Teachers should not be encouraged simply to do whatever they want. They should be given clear guidelines and boundaries that will help them direct their work on a daily basis.

The critical parameter, the criterion by which all behavior and decision making in the school must be assessed, is this question: Is this action or behavior consistent with our vision and values? While principals of effective learning communities promote autonomy, they are also vigilant, no-nonsense protectors of their schools' vision and values. They use the principles of "loose-tight" leadership. They can be "loose" on the particular strategies teachers use to advance vision and values, but they remain passionately "tight" on the fact that vision and values must be adhered to. They can be "loose" about what means are used to achieve an end, but they are unshakably "tight" on the end that must be achieved. This loose-tight leadership style can effectively be used, of course, only after the school has developed shared vision and values.

Principals who encourage individual autonomy without providing teachers with adequate information, support, and parameters will be making a fundamental error in leadership. Schools that allow each teacher to determine what will be taught, make no effort to monitor results, and provide no feedback on teaching efforts may rank high on the continuum of autonomy, but will never function as learning communities. Principals do not empower others by disempowering themselves. They cannot send the message that everything is acceptable; they must stand for something. First and foremost, they cannot support requests and behavior that are contrary to their schools' vision and values. They cannot limit their role to being middle managers or passive facilitators. They must lead, and this task requires them to be both ardent advocates of teacher autonomy and passionate promoters and protectors of vision and values. Empowered teachers and strong principals are not mutually exclusive goals. Schools that operate as learning communities will have both.

Responding to Resisters

Even in learning communities, principals will inevitably be confronted with those who resist change. In fact, in our work with principals across the country, we have found that the most frequent question that they ask is, "How should I respond to the teachers with bad attitudes, the teachers who resist all of our efforts to improve the school?" Principals often make one of three mistakes as they struggle with this problem.

They pay too much attention to the resisters. While principals should strive to develop vision and values that are embraced by every member of the staff, they must be prepared to settle for less. They can certainly hope that each teacher will be enthusiastic as the school sets sail on an improvement initiative, but if they wait for every teacher to get on board, it is likely that the ship will never leave port. While a strong consensus for vision and values is imperative, consensus does not necessarily mean unanimity. Principals of learning communities solicit input from everyone on the staff and always encourage spirited debate as a school charts its course toward improvement. They also take steps to ensure that differing points of view are presented and considered as the faculty struggles to reach a consensus. But once it is evident that the group supports a particular decision, principals of learning communities insist that everyone, including those who oppose it, act in alignment with it. They focus on advancing the cause rather than agonizing over those who are reluctant to join it.

They vilify resisters. Principals sometimes view themselves as the champions of progress and truth. From their perspective, teachers are either with them or against them. Such principals view teachers who oppose the change initiative as too lazy, too set in their ways, or too stupid to support the cause. Principals of learning communities resist this impulse to label teachers. They recognize that resistance is a natural and understandable human reaction to what people may perceive as disruption. They also realize that trying to eliminate resistance is futile. Throughout the change process, they will welcome and attend to the concerns of resisters. They understand that a willingness to consider different perspectives is critical to a learning community, and they recognize that their response to resisters could have a chilling effect on the atmosphere of freedom in which teachers may openly express a different point of view. While insisting that vision and values are upheld, they legitimize dissent and always seek to learn what lies behind it.

They focus on attitudes rather than on behaviors. A common question from principals concerned about the negative attitude of a staff member is, "What can I say to him that will change his attitude?" The most succinct answer is, "Nothing!" There is no pithy saying or exhortation that is likely to persuade a resister to change his or her attitude. Our attitudes are the result of our experience, and our experience is a product of our behavior. New experiences are needed for us to change our attitudes, and new experiences usually require us to use different behaviors. Thus, the effort to change attitude must begin with the effort to alter behavior in ways that result in new experiences. As psychologist Allen Wheelis (1973) writes, "Since we are what we do, if we want to change what we are, we must begin by changing what we do" (p. 13).

Principals of effective learning communities recognize that the most effective way to change negative attitudes is to focus on behavior. They understand that if they can change what people do, they are providing them with new experiences that can become a catalyst for transforming attitudes.

A high school principal's work with a science teacher illustrates this point. The faculty had adopted a value statement that stated, "We will expect our students to achieve the intended outcomes of our courses, and we will provide evidence of their mastery of those outcomes." The science teacher, Henry, balked at the statement, but it was endorsed over his objection. At the end of the next semester, 48% of his students received a D or F grade in his introductory science course. This distribution was consistent with his grading pattern for over a decade. The principal concluded that this grade distribution was inconsistent with faculty values and decided to discuss the issue with Henry.

The principal tried to present his concern as factually as possible and provided Henry with data, graphs, and charts that demonstrated how skewed these grades were compared to grades given by all of the other teachers who taught the course and all of the other teachers in the department. He demonstrated how the grades of students who had been transferred to Henry's class from other sections of the same course taught by other teachers invariably declined over time. He then reminded Henry of the faculty value statements in the hope that Henry would see the incongruity between the data and the values.

But Henry was still not convinced. Furthermore, Henry made it clear that the principal was in no position to comment on his students' grades because the principal had not spent time in the classroom. He reminded the principal that he had opposed the adoption of the value statements because they made teachers responsible for student success rather than placing the responsibility on the students, where it belonged. He attributed the discrepancy between his grade distribution and that of his colleagues to the fact that he was the sole defender of high standards in the department. Other teachers were inflating grades in order to placate whining students and demanding parents, but he would give only the grades that the students earned. He concluded that it was unlikely that the grades for his students would improve because students were generally lazy and unwilling to put in the effort necessary to be successful in his course.

The principal responded neither by denouncing Henry nor by urging him to change his attitude. Instead, he explained that Henry's approach was contrary to the commitments endorsed by the faculty and that some changes were in order. He directed Henry to present him with a copy of every lesson plan before it was taught to students. These plans were to stipulate the intended outcome for each lesson as well as the strategies Henry intended to use to enhance the clarity of the lesson and to check for student understanding. Henry was also to review every lab exercise, quiz, test, review sheet, and exam with the principal before distributing them to students in order to demonstrate that his assessments were aligned with his teaching. The principal advised Henry that he would be spending considerable time in Henry's classroom in order to provide him with timely feedback on his teaching methods and procedures. He concluded the conference by reminding Henry that the faculty had identified the commitments teachers must make if the school was to improve, and that it was imperative that Henry honor those commitments.

The principal put this plan into action immediately and monitored it carefully. Henry responded initially with anger and resentment. Over the course of the year, however, his students seemed to benefit from his newfound attention to clarity, more frequent checks for understanding, and the greater congruity between what he was teaching and testing. The principal encouraged Henry's efforts to incorporate the new strategies. He used the classroom observations as an opportunity to provide feedback on those efforts and frequently commended the improvements he was witnessing. Student grades improved dramatically. The students' success in Henry's class seemed to have a positive effect on their attentiveness and effort. For the first time, Henry's students outperformed the total group on the common, comprehensive exam at the end of the semester. These were new experiences for Henry—experiences that, over time, led to the softening of many of his negative attitudes.

This principal provides an excellent example of an appropriate response to resisters. He did not put the school's improvement initiative on hold because Henry was unwilling to endorse it. The initiative proceeded. Neither did he denigrate Henry for his opinions. He treated him with respect, even while he insisted that Henry make some changes. Most importantly, he focused on Henry's behavior rather than his attitude. He worked with Henry to change some important teaching behaviors in the hope of achieving different results that could motivate Henry to reexamine some of his earlier assumptions. While attitude is difficult to monitor, behavior is not. The principal could easily observe and evaluate changes in behavior, and that gave him an opportunity to reinforce some of the changes that occurred.

This strategy does not, of course, eliminate the natural frustration of working with those who are negative. It does not ensure conversions to the consensus view. It does, however, offer the best hope both for advancing an improvement initiative and for recruiting resisters to follow that initiative.

Finally, it is important to note that principals of successful learning communities do not hesitate to confront violations of the commitments articulated in shared visions and values. If the principal in this situation had been unwilling to discuss this issue with Henry, his inaction would have undermined his credibility within the entire school community. Faculty members would have concluded that the principal cared more about avoiding confrontation than about the collective commitment to improving their school. To be perceived by teachers as serious about change, principals must care enough to confront.

Principals of learning communities establish credibility by modeling behavior that is congruent with the vision and values of their school. Peter Drucker (1992) offers a succinct syllogism on leadership: "A leader, by definition, is someone who has followers" (p. 122). Without credibility and trust, there are no followers. Therefore, leaders must establish their credibility and earn the trust of others. For over two decades, James Kouzes and Barry Posner (1996) have received a consistent response when asking people what they look for in a leader—credibility. As they conclude:

> We want leaders who are credible. We must be able to believe in them. We must believe their word can be trusted, that they are personally excited and enthusiastic about the direction in which we are headed, and that they have the knowledge and skill to lead. We call it the first law of leadership: "If you don't believe in the messenger you won't believe the message." (p. 103)

Trust is certainly "the glue that holds organizations together" (Bennis & Townsend, 1995, p. 61). Principals of professional learning communities acquire trust the old-fashioned way—they earn it. They deliver on promises. They impose on themselves the highest standard of congruence between their words and deeds. They are consistent and predictable. They establish and focus on their priorities instead of flitting from innovation to innovation or defining their jobs as "putting out fires." They demonstrate conviction and courage by their willingness to stand up for their beliefs. They model the attitudes, behaviors, and commitments that they call upon others to demonstrate. They admit mistakes and change their behavior when necessary. They maintain their composure and respond professionally even in times of crisis or heightened emotions. They demonstrate competence in fulfilling the various responsibilities of their position. They understand that a well-intentioned visionary who cannot maintain a safe and orderly school environment will not earn the confidence of his or her faculty. But most important, principals of professional learning communities earn the trust of their staffs by adhering to the "golden rule of leadership . . . do what you say you will do" (Kouzes & Posner, 1996, p. 107).

Principals of learning communities are results-oriented. Schools are unlikely to develop the results orientation of a learning community without principals who are fixated on results. Effective leaders go beyond declaring intent: they turn aspirations into actions. They have an impatience that is born of urgency and are driven to "get on with it." They recognize that the ultimate test of a leader is results (Ulrich, 1996). Thus, principals of successful learning communities work with their staffs to articulate clear and measurable goals, to identify indicators that offer evidence of progress, and to develop systems for monitoring those indicators on a continuous basis. They are hungry for facts and constantly in search of meaningful data. They analyze results critically rather than resorting to "happy talk" and a search for a silver lining in data that suggest dark clouds. Tracy Kidder (1989) offers an excellent example of such "happy talk" in recounting a principal's speech to the faculty after learning that the students of their school had some of the worst scores in the state on a standardized test:

> I don't want to hear about test scores any more. I know what kids we got here. We can't bring them up to grade level no matter what we do. But can we improve instruction here? You bet we can. And we're doin' a good job. We really are. (p. 199)

If the principal of a school disregards, dismisses, or denies data that suggest a problem, there is little hope that the school will ever function as a professional learning community. Schools will become results-oriented and committed to continuous improvement only if principals use accumulated evidence to inform practice, celebrate success, and identify areas that need ongoing attention.

Living with Paradox

Michael Fullan contends that research on leadership has failed to provide the specificity and practical applications that offer clear direction even to well-intentioned principals. As he writes, "Principals who reviewed this literature in the hope of enhancing their effectiveness would be hard pressed to answer the question, 'so what do I do now, where do I start?'" (Fullan, 1995, p. 705). The complexity of the position makes it impossible to offer a simple guide to success. Principals must live with paradox—two competing demands that pull them in seemingly opposite directions. They must have a sense of urgency about improving their schools that is balanced by the patience that will sustain them over the long haul. They must focus on the future but must also remain grounded in the reality of the present. They must have both a long-term view and a keen, up-close focus on the present. They must be both "loose" and "tight" in their leadership style, encouraging autonomy while at the same time demanding adherence to shared vision and values. They must celebrate successes while perpetuating discontent with the status quo. They must be strong leaders who empower others.

Although it is impossible to reduce the conundrum of the principalship to a simple, step-by-step recipe, principals who are committed to helping their schools function as professional learning communities should keep the following 10 guidelines in mind:

1. **Attend to the building blocks of a professional learning community.** The effort to create a professional learning community must be based on a sense of shared mission, vision, values, and goals. Chapters 4 and 5 offer advice on how to address these topics.

2. **Communicate the importance of mission, vision, values, and goals on a daily basis.** A staff will come to regard mission, vision, values, and goals as meaningful and important only if the principal pays attention to them on a daily basis. Chapter 6 presents a communications audit that principals can use to assess the clarity of their communication.

3. **Create collaborative structures with a focus on teaching and learning.** One of the most consistent findings of the research on school improvement is the critical role that collaborative cultures play in the improvement process. Principals must build schools around collaborative teams that engage in a constant cycle of reflection, planning, experimentation, analysis of results, and

adaptation. They must provide teams with time for collaboration, a clear purpose, and the training and support that team members need to effectively collaborate. These issues are also addressed in Chapter 6.

4. **Shape the school culture to support a professional learning community.** The work of leading is the work of shaping organizational culture, and principals are uniquely situated to change the culture of their schools. They can help the faculty articulate the shared values that describe the intended culture in action. They can ask questions that prompt reflective dialogue among teachers. They can be the chief storytellers for their schools. Teddy Roosevelt's description of the presidency as a "bully pulpit" applies to the principalship as well. Principals can inundate their staff members with stories that illustrate the culture of a professional learning community. Finally, they can use celebration, ceremony, and ritual to remind staff members of what is valued and important in their school. Chapter 7 offers suggestions for shaping culture.

5. **Foster an approach to curriculum that focuses on learning rather than teaching.** A focus on learning rather than a focus on teaching represents a fundamental shift in the teacher-student relationship and causes significant changes in the daily operation of a school. Principals encourage this focus on learning when they work with teachers to establish processes that not only clarify what students must know and be able to do, but also clarify the strategies that enable the school to make valid conclusions regarding the degree of student learning. Chapter 8 addresses the issue of a learner-focused curriculum.

6. **Encourage teachers to think of themselves as leaders.** Great teachers demonstrate the qualities of great leaders— a clear sense of what must be accomplished, a gift for communication, an ability to motivate and inspire others, and a willingness to accept responsibility for results. Principals must foster this image of the teacher as a leader and demonstrate that they regard teachers as fellow leaders rather than as subordinates. The concept of teacher as leader is discussed in greater detail in Chapter 10.

7. **Practice enlightened leadership strategies.** Principals of learning communities use the concepts and strategies of shared decision making, individual and team empowerment, and "loose-tight" leadership described in this chapter. They do not regard the resistance of some faculty members as a reason for postponing an improvement initiative if there is clear consensus to proceed. They listen carefully to the concerns of resisters and strive to understand their perspectives. If change is in order, they focus on changing behavior rather than attitudes, knowing that attitudes are more likely to change when teachers have new experiences as a result of their new behavior.

8. **Establish personal credibility.** Principals of professional learning communities deliver on promises. They act in accordance with the attitudes, behaviors, and commitments that they ask others to demonstrate. They demonstrate competence in managerial tasks. They are consistent and predictable. They sustain focus on a few priorities, admit mistakes, and change behavior when necessary. They maintain composure and respond professionally even in times of crisis and heightened emotions.

9. **Be fixated on results.** Principals of learning communities work with their staff members to articulate clear and measurable goals, identify indicators that offer evidence of progress, and develop systems for monitoring those indicators on a continuous basis. They use the evidence to inform practice, celebrate successes, and identify areas that need further attention.

10. **Recognize that continuous improvement requires continuous learning.** Principals of professional learning communities understand that the continuous improvement of a school requires ongoing learning on the part of all the people within it. Therefore, they are committed to the professional development and renewal of each staff member. They are attentive to the content, process, and context of effective professional development practices. They help to establish external resources and networks that support and stimulate innovation in the school. They work with staff to ensure that opportunities for learning are not limited to special events or programs but rather are embedded in the daily work routine. They understand that developing the ability of others is one of their most important responsibilities. Chapter 12 addresses the issue of ongoing professional development in a professional learning community.

National Standards for Principals

The need for the collaborative processes that are endemic to a professional learning community does not diminish the need for effective leadership. In recognition of that fact, the Interstate School Leaders Licensure Consortium (ISLLC), acting under the auspices of the Council of Chief State School Officers, has adopted national performance standards for school leaders. Although the standards are stated in general terms, each one is accompanied by more specific comments on the knowledge, dispositions, and performances that indicate the standard is being met. According to ISLLC (1996), every school administrator is to serve as an educational leader who promotes the success of all students by:

- Facilitating the development, articulation, implementation, and stewardship of a vision of learning that is shared and supported by the school community.

- Advocating, nurturing, and sustaining a school culture and instructional program conducive to student learning and staff professional growth.

- Ensuring management of the organization, operations, and resources for a safe, efficient, and effective learning environment.

- Collaborating with families and community members, responding to diverse community interests and needs, and mobilizing community resources.

- Acting with integrity, fairness, and in an ethical manner.

- Understanding, responding to, and influencing the larger political, social, economic, legal, and cultural context.

The work of the ISLLC represents the first effort to articulate national standards for school administrators. Both the general standards and the more specific statements of knowledge, dispositions, and performances that support those standards are consistent with the principles of a professional learning community. Principals and administrative teams that hope to create professional learning communities in their schools should consider these standards seriously.

Dr. Kay Awalt was recognized by the United States Department of Education as a National Distinguished Principal in 1996. She offers the following reflection on the role of the principal in building a professional learning community.

Reflections by Kay Awalt
1996 National Distinguished Principal

Early in my administrative career, a principal friend engaged me in ongoing debate about the proper role of the principal. I proposed that the job required people who functioned as instructional leaders while she insisted that principals should view their position as building managers. She was tenacious in her efforts to convince this neophyte in the proper "ways of the principalship." Finally, relying on all the assertiveness I could gather, I turned to her and said, "I am sorry, but this is one area that you and I just cannot agree on. I happen to believe that a principal should be an instructional leader." That ended our debate. From that day on, while she focused on developing her skills as a manager, I concentrated on developing my ability to function as a leader. I have never regretted that decision!

Throughout my career as a principal, I worked with, learned with, and grew with teachers as we struggled to improve our school. We often had more questions than answers as we attempted to find the best ways to make a difference in the lives of our students. As I reflect on that experience, it is comforting to realize that we were doing what this book is advocating—empowering teachers, working collaboratively, and focusing on improved results. Yes, we made some mistakes, but we made them together and supported each other in our successes and failures. Successes were celebrated; failures were "windows" to better ways.

Although I was more likely to pose questions than to issue directives or make unilateral decisions, I considered myself a leader. I developed a philosophy of informing, involving, and leading. I made a conscious effort to keep staff informed of the challenges we were facing, current research for addressing those challenges, and the progress we were making. I was committed to involving teachers in goal setting and problem solving. We developed an advisory council of parents and teachers to give the school direction. We formed committees and divided responsibilities as we opened a new school and focused on its continuous improvement. We learned to conduct joint interviews and work together in determining who would join our staff. Above all, I tried to be a leader who served others, and service is what leadership is all about. Whatever I could do to enable teachers to reach their potential, I tried to accomplish. In my mind, developing others is the real challenge of leadership.

I can attest to the fact that school improvement does not happen overnight. It is a steady, constant examining of the concerns of parents, teachers, students, and the community. Some of our most productive ideas came from a combination of surveys, oral feedback, discussions of our advisory councils, and suggestions "outside the box." I learned to listen and to distinguish between practices and principles. I was willing to consider changes in almost any practice if we could identify a more promising idea, but in matters of principle I was committed to staying the course. In retrospect, I realize that I practiced the "loose" and "tight" leadership that the authors reference in this chapter. Did this approach make us a perfect school? No, but we were continually moving a good school toward becoming a better school.

When I attended the awards ceremony for the National Distinguished Principals program, I listened to principal after principal from all over the United States deliver the same message. Each indicated that his or her selection for the award would not have been possible without the efforts of parents, students, community leaders, and, above all, the teachers back home. That ceremony provided powerful evidence that principals cannot transform a school through their individual efforts. The effectiveness of a school is directly linked to its ability to create a learning community. Schools that are proactive, seeking, questioning, and curious will improve. That's a promise!

Summary

Principals cannot transform a school through their individual efforts. Creating a professional learning community is a collective effort, but that effort has little chance of success without effective leadership from the principal. Although past images of the principalship have focused on principals who were strong, assertive, and forceful leaders, the more promising contemporary view calls for principals who can work collaboratively with others in building consensus. This chapter describes five characteristics of effective principals and offers ten suggestions that can help principals integrate the different elements of a professional learning community. It summarizes the national standards for school leaders developed by the Interstate School Leaders Licensure Consortium and concludes with reflections on the principalship from a National Distinguished Principal.

Chapter 10

Teaching in a Professional Learning Community

Community begins with a shared vision. It's sustained by teachers who, as school leaders, bring inspiration and direction to the institution. Who, after all, knows more about the classroom? Who is better able to inspire children? Who can evaluate, more sensitively, the educational progress of each student? And who but teachers create a true community for learning? Teachers are, without question, the heartbeat of a successful school.

—Ernest Boyer (1995, p. 31)

The bottom line is that there is just no way to create good schools without good teachers. Those who have worked to improve education over the last decade have learned that school reform cannot be "teacher-proofed." Success in any aspect of reform—whether it is creating standards, developing more challenging curriculum and assessments, implementing school-based management, or inventing new model schools and programs—depends on highly skilled teachers working in supportive schools that engender collaboration with families and communities.

—*What Matters Most: Teaching for America's Future*
(National Commission on Teaching and
America's Future, 1996, pp. 9–10)

I t is no accident that the word "professional" appears in the title of this book. Ultimately, the success of any initiative to create a learning community will depend upon the competence and commitment of the professionals in that school, particularly its teachers. Schools are effective because of their teachers, not in spite of them. Even the most well-conceived improvement programs fall flat if teachers lack the skills to implement them. Teachers must bring the principles of the learning community to life in their individual classrooms. Situated in the classroom—the critical focal point of the learning community—teachers are essential to any meaningful reform effort and are in the best position to have a positive impact on the lives of children. As Lee Shulman (1996) writes:

> *The teacher must remain the key. . . . Debates over educational policy are moot if the primary agents of instruction are incapable of performing their functions well. No microcomputer will replace them, no television system will clone and distribute them, no scripted lessons will direct and control them, no voucher system will bypass them.* (p. 5)

Yet, despite the critical importance of teachers to the effectiveness of a school, the factory model has traditionally regarded teachers as functionaries rather than as professionals. Professions such as medicine, law, accounting, or architecture have structures in place to ensure the competence of their members. Candidates must graduate from an accredited professional school that provides current knowledge and effective training practices. Only those who can pass challenging licensing examinations that test their knowledge and skill are allowed to practice. Then, to qualify for advanced certification, they must devote years of additional study and practice in preparation for rigorous performance tests that measure their ability to meet increasingly demanding standards of competence. Accountants, for example, must pass stringent qualifying examinations in order to be designated as certified public accountants; similarly, doctors must qualify for board certification in their areas of specialty. All of these professionals are expected to remain current in their fields throughout their careers.

But existing practices for teaching stand in sharp contrast to the structures and standards of other professions. Accreditation is not required of teacher education programs, and only about 500 of the 1,200 teacher education programs in the United States have received professional accreditation through the National Council for Accreditation of Teacher Education (NCATE). Roughly one in four American teachers lacks the qualifications for his or her job. More than 12% of new hires enter the classroom without any formal training, and another 14% arrive without fully meeting state standards. Nearly a quarter of all secondary school teachers do not have even a minor in the area of their main teaching assignment (National Commission on Teaching and America's Future, 1996). As the national commission charged to examine this problem concludes:

> *Although no state will permit a person to write wills, practice medicine, fix plumbing, or style hair without completing training and passing an examination, more than forty states allow districts to hire teachers who have not met these basic requirements. Most states pay more attention to the qualifications of veterinarians treating America's cats and dogs than to*

*those of the people educating the nation's children
and youth.*

—National Commission on Teaching and
America's Future (1996, p. 9)

Traditionally, those who have entered the teaching profession have had little opportunity for advancement unless they have left the classroom. Entering novices have exactly the same responsibilities as 30-year veterans. Furthermore, in many states there is absolutely no requirement for advanced training once a teacher has received initial certification. The only requirement to retain a teaching certificate in these states is a minimal annual fee. Teaching is a profession in need of professionalization.

An effective framework for this professionalization has been developed by the National Commission on Teaching and America's Future (1996):

> *The first priority is reaching agreement on what teachers should know and be able to do to help students succeed. Unaddressed for decades, this task has recently been completed by three professional bodies, the National Council for the Accreditation of Teacher Education (NCATE), the Interstate New Teacher Assessment and Support Consortium (INTASC), and the National Board for Professional Teaching Standards (NBPTS). Their combined efforts to set the standards for teacher education, beginning teacher licensing, and advanced certification outline a continuum of teachers' development throughout their careers. (p. 18)*

The framework for the professionalization of teaching includes the following:

Accreditation. All teacher preparation programs should be required to meet NCATE standards. Programs that do not meet these basic standards should be closed.

Licensing. All beginning teachers should be required to meet the standards identified by INTASC in order to receive an initial teaching license. These standards specify what beginning teachers should know and be able to do as they enter the profession. New teachers should also be provided with an expert mentor as they begin their career.

Certification. The teaching profession should be based on a continuum of expertise that uses the standards established by NBPTS as benchmarks for performance. Teachers should have the opportunity to qualify for advanced certification based on their ability to meet these standards, and they should also be rewarded for doing so. All teachers should be expected to update their skills throughout their careers, and ongoing professional development should be a part of their daily work through joint planning, study groups, peer coaching, and research.

The standards articulated in this framework advance the concept of the school as a professional learning community and emphasize the critical role of the teacher within that community. They demand the attention of educators. Professional teachers should study the INTASC and NBPTS standards intensely and then should use them as benchmarks when reflecting on their own performance. The following brief summaries are presented to stimulate further exploration and inquiry into these landmark documents for the teaching profession.

INTASC Standards

The Interstate New Teacher Assessment and Support Consortium has established both performance standards for beginning teachers and examinations to measure these standards. The consortium is based on 10 principles, which in turn extend to three sets of standards: knowledge standards, disposition standards, and performance standards. The 10 INTASC principles are listed below.

1. The teacher understands the central concepts, tools of inquiry, and structures of the discipline(s) he or she teaches and can create learning experiences that make these aspects of subject matter meaningful for students.

2. The teacher understands how children learn and develop, and can provide learning opportunities that support their intellectual, social, and personal development.

3. The teacher understands how students differ in their approaches to learning, and can create instructional opportunities that are adapted to diverse learners.

4. The teacher understands and uses a variety of instructional strategies to encourage students' development of critical-thinking, problem-solving, and performance skills.

5. The teacher uses an understanding of individual and group motivation and behavior to create a learning environment that encourages positive social interaction, active engagement in learning, and self-motivation.

6. The teacher uses knowledge of effective verbal, non-verbal, and media communication techniques to foster active inquiry, collaboration, and supportive interaction in the classroom.

7. The teacher plans instruction based on knowledge of subject matter, students, the community, and curriculum goals.

8. The teacher understands and uses formal and informal assessment strategies to evaluate and ensure the continuous intellectual, social, and physical development of the learner.

9. The teacher is a reflective practitioner who continually evaluates the effects of his or her choices and actions on others (students, parents, and other professionals in the learning community) and who actively seeks out opportunities to grow professionally.

10. The teacher fosters relationships with school colleagues, parents, and agencies in the larger community to support students' learning and well-being.

These principles and their companion standards represent an important resource for helping new teachers as they enter the profession. The principles can also serve as the basis for a faculty's collaborative dialogue on teaching. Finally, they represent a useful tool both for individual self-evaluation and for the formal evaluation processes of a school.

NBPTS Standards

While INTASC set entry-level standards for teachers, the National Board of Professional Teaching Standards was established in 1987 to certify experienced teachers. The standards developed by the board are based on a set of general principles as well as discipline-specific standards that focus on the knowledge, skills, dispositions, and professional judgments of a teacher. These areas are assessed through a variety of means, including portfolios, videotapes, and exercises designed to assess the teaching practices of each candidate for certification.

While NBPTS has succeeded in establishing rigorous benchmarks and assessment procedures that give teachers an opportunity to be nationally certified, its process is so extensive and expensive that it is unrealistic to make NBPTS certification a career goal for all experienced teachers. The National Commission on Teaching and America's Future confirmed that the NBPTS process could not impact teachers on a wide-scale basis when the board established the goal of certifying only one teacher in each school district in the nation over the next decade. There is little to suggest that national certification for a single teacher will have a significant impact on a school district or school. However, the standards articulated by NBPTS could and should drive the efforts of local schools and school districts to enhance the performance of all of their teachers.

The core propositions of NBPTS include the following:

Teachers are committed to students and their learning. Board-certified teachers are dedicated to making knowledge accessible to all students. They act on the belief that all students can learn. They treat students equitably, recognizing the individual differences that distinguish their students from one another and considering these differences in their practice. They adjust their practices as needed, based on observation and knowledge of their students' interests, abilities, skills, knowledge, family circumstances, and peer relationships.

Accomplished teachers understand how students develop and learn. They incorporate the prevailing theories of cognition and intelligence into their practice. They are aware of the influence of context and culture on behavior. They develop students' cognitive capacity and their respect for learning. Equally important, they foster students' self-esteem, motivation, character, and civic responsibility and their students' respect for individual, cultural, religious, and racial differences.

Teachers know the subjects they teach and how to teach those subjects to students. Board-certified teachers have a rich understanding of the subject(s) they teach and of how knowledge in their subject is created, organized, linked to other disciplines, and applied in real-world settings. While faithfully representing the collective wisdom of our culture and upholding the value of disciplinary knowledge, they also develop the critical and analytical capacities of their students.

Accomplished teachers have a command of the specialized knowledge of how to convey and reveal subject matter to students. They are aware of the preconceptions and background knowledge that students typically bring to each subject and of strategies and instructional materials that can be of assistance. They understand where difficulties are likely to occur, and they modify their practice accordingly. Their instructional repertoire allows them to create multiple paths to the subjects they teach, and they are adept at helping students learn how to pose questions and find answers to solve their own problems.

Teachers are responsible for managing and monitoring student learning. Board-certified teachers create, enrich, maintain, and alter instructional settings to capture and sustain the interest of their students and to make the most effective use of time. They also are adept at enlisting their colleagues' knowledge and expertise to complement their own.

Accomplished teachers command a range of generic instructional techniques, know when each is appropriate, and can implement them as needed. They are as aware of ineffectual or damaging practice as they are devoted to effective and elegant practice.

They know how to engage groups of students to ensure a disciplined learning environment, and they know how to organize instruction to meet the schools' goals for students. They are adept at setting norms for social interaction among students and between students and teachers. They understand how to motivate students to learn and how to maintain their interest even in the face of temporary failure.

Board-certified teachers can assess the progress of individual students as well as that of the class as a whole. They employ multiple methods for measuring student growth and understanding and can clearly explain student performance to parents.

Teachers think systematically about their practice and learn from experience. Board-certified teachers are models of educated persons who exemplify the virtues they seek to inspire in students: curiosity, tolerance, honesty, fairness, respect for diversity, and appreciation of cultural differences. Such teachers also exemplify the abilities their students must demonstrate if they are to grow intellectually: the ability to reason and consider multiple perspectives, to be creative and take risks, and to adopt an experimental and problem-solving orientation.

Accomplished teachers use their knowledge of human development, subject matter, and instruction and their understanding of their students to make principled judgments about sound practice. Their decisions are not only grounded in the literature, but also in their experience. They engage in lifelong learning, which they seek to encourage in their students.

Striving to strengthen their teaching, board-certified teachers critically examine their practice, seek to expand their repertoire, deepen their knowledge, sharpen their judgment, and adapt their teaching to new findings, ideas, and theories.

Teachers are members of learning communities. Board-certified teachers contribute to the effectiveness of their schools by working collaboratively with other professionals on instructional policy, curriculum development, and staff development. They can evaluate school progress and the allocation of school resources in light of their understanding of state and local educational objectives. They are knowledgeable about specialized school and community resources that can be engaged for their students' benefit, and are skilled at employing such resources as needed.

Accomplished teachers find ways to work collaboratively and creatively with parents, engaging them productively in the work of the school (National Board for Professional Teaching Standards, 1994, pp. 7–8).

This brief summary of the work of INTASC and NBPTS is not intended to provide a comprehensive overview of their findings, but rather to reinforce the fact that professional benchmarks have, at long last, been established for teaching. Members of a professional learning community will strive to uphold the highest standards of their profession. The work of INTASC and NBPTS simply articulates these high standards and offers educators a continuum of professional development to guide them throughout their teaching careers. Currently, this work has received scant attention from practicing educators; in fact, most do not know these standards exist. One of the distinguishing characteristics of a professional learning community will be the collective attention that is given to analyzing and advancing the highest standards of the profession.

The Practice of Teaching

Those who devote their careers to the legal and medical professions often describe their experience in terms of "practice." It is quite common to hear the phrase, "I have been practicing medicine for 20 years." The term "practice" in this context suggests a recognition that a professional must be a lifelong learner constantly seeking ways to become more effective in his or her field. When educators refer to "practice teaching," however, they are typically referring to the nine-week period in their senior year of college during which they were expected to learn everything there is to know about teaching.

If teachers are to help transform their schools into professional learning communities, they must recognize their obligation to continue to "practice" and to explore the art and science of teaching for their entire careers. Furthermore, they must conduct the practice of their profession in ways that will distinguish them from their more conventional colleagues. Chapter 2 discusses some of these key differences: making a commitment to shared mission, vision, values, and goals; engaging in collective inquiry; working in collaborative teams; experimenting; making a commitment to both personal and organizational improvement; and focusing on results. These differences are crucial, and if they are "practiced" effectively, they will change the art of teaching in six significant ways.

1. Professional teachers emphasize learning rather than teaching. The focus of traditional schools is teaching; the focus of the professional learning community is student learning. The difference is much more than semantics. It represents a fundamental shift in the teacher-student relationship. This new relationship would not allow for the familiar teacher lament, "I taught it—they just did not learn it."

Professional teaching requires much more than presentation or coverage of material. It requires learning that is both measurable and measured. Teachers in professional learning communities recognize that teaching has not occurred until learning has occurred, and they act accordingly. Their emphasis, therefore, is not simply on covering material but rather on engaging students in the consideration of essential content in ways that will help them develop a deep understanding of that content. The traditional teacher responds to a student who has failed to learn by asking, "What is wrong with this student?" Professional teachers ask, "How could the content or instructional strategies be modified so that the student can learn what was intended?" (Schlechty, 1997, p. 146). This attentiveness to student learning is one of the core characteristics of schools with strong professional communities (Louis, Kruse, & Marks, 1996, p. 181).

2. Professional teachers emphasize active student engagement with significant content. Professional teachers recognize the importance of students becoming actively engaged with significant content. Learning involves action, and most of what students learn comes from what they do. Yet the challenge confronting teachers is not simply to ensure that students are engaged in tasks. Teachers have always assigned tasks to students. The real question is how to engage students in the exploration of significant content in real and meaningful ways over the sustained period of time that is necessary for students to reach high levels of proficiency.

Professional teachers meet this challenge in two ways. First, they avoid the trivialization of content and focus on the most essential and significant content. Second, they create a classroom environment in which learners are actively engaged in acquiring knowledge and applying it in meaningful situations.

Phil Schlechty (1997) contends that teachers can create an environment of active student engagement if they design work and activities that are characterized by the following properties:

- The work or activity is product-focused.

- The standards for assessing the product(s) associated with the activity are clear to students, and the students find them compelling.

- Students are provided with opportunities to fall short of the standards on initial tries without suffering adverse consequences.

- The work is designed so that student performances are affirmed.

- The work is designed so that affiliation with others is encouraged and supported.

- Novelty and variety are present in the task structure.

- The work is designed so that students have choice in what they do, although this does not mean they have choice in what they learn.

- The tasks have a sense of realness and authenticity about them.

- Knowledge and information are integrated as opposed to segmented.

- The content presented is rich and significant. (p. 170–171)

3. Professional teachers focus on student performance and production. Traditional teachers develop their plans with a focus on their own activities: "First, I will present an overview. Then I will lecture." However, teachers in professional learning communities develop plans that focus on what their students will be doing. Their emphasis is on student performance and production in a real-world context. As David Perkins (1992) argues, student understanding implies not only that students possess certain knowledge, but also that they they are able to do something with the knowledge they have gained. In schools that function as professional learning communities, students are asked to do the work of scientists, musicians, business entrepreneurs, politicians, mathematicians, attorneys, novelists, physicians, designers, historians, critics, etc. (Newmann et al., 1996).

This emphasis on doing means that students are expected to produce a polished product using the performance criteria of the discipline as a standard. Exhibitions, demonstrations, portfolios, and projects are commonplace. Instead of asking, "What will I be doing?" teachers in professional learning communities are more likely to ask such questions as, "How can the performances and products be made more authentic?" "What standards should students be expected to meet?" and "What audiences should review and critique student work?" Authentic, meaningful performance thus becomes a central tenet of their efforts to develop curriculum and assess student achievement. Furthermore, this tenet motivates students because it addresses such questions as, "Why are we doing this?" and "What are we to accomplish?"

4. Professional teachers routinely collaborate with their colleagues. The point that a collaborative culture is a *sine qua non* of a professional learning community has been made repeatedly throughout this book; however, a chapter on professional teaching must reinforce that point once again. While traditional teachers labor in isolation, the teachers of a professional learning community share ideas about practice.

Furthermore, teachers in a professional learning community recognize their obligation to work together on schoolwide issues. They take an interest in the entire school. They recognize that the solutions to some school problems require collective action, and they accept personal and professional responsibility for contributing to those solutions. This willingness to examine issues outside of individual classrooms and to seek solutions together is a major factor in the success of a professional learning community. As Donahoe (1993) writes:

> *Every member of the teaching and classified staff must have an active role in restructuring for school improvement. Schools that restructure by forming a representative executive committee or leadership council do not significantly change the isolated roles of teachers within the organization. Schools are small enough to function as a form of direct rather than representative democracy.* (p. 300)

When teachers are not involved in the decision-making processes of their schools, the atmosphere of detachment and isolation that erodes the profession is reinforced. Collaborative processes not only result in better decisions but also foster the sense of community that is an integral part of school improvement.

5. Professional teachers are students of teaching and consumers of research. Professionals in any field are expected to stay current—to learn about emerging concepts of "best practice." But they are not expected to suspend their professional judgment and embrace every new theory or idea that is presented. New concepts warrant consideration, experimentation, debate, and assessment before they become part of standard practice. The ongoing analysis of advances in research on curriculum and teaching is vitally important in improving schools; however, this analysis requires that teachers function both as "students of teaching" and as "consumers of research."

Many schools offer extensive professional libraries that are well stocked with books and journals reporting on current educational research. But simply providing teachers with access to timely materials and current research findings is not enough. Schools that function as professional learning communities create systematic processes to facilitate the consideration of research findings either by the entire faculty or by groups of teachers.

The consumer-validation approach to educational research (Eaker & Huffman, 1980) is an example of one such system. It is based on the premise that teachers should test an innovation in their classrooms before they embrace it, and it calls for teachers to act as "investigators" of research before becoming its "consumers." The consumer-validation procedure includes three steps:

1. *Research reporting seminars.* The primary purpose of these seminars is to provide a small group of teachers with a clear understanding of research findings on a particular topic, such as time on task, questioning strategies, or classroom management. The findings are synthesized and presented as clearly and concisely as possible. Teachers are then invited to brainstorm specific activities or strategies for implementing the research findings in their classrooms.

2. *Classroom implementation.* During the next three to four weeks after the seminars, teachers apply the research by initiating some of the strategies or activities that were identified in the brainstorming sessions. Then teachers are asked to reflect on and evaluate the results of their efforts. Forms are provided to help teachers describe the activities and strategies they tried and to record their reactions to what occurred.

3. *Sharing sessions.* In this final stage, the seminar groups reconvene, and teachers share their findings. These sessions serve several important purposes. First, the pooling of information provides teachers with new ideas to try in their own classrooms. Second, the sessions are motivational because the "testimonial" of a colleague is of tremendous value in motivating teachers. Finally, the sessions provide teachers with a forum for discussing teaching practices with each other.

A number of sources can be used to stimulate this kind of analysis and to encourage dialogue about teaching. The *Handbook of Research on Improving Student Achievement* (Cawelti, 1995) offers a summary of both generic and discipline-based teaching practices that are correlated with student achievement. In *The Quality School,* William Glasser (1992) applies the principles of total quality management to the classroom and suggests six conditions for quality school work. *Teaching from a Research Knowledge Base* (Bellon, Bellon, & Blank, 1992) provides an excellent review of the research on effective teaching and includes over 100 classroom scenarios to help bridge the gap between research and practice. The *Effective Schools Research Abstract Series,* published monthly by Effective Schools Products, reviews recent research findings related to school improvement and classroom instruction. The research is presented in jargon-free terminology that summarizes what the researchers did, what they found, and the implications for school improvement.

The Northwest Regional Educational Laboratory (1990b) offers a summary of classroom characteristics and practices associated with improvements in student performance. The findings of this concise report are presented below as an example of the wealth of information that is available to teachers who are willing to seriously discuss their work.

Instruction is guided by a preplanned curriculum.

Learning goals and objectives are developed and prioritized according to district and building guidelines, selected or approved by teachers, sequenced to facilitate student learning, and organized or grouped into units or lessons.

Unit or lesson objectives are set in a timeline so that the calendar can be used for instructional planning.

Instructional resources and teaching activities are identified, matched to objectives and student developmental levels, and then recorded in lesson plans. Alternative resources and activities are identified, especially for priority objectives.

Resources and teaching activities are reviewed for content and appropriateness and are modified according to experience to increase their effectiveness in helping students learn.

Students are carefully oriented to lessons.

Teachers help students get ready to learn. They explain lesson objectives in simple language and refer to the objectives regularly throughout lessons in order to maintain focus.

Objectives may be posted or handed out to help students maintain a sense of direction.

Teachers check to see that objectives are understood.

The relationship of a current lesson to previous study is described. Students are reminded of key concepts or skills previously covered.

Students are challenged to learn, particularly at the onset of difficult lessons. Students know in advance what is expected and are ready to learn.

Instruction is clear and focused.

Lesson activities are previewed; clear written and verbal directions are given; key points and instructions are repeated; student understanding is checked.

Presentations, such as lectures or demonstrations, are designed to communicate clearly to students; digressions are avoided.

Students have plenty of opportunity for guided and independent practice with new concepts and skills.

To check understanding, teachers ask clear questions and make sure all students have a chance to respond.

Teachers select problems and other academic tasks that are well matched to lesson content so student success rate is high. Precise work assignments also provide variety and challenge.

Homework is assigned that students can complete successfully. It is typically given in small increments and provides additional practice with content covered in class. Work is checked, and students are given quick feedback.

Parents help keep students involved in learning. Teachers let parents know that homework is important and give them tips on how to help students keep working.

Learning progress is monitored closely.

Teachers frequently monitor student learning, both formally and informally.

Teachers require that students be accountable for their academic work.

Classroom assessments of student performance match learning objectives. Teachers know and use test-development techniques to prepare valid, reliable assessment instruments.

Routine assessment procedures make checking student progress easier. Students hear results quickly; reports to students are simple and clear so they can understand and correct errors; reports are tied to learning objectives.

Grading scales and mastery standards are set high to promote excellence.

Teachers encourage parents to keep track of student progress.

When students do not understand, they are retaught.

New material is introduced as quickly as possible at the beginning of the year or course, with minimum review or reteaching of previous content. Key prerequisite concepts and skills are reviewed thoroughly but quickly.

Teachers reteach priority lesson content until students show they have learned it.

Regular, focused reviews of key concepts and skills are used throughout the year to check on and strengthen student retention.

Class time is used for learning.

Teachers follow a system of priorities for using class time and allocate time for each subject or lesson. They concentrate on using class time for learning and spend very little time on non-learning activities.

Teachers set and maintain a brisk pace for instruction that remains consistent with thorough learning. New objectives are introduced as quickly as possible; clean start and stop cues help pace lessons according to specific time targets.

Students are encouraged to pace themselves. If they do not finish during class, they are expected to work on lessons before or after school, during lunch, or at other times so they can keep up with what is going on in class.

There are smooth, efficient classroom routines.

Classes start quickly and purposefully; teachers have as-signments or activities ready for students when they arrive. Materials and supplies are ready, too.

Students are required to bring the materials they need to class each day; they use assigned storage space.

Administrative matters are handled with quick, efficient routines that keep class disruptions to a minimum.

There are smooth, rapid transitions between activities throughout the day or class.

Standards for classroom behavior are explicit.

Teachers let students know that there are high standards for behavior in the classroom.

Classroom behavior standards are written, taught, and reviewed from the beginning of the year or the start of new courses.

Rules, discipline procedures, and consequences are planned in advance. Standards are consistent with or identical to the building code of conduct.

Consistent, equitable discipline is applied to all students. Procedures are carried out quickly and are clearly linked to students' inappropriate behavior.

Teachers stop disruptions quickly, taking care to avoid disrupting the whole class.

In disciplinary action, the teacher focuses on the inappropriate behavior, not on the student's personality.

There is no lack of research for those who seek to promote discussion of effective teaching. The issue is whether or not educators are prepared to accept their responsibilities to work together to become proficient consumers of that research. A professional learning community will fulfill that responsibility by ensuring that frequent and focused discussions on teaching and learning are the standard practice in its school.

6. Professional teachers function as leaders. At one point in our workshops, we often divide participants into two separate groups. The individuals in the first group are asked to think of the very best leader they have ever worked with and then to develop a list of descriptors for that individual. Members of the second group are asked to think of the very best teachers they ever had and then to describe the qualities of those teachers. When the separate groups reunite and report their findings, invariably the qualities that each group has identified are almost identical:

> *He had a contagious enthusiasm.*
>
> *She had a clear sense of what she wanted to accomplish.*
>
> *She knew how to communicate in our terms.*
>
> *He believed in me and gave me confidence in myself.*
>
> *He was passionate about it. You could not remain detached around him.*
>
> *She never gave up on me. She was tenacious.*
>
> *He was a tremendous motivator.*
>
> *She was challenging, but she made it fun to meet the challenge.*
>
> *He was energizing. It was just great to be around him.*
>
> *He was consistent and fair. You always knew where you stood.*
>
> *You always knew she wanted you to succeed.*
>
> *He had the ability to connect with others, to establish powerful personal relationships.*

As John Gardner (1986) observes, "every great leader is clearly teaching—and every great teacher is leading" (p. 19).

The task of a teacher is similar to the task of any leader. Like leaders of any enterprise, effective teachers recognize that they will be unable to carry out the other tasks of leadership unless they clearly understand what they want to accomplish. They have a clear sense of the knowledge, skills, attitudes, and behaviors that they want students to demonstrate in their classes, and they can mentally rehearse strategies to bring about the desired results. Their clarity of purpose enables them to structure each unit of instruction to contribute to the overarching goals.

Leaders must also be effective communicators. Effective teachers master the technical aspects of instruction that enhance clarity, but more important, like all great leaders, they recognize that what they pay attention to is a powerful means of communicating what is truly significant. They monitor student achievement of essential outcomes and respond when students are experiencing difficulty. They confront students who do not give their best efforts and celebrate those who do. They model the enthusiasm and passion for learning that they hope to instill in their students. They recognize the power of example.

Leaders are judged on the basis of results that cannot be achieved solely by their own efforts. Ultimately, the effectiveness of leaders is evaluated not on the basis of what they do themselves, but rather on what they have motivated others to do. Effective teachers are also results-oriented. Their planning centers not on what they will do, but on what their students are to do. And in the final analysis, their impact is assessed on the basis of what their students have achieved.

John Gardner (1988) contends that "the taking of responsibility is at the heart of leadership" (p. 14). Great leaders do not pass the buck. Effective teachers, like great leaders, are willing to accept responsibility for their students because they believe that they can affect student learning. This sense of self-efficacy serves as a powerful motivator for it leads teachers to conclude that they can and should make a significant difference in the lives of their students. They strive to function as "transformational leaders" who transform or change in a positive way their colleagues, students, and organizations. They expect their students to be successful, and they work hard to realize that expectation because they are driven by the belief that "at their best, teachers, like other leaders, shape relationships that make a measurable difference in others lives" (Bolman & Deal, 1995, p. 3).

Finally, great leaders bring great passion to their work that enables them to persist in the face of setbacks. The same is true of great teachers. As Andy Hargreaves (1997) writes:

> *Good teaching is not just a matter of being efficient, developing competence, mastering technique, and possessing the right kind of knowledge. Good teaching also involves emotional work. It is infused with pleasure, passion, creativity, challenge, and joy. It is a passionate vocation.* (p. 12)

The way in which a role is defined will have an enormous impact upon how that role is carried out within an organization. The factory model's view of the teacher as a semi-skilled worker with virtually no autonomy has adversely affected the work of teachers within schools for decades. Clearly that role must be redefined. New analogies have been proposed—the teacher as diagnostician, social worker, parent, entertainer, and so on. But in the professional learning community, the only appropriate analogy for teachers is the teacher as leader.

The concepts of "teacher as leader" and "professional learning community" can be powerful forces for school improvement, but they can just as easily serve as clichés that have little effect on actual practice. Concepts need to be brought into sharp focus if they are to influence the culture of any organization. The following reflections of Terry Weeks, a National Teacher of the Year, help to bring the concepts of the teacher as leader at work in a professional learning community into sharper focus.

A Professional Community of Learners:
Reflections by Terry Weeks
1988 National Teacher of the Year

The passion for teaching that pulled me toward the profession as a young boy began to evaporate early in my career. Before long, the sound of the ticking clock at the start of *60 Minutes* was enough to trigger immediate nervous tension because first period was now only hours away. The zeal was gone because I had wandered off the path that I intended to follow the day I accepted the keys to my first classroom.

Looking back on it now, I think my problems started when I veered off the road of sound practice and went in search of the path of least effort. The former offered possibilities; the latter offered relaxation. For instance, I discovered it was much easier to plan a lesson where I did all the talking. It was relatively easy to gather facts for distribution. It took much longer to plan for meaningful pupil participation. Lecturing was safe; student interaction was risky. Soon the quality of a good lesson was determined by my performance. I had created a community with just one key player—me—and I was lonely. I have since discovered that the slump I experienced is not that uncommon in the teaching profession. Some would even argue that the track I was on could be called the road most traveled.

Fortunately, there is a way to get back to the path we intended to follow when we embarked on our career in teaching. All we have to do is follow the signs that lead to a professional community of learners. Be forewarned, however—making this journey will involve pulling up one's roots. We will have to say goodbye to some old friends: the constant lecture, the daily worksheet, working in isolation, and the comfort of doing things the way we have always done them. Yet, the experience may very well introduce us to new practices that have the potential to energize us in a most dramatic fashion.

In several ways, our trip will be similar to those taken by the pioneers who blazed trails to America's heartland. It begins with a deep commitment that the destination is worth the effort. The frontiersmen embarked on their missions because they believed there was a better way of life within their grasp. They were confident that the struggles and growing pains would pale in comparison to the luxuries associated with a fresh start. As teachers, our first step begins with a genuine desire to seek a better way of doing things, to truly believe that new paths to learning are worth exploring.

Once they decided to pull up roots, the pioneers were forced to make some tough decisions about what should be carried with them. Many of their belongings had to be left behind. We, too, should give careful consideration to baggage that we can do without. Perhaps the first thing we should leave is all the answers. In a learning community, an open mind is a valuable asset. Members approach their tasks by exploring the possibilities before them. They engage in frequent dialogue, and questioning is constant. What knowledge is of greatest worth? What do we want our students to be able to accomplish? How is society changing? What skills are needed for the future? How do young people learn? Which activities are best to enhance conceptual understanding? These, and other vehicles of inquiry, establish an environment where the measure of success is determined not by the performance of the teacher, but by what the students are able to achieve.

Stagnation is another item that can be left behind. In a community of learners, members are always pressing ahead, always trying to improve. They stay abreast of current research, they read new books, and they share this new knowledge as they work in collaborative teams. In addition, they are not afraid to try new techniques. One thing that sets them apart from others is the manner in which they handle failed attempts. Instead of discarding the entire idea, pledging "never to try that again," they reflect on the experience and examine whether a little bit of fine-tuning is all that is needed. Often they invite the opinions of colleagues in this process.

A narrow view will not be needed on this journey. It will be replaced with a more global vision in which individuals see themselves as connected to the total school. Time use, the physical condition of the school, attendance and drop-out rates, and the level of parental involvement will no longer be "someone else's responsibility." These concerns, and others, become joint property. The exciting aspect is that collective ownership empowers teachers to become real leaders within the school setting.

Another practice that can remain behind is nonreflective decision making. In a community of learners, future directions are carefully plotted. Data collection is an ongoing process and includes examinations of pupil behaviors, test scores, performance-based assessments, and other measurements deemed appropriate. Community members meet and discuss what is revealed by this information; and since the data are tied to what students are able to do, concerns related to pupil outcomes become the foundation upon which the community is built.

Most people who enter the teaching profession are driven by a burning desire to make a positive difference. When we accept the keys to our first classroom, the flame inside us burns bright with hope and enthusiasm. All too often, our working environment and changing attitude robs the flame of much-needed oxygen. It does not have to be that way! Active membership in a professional learning community can rekindle the flame and revitalize us. The reason: energy stays focused where it should be—on the students.

The story is told of a young World War II soldier who decided to take a short walk in camp the night before a major battle. General Dwight D. Eisenhower approached and quietly walked beside the young man. The general's identity went undetected. "What are you thinking about, son?" asked the general. "I guess I'm afraid," was the reply. "Well, so am I," said Eisenhower. "Let us walk together and perhaps we will draw strength from each other." Perhaps one of the primary benefits of membership in a professional community of learners is that we do not have to fight our battles alone. By walking together, we too will be able to draw strength from one another.

Summary

Teachers represent the heartbeat of a school, and the changes essential to school improvement must be manifested by individual teachers at the classroom level. It is impossible to create good schools without good teachers, just as it is impossible to create professional learning communities without teachers who function as professionals. The recent work of the Interstate New Teacher Assessment and Support Consortium and the National Board for Professional Teaching Standards has articulated standards for what teachers should know and be able to do. Teachers who meet these standards will:

- Emphasize learning rather than teaching.

- Design curriculum and instruction that result in active student engagement with significant content.

- Focus on student performance and production in developing curriculum and assessment strategies.

- Collaborate with colleagues on teaching and learning as well as schoolwide issues.

- Consider themselves lifelong students of teaching and consumers of the research affecting their profession.

- Accept responsibility for creating the conditions that enable each student to be successful.

- Function as transformational leaders—leaders who believe in their ability to make a difference both in the lives of their students and the effectiveness of their schools.

Those who are trying to transform their schools into professional learning communities should consider these standards seriously.

Chapter 11

The Role of Parents in a Professional Learning Community

The research is abundantly clear: nothing motivates a child more than when learning is valued by schools and families/community working together in partnership. . . . These forms of [parent] involvement do not happen by accident or even by invitation. They happen by explicit strategic intervention.

—Michael Fullan (1997a, pp. 42–43)

To educate children without a deep partnership of teacher and parent is hopeless.

—Patrick Dolan (1994, p. 159)

Involving parents in the education of their children is highly desirable. As the United States Department of Education (1995a) concludes, "Thirty years of research make it clear: parents and families are pivotal to children's learning" (p. 19). The most comprehensive survey of research on parental involvement is a series of publications developed by Anne Henderson and Nancy Berla. The following conclusions represent just some of the findings emerging from that research:

- *When parents are involved, students achieve more, regardless of socioeconomic status, ethnic/racial background, or the parent's education level.*

- *The more extensive the parent involvement, the higher the student achievement.*

- *When parents are involved, students exhibit more positive attitudes and behavior, are more likely to graduate, and are more likely to attend post-secondary education.*

- *The benefits of involving parents are not confined to the early years; there are significant gains at all ages and grade levels.*

- *The most accurate predictor of a student's achievement in school is the extent to which that student's family is able to (1) create a home environment that encourages learning; (2) communicate high, yet reasonable, expectations for their children's achievement and future careers; and (3) become involved in their children's education.*

—Henderson (1987); Henderson & Berla (1995)

These findings have led the United States Congress to adopt a national goal that calls on every school in America to increase parental involvement and participation in promoting the social, emotional, and academic growth of children (United States Department of Education, 1995a).

Despite the apparent unanimity regarding the important role that parents can play in the educational process, both educators and parents continue to struggle in their efforts to define exactly what that role should be. Educators often appear to be schizophrenic on the topic. Teachers in urban and rural areas are likely to complain of parental indifference, while teachers in suburban areas tend to complain of parental overzealousness or undue influence.

A recent survey of teachers and parents yielded confusing results. While 90% of teachers agreed that parental involvement was needed in their schools, only 32% of the teachers felt it was their responsibility to involve parents, and 50% said they did not have enough time to do so. Almost 90% of the teachers supported the idea of parent volunteers in schools, but 70% of the parents indicated that they had never been invited to volunteer. Only 3% of the teachers felt that parents were genuinely interested in being involved in the educational process, but 80% of the parents surveyed indicated that they would like to be more involved in the school (Center on Families, Communities, Schools and Children's Learning, 1994, pp. 2–4).

Parents also send mixed messages. While they may acknowledge the importance of their involvement in the education of their children, they often do not act on that knowledge. A recent survey by the National Center for Educational Statistics found that only 60% of parents had spoken to their child's teacher or counselor, and only 29% had visited classes in the preceding year. Over 90% of the parents reported that lack of time was a major obstacle in their becoming more involved (Gutman, 1995).

Furthermore, parental involvement declines dramatically as students move from the elementary grades through middle school and high school (Center on Families, Communities, Schools and Children's Learning, 1994). As children get older and seek greater independence, they often make it clear that they do not want their parents involved in their schools. Uncertain of how to respond to the adolescents in their homes, many parents are more than willing to turn them over to the school and hope for the best. As a result, parents are much less involved in their children's education at a time when there is a need for increased parental involvement in their children's lives.

Parents as Partners

There are clear benefits to creating an effective partnership in the business world. A partner can bring specific skills and expertise to the enterprise, offer a different perspective on issues, increase available resources, serve as a source of support in difficult times, and help to achieve mutual goals. Parents can fulfill all of these roles in an effective partnership with schools. Certainly students benefit from parental involvement, but schools benefit as well. While educators may have expertise in content and pedagogy, parents' knowledge of their own children can be extremely helpful to teachers as they try to meet their students' needs. Parents can also help educators view their schools from a different perspective—that of the paying customer. When parents view the school in a positive way, they are more likely to provide the necessary financial support for quality education.

Furthermore, parents who are positive about a school can serve as advocates for its improvement efforts. As Patrick Dolan (1994) writes, "If parents are with you, they will bring the community with them. If they are not, they will stop you dead. . . . You need their protection when hostile winds begin to blow" (p. 157). Finally, while there may be differences of opinion from time to time, parents and educators share the same goal—the eventual success of the child. Thus, parents represent a potentially powerful ally in the effort to create a school that functions as a professional learning community. When educators make a systematic effort to link the school with parents, they are building a support system for both enhanced student achievement and an effective learning community (Marks, Doane, & Secada, 1996).

There is, however, a tendency for educators to define their partnership with parents in narrow terms: "It is our job to make the decisions; it is your job to support them." Not many people will be attracted to a "partnership" that asks them to provide the finances for the operation yet demands their unquestioning support of all decisions made by their partner. Good partnerships should be mutually beneficial. Defining the possibilities and parameters of a meaningful, mutually beneficial partnership with parents certainly represents a significant challenge for schools, but schools that operate as professional learning communities will respond to that challenge.

A Framework for School-Parent Partnerships

The National Parent Teacher Association has used a framework developed by the Center on School, Family, and Community Partnerships to identify national standards for parental involvement. These standards have been endorsed by more than 30 professional organizations, including the American Federation of Teachers, the National Education Association, the National Association of Elementary School Principals, the National Association of Secondary School Principals, the National Middle School Association, and the National School Board Association. The standards fall into six categories.

Standard One—Communicating

Communication between the home and school is regular, two-way, and meaningful. Timely, two-way communication is critical to any partnership. Partners require communication that allows for a sharing of ideas and concerns, establishment of mutual goals, clarification of expectations, and regular follow-up. Parents can be more productive partners if schools:

- Provide parents with clear information regarding course expectations and offerings, student placement, school activities, student services, and optional programs.

- Establish times for conferences that are convenient for working parents.

- Develop routine procedures to allow parents to review the work of their children on a regular basis—for example, using a folder to send student work home each week and providing a place for parent comments on the front cover.

- Provide parents with a handbook that clarifies what they can expect from the school, what the school asks of them, and how they can raise a concern or question.

- Use technology such as e-mail and voice mail to enable parents to get messages to teachers when they are in class.

- Constantly solicit parent opinions on the operation of the school through annual surveys or class assignments that ask students to survey parents about the school and areas needing improvement. (Phone surveys of a randomly selected sampling of parents generally provide more useful information than mailings.)

- Create a variety of forums for parents to discuss their ideas and concerns with educators. These might include such activities as parent breakfasts or luncheons at the school, neighborhood coffees in the evening, and school information booths in public places such as shopping malls or grocery stores.

- Publish a parent newsletter that advises parents of events and initiatives at the school. (For an example of an award-winning parent newsletter, contact Stevenson High School, One Stevenson Drive, Lincolnshire, IL 60069.)

Research indicates that when parents receive frequent and effective communication from their children's school, their involvement increases, their overall evaluation of educators is more favorable, and their attitudes toward the school and its program improves (National PTA, 1997). Therefore, schools should strive to enhance the frequency and effectiveness of their communication with parents. In doing so, they should be mindful of the following:

Communication is most powerful when it is timely. No one benefits when parents receive information so late that their ability to respond is limited or when parental concerns are allowed to fester without being expressed. The policy in one high school called for teachers to notify parents of the academic performance of their children at the midpoint of each nine-week grading period, but only if the student was failing at that time. As a result, most parents in this district received their first notification of student progress when report cards were sent home in the 10th or 11th week of an 18-week semester. At that point, the majority of each grade had already been determined. When parental frustration over this policy became apparent, the school had to acknowledge that it was not fulfilling its responsibility to provide parents with timely communication. The faculty addressed the problem by replacing the two nine-week grading periods with three six-week periods and sending progress reports home on each student at the midpoint of each of the three grading periods. This enabled parents to receive information on the progress of their children every three weeks. As a result, the percentage of students receiving Ds or Fs as final course grades was cut by two-thirds, and the academic achievement of students improved dramatically. Since then, this school has also used technology to develop a weekly progress report for students who are experiencing academic difficulty. Because a partnership cannot be effective if one of the partners is "left in the dark," the professional learning community provides parents with timely information.

The principal of another school was struck by the vehemence of some parents when they notified him of their complaints. Upon investigation, he found that these parents had often allowed an issue to fester because they either did not know how or with whom to raise the issue. The principal responded by developing a parent hotline that allowed parents to call in with a concern as soon as it developed and that assured them of a response within 24 hours. Time is of the essence when it comes to the communication between school and parents.

Communication protocols should not place excessive demands upon teachers. The changes in the grading and progress report system described above were made possible only because the school had developed reporting procedures that did not make great demands on teachers. Teachers were asked to identify the comments that they would like to send to parents. The list they developed included 99 different possibilities—everything from "current grade is B" and "makes positive contributions to class discussions" to "is in danger of failing" and "call me—we need to talk." These statements were then put into a computer database that made sending a progress report as simple as assigning a number or two to each student on a computerized class list. Schools must learn to use the power of technology to enhance communication. Communication strategies that are based on the premise of expanding a teacher's workload are bound to fail.

Communication should celebrate success as well as identify concerns. Several years ago, contestants on the television program *Family Feud* were asked the following question: "You are a parent who has just received a phone call from your child's school. Why has the school called?" Contestants were to guess the studio audience's most frequent responses to that question. The five most common answers were:

1. He is failing.

2. He has misbehaved.

3. He is missing assignments.

4. He is ill or injured.

5. He is truant or tardy.

According to this sampling of parents, the best and most "neutral" message that they can hope to receive when getting a call from school is that their child is sick. Not one of the members of the audience or any of the 10 contestants suggested that the school might be calling with a positive message. What is wrong with this picture? Certainly schools must notify parents of concerns; however, there is an enormous imbalance in the messages that educators send home. An institution created to promote the success of its clients should certainly advise students and parents of achievement, improvement, and triumphs, as well as concerns.

Communication must be two-way. Many schools define effective communication in terms of strategies and instruments for getting messages from the school out to parents. They focus on what parents need to know. These schools understand half of the equation. All communication must be two-way if it is to be effective. A professional learning community will be intensely interested in the information, observations, and perceptions that parents can bring to the partnership and will develop systematic procedures for hearing what parents have to say. Its members will remember Covey's rule of communication: "Seek first to understand, then to be understood" (1989, p. 237).

Standard Two—Parenting

Parenting skills are promoted and supported. Parents offer educators valuable information and insights about their children, but they can also benefit from the expertise of educators who are likely to be more familiar with the general characteristics (and challenges) of children at different ages. Mrs. Jones may be an expert on her daughter Sally, but she may not be an expert on what Sally is going through during the middle school years. Parents can be more productive partners if schools:

- Support parents with training, resources, and other services.

- Provide workshops or programs that help parents with parenting issues such as communication, discipline, peer pressure, study habits, drug and alcohol abuse, single parenting, etc.

- Provide transportation and child-care services to encourage parents to attend these workshops and programs.

- Offer parents suggestions for establishing expectations and routines with their children. For example, student achievement is correlated with three factors that parents can control: preventing student absenteeism, having reading materials in the home, and limiting television viewing (Gutman, 1995).

- Link parents to programs and resources within the community that provide support services to families.

Almost every parent has occasionally felt overwhelmed and outmatched in the course of raising a child. Most will welcome research-based information on parenting, and schools are in a position to provide them with that information.

Standard Three—Student Learning

Parents play an integral role in assisting student learning. Student learning increases when parents are involved in the process by helping at home. However, most parents need guidance on how they can be most helpful. Everyone benefits when schools explain to parents the skills their children are to learn and also provide specific strategies a parent can use to participate in their child's development of those skills. Parents can be more productive partners if schools:

- Inform parents of the specific learning expectations for students in each subject at each grade level.

- Provide parents of elementary and middle school children with school-developed curriculum guides and learning packets for each course or grade level that suggest how parents can foster learning of particular concepts at home.

- Develop procedures that enable parents to monitor homework, provide appropriate assistance, and give feedback to teachers. For example, schools can tell parents what to look for in each assignment and invite parents to make a quick check-off response such as:

  ____ My child understands and can correctly apply this skill.

  ____ My child needed help on this but seems to understand the lesson.

  ____ My child needs further instruction or help on this skill/lesson.

- Use technology to establish "homework hotlines" that offer parents reminders of the homework that has been assigned and suggestions for helping students complete the homework.

- Assign interactive homework that will require students to discuss and interact with their parents about what they are learning in class.

- Involve parents in setting student goals each year and in planning for postsecondary education and careers.

- Ask parents to take an active role in reviewing student portfolios according to standards articulated in a scoring rubric.

- Suggest recommended books that parents might read aloud to their children or encourage their children to read for themselves.

Parents represent the "unutilized labor force of schooling" (Gerstner et al., 1994, p. 80). They can reinforce what students are learning if schools will simply provide them with the information, materials, and guidance that will enable them to function as teacher aides in their own homes.

Standard Four—Volunteering

Parents are welcome in the school, and their support and assistance are sought. Both the financial and human resources of most schools are already overtaxed, as educators struggle to achieve their goals and meet the needs of each student. Parent volunteers can represent a valuable asset in that struggle. Furthermore, parent volunteers are more likely to express confidence in the school and to serve as its advocates. Parents can be more productive partners if schools:

- Survey parents regarding their interests, talents, and availability.

- Develop a program for using volunteers as tutors, mentors for children at risk, translators for students who need help in learning to speak English, chaperones for community service projects undertaken by students, assistants for clerical support personnel, etc.

- Develop a training and orientation program for all new parent volunteers.

- Create opportunities for parents who may be unavailable during the school day to help the school in other ways, such as reading aloud for books on tape.

- Develop a speakers' bureau or pool of parents with particular talents or interests that teachers can use to enhance curriculum development or to lead a lesson.

- Use parents to organize and implement special events, such as career days, fine arts programs, graduation celebrations, etc.

- Develop feedback forms that enable volunteers to reflect on their experience, and analyze the results in an effort to make the experience more satisfying.

The most effective step a school can take to foster parent volunteers is to create a position for a volunteer coordinator. Parent associations often engage in fund-raising projects to provide a school with playground equipment, new computers, or instruments for the band. While these projects may be worthwhile, they are unlikely to have as much impact as using the funds to provide a stipend for an individual who will recruit and coordinate volunteer services to the school. One school that used the financial support of its parent association to fund such a position had a dramatic increase in the number of hours that parents provided the school in volunteer services. If schools make a conscious effort to use parent volunteers, and teachers and administrators are creative in how they they are used, parent volunteers can contribute a great deal to a professional learning community.

Standard Five—Making Decisions

Parents are full partners in the decisions that affect their children. Partnerships work best when there is mutual respect and each partner can participate in the decision-making process. When schools view parents as partners and engage them in decision-making processes, they realize higher levels of student achievement and greater public support (National PTA, 1997). The involvement of parents, as individuals or as representatives of others, is beneficial in collaborative decision-making processes on issues ranging from course selection and discipline policies to schoolwide improvement initiatives. Parents can be more productive partners if schools:

- Include parent representatives in the process of identifying the mission, vision, values, and goals of the schools.

- Develop and use processes to solicit more broad-based parental input on mission, vision, values, and goals.

- Include parents on decision-making and advisory task forces and committees and provide them with the necessary information and training to make informed decisions.

- Facilitate active parent participation in the decisions that affect their children, such as student placement, course selection, and individualized educational plans.

- Work with parents to identify the student and school performance data that parents find most relevant and then provide them with that data on a regular basis.

- Provide well-publicized processes that enable parents to raise issues or concerns, appeal decisions, and propose initiatives.

- Solicit parental input in the evaluation of the programs, policies, and procedures of the school.

- Advise parents of changes in programs, policies, and procedures that have been made as a result of parental input or involvement.

- Inform parents of local, state, or national issues that impact education.

Parents are more likely to feel ownership in a school and its programs when they have a voice in key decisions. Schools must both use decision-making processes that solicit parental input and provide parents with the information they need to make informed decisions.

Standard Six—Collaborating with the Community

Community resources are used to strengthen schools, families, and student learning. If a partnership relies exclusively on the talents and assets of its partners, it will severely limit what it might accomplish. Partners need to establish networks with people of similar interests as well as with specialists who offer particular expertise or resources that are beneficial to the partnership. While parents and schools can and should form an active partnership, they should not overlook or exclude other individuals or agencies in the community that have an interest in children and that might contribute significantly to the attainment of educational goals. If schools collaborate with the wider community, they can help families connect to area resources, link educational programs with the realities of the workplace, create community service opportunities for students, respond to the needs of adult learners, and make a more effective contribution to the community. The school-parent partnership will be more productive if schools:

- Coordinate and distribute information regarding cultural, recreational, academic, health, social, and other resources for families in the community.

- Work with community partners to organize special programs and events, such as health fairs, technology nights, summer recreational programs, job fairs, etc., to inform families of community resources and services.

- Develop partnerships with area businesses and service groups to create a speakers bureau, coordinate job shadowing and mentoring experiences for students, and provide businesses with access to school facilities and personnel.

- Establish "pen pal" or e-mail relationships between students and senior citizens and/or business representatives.

- Create community service opportunities for students.

Schools are typically viewed as institutions that provide educational services to the youth of the community, Monday through Friday, from September to June. Instead, schools should be regarded as valuable resources that can make a significant contribution to the entire community. Adlai Stevenson High School in Lincolnshire, Illinois, has made a concerted effort to function as a resource that serves the entire community throughout the entire year. It offers educational services for all ages. The school provides learn-to-swim classes for infants, a full-time day-care center for three- and four-year-olds, an extensive summer program, and athletic and recreational camps for children of all ages. It has also developed agreements that enable it to serve as a satellite campus for the community college, for a state university, for a private college, and for multi-university programs that offer everything from associate to graduate degrees. Finally, it provides leisure, recreational, and noncredit educational programs for the adults in the area.

Stevenson is also an active partner with other community agencies. It coordinates blood drives with the health department to serve as the primary source for blood donations in the county and works with Big Brothers and Big Sisters to "adopt" over 200 needy families each Christmas. It hosts the monthly meetings of the community coalition that combats drug and alcohol abuse and works with an area foundation to offer an annual Fine Arts Series to the community. Additionally, Stevenson has developed partnerships that allow hundreds of students to become involved in community service projects—everything from sponsoring a Special Olympics and working in soup kitchens to organizing social activities for residents of nursing homes, conducting environmental protection studies, and tutoring younger students.

Finally, Stevenson has established an active school-business partnership that provides students with opportunities for job shadowing and mentoring. It also works with employers to identify training needs and then coordinates with its higher education partners to provide programs on the Stevenson campus that meet those needs.

Schools can and should make a significant contribution to efforts to enhance the quality of life in their communities. They can and should consider how they can serve all of their "customers." However, the primary business of schools is the business of teaching and learning, and teaching and learning must remain the focus. Special programs and participation in social services should be self-sustaining and should not divert resources from the educational program. Furthermore, while schools can assist other agencies in their efforts to meet community needs, they should never take on the primary responsibilities for meeting those needs. As the Committee for Economic Development (1994) writes:

> *Many look to the school instead of to the parents and community as the front line of defense against every social or health problem. . . . [Social] services may be placed in the schools, they may be delivered through the schools, but they should not be made the responsibility of the schools.* (p. 5)

Schools must not lose sight of the fact that the greatest contribution they can make to any community is to ensure that its children achieve critical academic goals.

Summary

While there is an abundance of research establishing the fact that parents' involvement in the education of their children is highly desirable, parents and educators continue to struggle in their efforts to define exactly what that role should be. The best model for the relationship between the school and parent is the model of a business partnership—a relationship in which each party is expected to bring specific skills and expertise to the enterprise, to offer a different perspective on issues, to offer support in difficult times, and to contribute toward the achievement of mutual goals. The National PTA has used a framework developed by the Center on School, Family, and Community Partnerships to identify the following six standards for a partnership between schools and parents:

Standard One—Communicating: Communication between the home and school is regular, two-way, and meaningful.

Standard Two—Parenting: Parenting skills are promoted and supported.

Standard Three—Student Learning: Parents play an integral role in assisting student learning.

Standard Four—Volunteering: Parents are welcome in the school, and their support and assistance are sought.

Standard Five—Making Decisions: Parents are full partners in the decisions that affect their children.

Standard Six—Collaborating with the Community: Community resources are used to strengthen schools, families, and student learning.

Schools that function as learning communities will recognize the power of an effective partnership with parents and will develop specific strategies to create that partnership.

Chapter 12

Staff Development in a Professional Learning Community

Research and experience have taught us that wide-spread, sustained implementation of new practices in classrooms, principal's offices, and central offices requires a new form of professional development. This staff development not only must affect the knowledge, attitudes, and practices of individual teachers, administrators, and other school employees, but it also must alter the cultures and structures of the organization.

—Dennis Sparks and Stephanie Hirsh (1997, pp. 1–2)

The terms "staff development," "inservice," and "professional development" are likely to engender negative reactions in veteran educators. For many teachers, these terms are synonymous with occasional day-long workshops where they sit passively while an alleged expert "exposes" them to new ideas or practices. The program is then assessed on the basis of the "happiness quotient"—the level of teacher satisfaction with the presentation—rather than on its impact on teaching and learning. This traditional approach to staff development is fragmented, unfocused, and does not address schoolwide problems or priorities. The creation of professional learning communities requires a radical rethinking of the purpose and activities of staff development and a new understanding of its contribution to individual and organizational renewal.

Standards for Staff Development

It has been emphasized throughout this book that national standards are a major resource for school improvement. The National Staff Development Council (NSDC) has worked in cooperation with 11 other national educational organizations to identify standards for professional development that provide benchmarks by which schools can assess their programs. The standards are organized into three categories: content, process, and context. Content addresses the "what" of staff development—the actual skills or knowledge that educators need to possess or acquire. Process addresses the "how" of staff development—the means by which educators will acquire the knowledge and skills. Context refers to the organization, system, or culture that supports staff development initiatives.

The NSDC standards for content, process, and context are accompanied by supporting rationale, examples, anticipated outcomes, and discussion questions. A brief summary of the standards for elementary schools is presented below. Similar standards are available for middle schools and high schools.

Content

Effective elementary school staff development:

- increases administrators' and teachers' understanding of how to provide school environments and instruction that are responsive to the developmental needs of children in grades pre-kindergarten through six.

- facilitates the development and implementation of school- and classroom-based management that maximize student learning.

- addresses diversity by providing awareness and training related to the knowledge, skills, and behaviors needed to ensure that an equitable and quality education is provided to all students.

- enables educators to provide challenging, developmentally appropriate curricula that engage students in integrative ways of thinking and learning.

- prepares teachers to use research-based teaching strategies appropriate to their instructional objectives and their students.

- prepares educators to demonstrate high expectations for student learning.

- facilitates staff collaboration with and support of families for improving student performance.

- prepares teachers to use various types of performance assessment in their classrooms.

Process

Effective elementary school staff development:

- provides knowledge, skills, and attitudes regarding organization development and systems thinking.

- is based on knowledge about human learning and development.

- provides for the three phases of the change process: initiation, implementation, and institutionalization.

- bases priorities on a careful analysis of disaggregated student data regarding goals for student learning.

- uses content that has proven value in increasing student learning and development.

- provides a framework for integrating innovations and relating those innovations to the mission of the organization.

- requires an evaluation process that is ongoing, includes multiple sources of information, and focuses on all levels of the organization.

- uses a variety of staff development approaches to accomplish the goals of improving instruction and student success.

- provides the follow-up necessary to ensure improvement.

- requires staff members to learn and apply collaborative skills to conduct meetings, make shared decisions, solve problems and work collegially.

- requires knowledge and use of the stages of group development to build effective, productive, collegial teams.

Context

Effective elementary school staff development:

- requires and fosters the norm of continuous improvement.

- requires strong leadership in order to obtain continuing support and to motivate all staff, school board members, parents, and the community to be advocates for continuous improvement.

- is aligned with the school and district's strategic plans and is funded by a line item in the budget.

- provides adequate time during the work day for staff members to learn and work together to accomplish the school's mission and goals.

- is an innovation in itself that requires study of the change process. (1995, pp. 5–6)

The United States Department of Education (1995b) has also attempted to identify standards for professional development that are based on the best available research and exemplary practices. Its findings are presented below.

The mission of professional development is to prepare and support educators to help all students achieve at high standards of learning and development. Successful professional development:

- focuses on teachers as central to student learning, yet includes all other members of the school community.

- focuses on individual, collegial, and organizational improvement.

- respects and nurtures the intellectual and leadership capacity of teachers, principals, and others in the school community.

- reflects best available research and practice in teaching, learning, and leadership.

- enables teachers to develop further expertise in subject content, teaching strategies, uses of technologies, and other essential elements in teaching to high standards.

- promotes continuous inquiry and improvement embedded in the daily life of the schools.

- is planned collaboratively by those who will participate in and facilitate that development.

- requires substantial time and other resources.

- is driven by a coherent long-term plan.

- is evaluated ultimately on the basis of its impact on teacher effectiveness and student learning; and this assessment guides subsequent professional development efforts.

In *Teachers Take Charge of Their Learning* (1996), the National Foundation for the Improvement of Education (NFIE) also attempts to define the elements of an effective professional development program. Its conclusions are presented below.

An effective professional development program is one that:

- has the goal of improving student learning at the heart of every school endeavor.

- fosters a deepening of subject matter knowledge, a greater understanding of learning, and a greater appreciation of students' needs.

- helps teachers and other staff meet the needs of students who learn in different ways and who come from diverse cultural, linguistic, and socioeconomic backgrounds.

- provides adequate time for inquiry, reflection, and mentoring, and is an important part of the normal working day.

- is rigorous, sustained, and adequate to the long-term change of practice.

- is directed toward teachers' intellectual development and leadership.

- is teacher designed and directed, incorporates the best principles of adult learning, and involves shared decisions designed to improve the school.

- balances individual priorities with school and district needs.

- makes best use of new technologies.

- is site-based and supportive of a clearly articulated vision for students.

These standards and supporting documents can serve as very useful instruments in auditing the professional development practices of a school and/or district. When considered together, they suggest the changes that must be made in traditional practices in order to provide staff development programs that support and enhance a learning community.

The Purpose of Staff Development Programs in a Professional Learning Community

Throughout this book, we have argued that professional learning communities are committed to results-driven education. They move beyond prescribing courses and specifying seat time to articulating specifically what students should know and be able to do as a result of their education. The premise that schools must focus on results leads to the corollary assumption that the purpose of a comprehensive staff development program is to improve the ability of educators to help all students achieve the intended results of the school. As Dennis Sparks and Stephanie Hirsh (1997) write:

> In a logical progression, results-driven education for students requires results-driven staff development for educators. . . . Staff development's success will be judged not by how many teachers and administrators participate in staff development programs or how they perceive its value, but by whether it alters instructional behavior in a way that benefits students. (p. 5)

This focus on student results means that a professional learning community assigns a higher priority to building the collective capacity of the group than the knowledge and skills of individuals (Louis, Kruse, & Raywid, 1996). Many schools approach professional development from the perspective that the school will be improved if they can provide incentives to individuals to learn and grow independently. Thus, they encourage teachers and principals to earn advanced degrees from a myriad of universities or to attend a potpourri of workshops that may have little to do with the school's improvement initiatives. The flaw in this approach is that individual learning does not ensure organizational learning or an enhanced ability to achieve a common purpose.

In the struggle between an individual who has acquired greater insight and a system that is unwilling to change, the system will usually win. Furthermore, effective organizations are attentive to developing "group IQ." While a group can be no "smarter" than the sum total of the strengths of individual members, it can be "dumber" if its internal workings do not allow members to share their talents (Goleman, 1995). A learning community requires more than individual knowledge. It requires developing the ability of the group to work together to solve problems and renew its school. An effective staff development program will address this collective capability and enhance the group IQ.

The Content of Staff Development Programs in a Professional Learning Community

Staff development content is based on research. In Chapter 4 we asserted that a professional learning community will always begin its exploration of an issue by gathering relevant background information and compiling the best thinking on that issue. In keeping with that principle, the staff development programs of professional learning communities are based on the best available research and exemplary practices. If teachers are asked to devote their time and energy to a new program or practice, there should be compelling evidence that the innovation actually makes a difference in teacher effectiveness and the success of students. The research of the past quarter-century has provided considerable insight into "what works," and yet the professional development programs of many schools ignore this research. Their error is less a result of not knowing what to do and more a result of not using what is known.

The professional learning community bridges the gap between research and practice. Whether the topic is the developmental needs of students, classroom-based management, teaching strategies for specific instructional objectives, authentic assessment, or the many other areas that can impact the ability of a school to achieve its intended results, the professional learning community uses a research-based staff development program.

Staff development content focuses on both generic and discipline-specific teaching skills. General teaching strategies such as mastery learning and problem-based learning will continue to have their place in staff development programs. There is, however, increasing awareness of the benefits of training programs that offer particular pedagogical approaches and applications for specific content areas such as mathematics, science, social studies, and language arts (Sparks & Hirsh, 1997). For example, a nationally recognized high school builds its staff development program on three general strands that apply to all classrooms, such as student-centered instruction, authentic assessment, and integration of technology. Each strand runs for at least three years. Initial investigation of each topic is typically conducted in general sessions with teachers from multiple disciplines. Eventually, however, teaching teams work together to develop ideas and strategies for implementing the training in their specific disciplines or courses. Training programs are more effective when they include provisions for assisting educators in transferring general concepts to their particular assignments.

Staff development content expands the repertoire of teachers to meet the needs of students who learn in different ways. If the purpose of staff development is to enable the school to help all students achieve an education, and if students learn in different ways, it must follow that an effective staff development program will expand the teachers' repertoire of skills to address the diverse learning styles of students.

The Process of Staff Development in a Professional Learning Community

The process of staff development is attentive to the tenets of good teaching. The qualities of good teaching discussed in Chapter 10 should be evident in staff development programs. Ironically, this is seldom the case. As the National Commission on Teaching and America's Future (1996) reports:

> There is a mismatch between the kind of teaching and learning teachers are now expected to pursue with their students and the teaching they experience in their own professional education. Teachers are urged to engage their students in actively building their understanding of new ideas; to provide opportunities for practice and feedback as well as for inquiry, problem solving, collaboration, and critical reflection; to connect knowledge to students' developmental stages and personal experiences; and to carefully assess student learning over time. These desirable characteristics of teaching are usually absent in the learning afforded to teachers. There are few parallels between how teachers are expected to teach and how they are encouraged to learn. (p. 84)

The attention to different learning styles, focus on authentic problems, opportunities for guided practice, and chance to work with others that reflect good teaching also reflect good staff development and are evident in the professional learning community.

The process of staff development provides the coaching critical to mastery of new skills. Nearly all teachers are able to develop mastery of new curricular and instructional practices if the training they receive includes:

- Presentation and explanation of the theory behind the practice.

- Demonstration.

- Opportunities for initial guided practice.

- Prompt feedback about their efforts.

- Sustained coaching. (Showers, Joyce, & Bennett, 1987)

Coaching—the provision of ongoing feedback and support—promotes the sustained practice, reflection, and dialogue that then foster the acquisition of new knowledge and skills. As one study concludes, "Until alternatives are developed, coaching or its equivalent appears to be essential if the investment in [educator] training is not to be lost" (Showers, Joyce, & Bennett, 1987, p. 57).

The process of staff development results in reflection and dialogue. Many training programs call for teachers to unthinkingly follow a cookbook approach to the complex task of teaching. Staff development programs should be designed to develop thoughtful professionals who have the ability to assess and revise their own actions in order to improve the likelihood of success for their students. Carl Glickman (1986) describes this ability to make assessments of and revisions to an immediate concrete experience as "abstract thought." Training promotes this abstract thought when it provides teachers with the opportunity to reflect on their attempts to implement new strategies.

Creating small, supportive groups in which teachers are encouraged to discuss their questions, concerns, and ideas about a new program also enhances the successful implementation of a program. Giving teachers this opportunity to discuss problems reduces their sense of isolation. Furthermore, the small-group format of many professional development programs provides a forum for sharing success stories and testimonials that can fuel the school's improvement initiative. Effective staff development looks more like a collective study of the teaching and learning process than a series of presentations.

The process of staff development is sustained over a considerable period of time. In her study of innovative organizations, Rosabeth Moss Kanter (1983) found that one of the most common mistakes of companies that were unsuccessful in their attempts at innovation was failure to see the project through to its conclusion. The same failure is evident in traditional staff development programs. Many school districts take great pride in the array of staff training that has been provided. As one energetic principal proudly announced, "This year we have trained all our staff in the 'Seven Habits of Highly Effective People,' assertive discipline, cooperative learning, portfolio assessment, and integrating technology into their teaching." It was February. This potpourri approach that exposes teachers to a little of this and a little of that does not affect their practice. Mastery takes time, and teachers benefit when there is a sustained, multi-year commitment to training.

The process of staff development is evaluated at several different levels. If the purpose of staff development is improved results for students, staff, and the school as an organization, it is no longer justifiable to assess the effectiveness of a staff

development program solely on the basis of participant satisfac
tion. This narrow assessment strategy does not provide a reliable predictor of either willingness to implement or impact on
learning. Evaluation must assess results.

The Xerox Corporation assesses the impact of its training
programs by probing for information at four different levels.
The Xerox model (Elam, Cramer, & Brodinsky, 1986) can easily
be applied to schools.

Question	Method of Data Collection
Did participants enjoy the training?	Questionnaire
Did participants learn intended skills?	Create a task situation for the participants to complete and have them evaluate their performance.
Did participants use their skills on the job?	Observers determine whether new skills are being applied in the workplace.
Did the program affect the bottom line?	Collection of observable, verifiable, tangible facts that show specific profit or performance results.

The focus on results does not mean that the burden of
school improvement rests exclusively on a staff development
program. As Sparks and Hirsh (1997) write:

> *Factors such as district and school leadership, the*
> *application of academic standards, and the quality of*

the curriculum and assessment process are also criti-cal to improving achievement. Systems theory makes it clear that student learning is the result of complex interactions among the various parts of the system (some of which the school has little or no influence over) and that all of these parts must be critically examined to determine their influence on one another and on student learning. (p. 41)

The interconnectedness of the elements affecting teaching and learning makes it impossible to attribute either improvements or problems to a single area. Nevertheless, when evaluating staff development or any of the areas affecting student achievement, educators must keep their eye on the prize—improved results.

The Context of Staff Development in a Professional Learning Community

The context of staff development focuses on the school level and has strong support from the central office. Professional development is most effective when it engages the entire staff of a particular school in an effort to achieve incremental improvements related to a set of common objectives over a three- to five-year period (Sparks & Hirsh, 1997). Traditional models of professional development tend to be district-focused and district-driven. But the appropriate focus should be on the individual school because the local school site provides the best context for effective staff development.

The importance of school-focused staff development does not diminish the critical role that the district office must play in the school improvement process. Effective leadership at the district level can mean the difference between successful and unsuccessful improvement initiatives. There is considerable evidence that individual schools will be unlikely to sustain a change process without the leadership and support of the district (Fullan, 1993; Schlechty, 1997; Wehlage, Osthoff, & Porter, 1996). As Schlechty (1997) writes, "only through revitalizing and redirecting the action of district level operations can the kind of widespread and radical change that must occur become possible" (p. 78).

The solution to this apparent contradiction between school-based staff development and district-led staff development is once again found in the concept of "loose-tight" leadership. A district office can be "loose" on the particular staff development initiatives that the faculty of each school elects to pursue, provided that the initiative is designed to develop the capacity of an individual school to function as a professional learning community. In one school, this might mean the emphasis is on training in collaboration. In another, the training may be designed to help staff make curricular decisions. In yet another, the emphasis could be on developing valid assessments of student performance. Although the areas of emphasis may differ, each should help the school evolve as a professional learning community.

District offices help individual schools create effective staff development programs and sustain school improvement initiatives when they:

Promote shared vision and values by:

- Developing a compelling vision of district schools and helping each school translate that general vision into its local context.

- Linking district goals to the vision and requiring each school to do the same.

- Screening initial applicants for positions in the school on the basis of their fit with the vision and values of that school.

- Insisting that schools articulate the link between their professional development plan and their vision and goals.

Foster collective inquiry by:

- Posing the questions that focus the attention of a school on the central issues of a professional learning community, and engaging staff in the consideration of those questions.

- Synthesizing and sharing research and best practice and providing that information to staff on an ongoing basis.

- Building links between schools and external sources of information and research such as professional organizations.

- Providing the local school site with the authority to make decisions. (People are not inclined to inquire into issues unless they feel they can act on their conclusions.)

Promote collaboration by:

- Providing time in the school day and school year for teachers to work together on issues of teaching and learning.

- Developing structures that help teachers determine the purpose of their collaboration and the results it should produce.

- Training staff in collective inquiry, team building, establishing group norms, and reaching consensus.

- Insisting that schools use a staff development training model that incorporates guided practice and coaching.

- Modeling collaboration with other community agencies and with the schools themselves.

Encourage experimentation by:

- Conducting districtwide action research projects.

- Providing incentives for experimentation.

- Recognizing innovators.

Build continuous improvement processes in district and school routines by:

- Establishing a cycle of setting goals, reflecting, planning, experimenting, analyzing results, and revising plans as the standard procedure in the district and its schools.

- Requiring each member of the district to develop personal professional improvement plans.

- Anchoring changes in the culture of the district and schools so that they are sustained despite changes in personnel.

- Citing and celebrating improvements and then identifying new and more challenging goals.

Focus on results by:

- Working with schools to identify the knowledge and skills each student is to acquire in each grade level and/or course.

- Developing varied assessment procedures that provide teachers with the information and feedback they need to make informed decisions on their practice.

- Conducting ongoing market research of parents and community members and sharing the results with the schools.

- Asking, "What are the results we seek?" and "How will we know if we have achieved them?" when considering any new improvement initiative—and requiring schools to do the same.

- Centering district goals on improved student performance.

- Providing periodic reports on the progress being made toward district goals.

Advocates of site-based school improvement typically call on the districts to provide the resources and support that enable schools to engage in the difficult work of improvement. But simply telling districts to supply its schools with the resources they need is not very useful. Most districts simply do not have the resources to meet all requests or to do all that needs to be done. The issue then becomes targeting resources towards areas that offer the greatest leverage. When a district focuses on helping its educators develop their ability to function as members of a professional learning community, the district will realize the greatest dividends from its investment. The focus on the professional learning community also enables districts to provide a framework for individual school improvement that offers tremendous autonomy to individual schools.

The context of staff development is job-embedded. Traditional schools think of staff development in terms of workshops. This approach suggests that educators learn best when they leave their schools to attend training sessions. In contrast, professional learning communities think of staff development in terms of the workplace, and that, to paraphrase Robert Frost, makes all the difference. As John Kotter (1996) writes:

> *Because we spend so many of our waking hours at work, most of our development takes place—or doesn't take place—on the job. This simple fact has*

enormous implications. If our time at work encour-
ages us and helps us to develop, we will eventually
realize our potential. Conversely, if time at work does
little or nothing to develop our skills, we will never live
up to our potential. (p. 165)

In the right school context, learning is so deeply embedded in the daily work of educators that it is difficult to distinguish between where the work ends and the learning begins. Teachers are engaging in a powerful form of staff development each time they work together to develop curriculum and assessment strategies; engage in the ongoing cycle of inquiry, reflection, dialogue, action, analysis, and adjustments in order to improve results; and give one another feedback as they practice new skills. Creating this context of job-embedded learning offers the most promising strategy for effective staff development.

Any consultant or facilitator who has tried to help a school launch some aspect of school improvement has seen the phenomenon of school context at work. Two schools initiate major professional growth programs designed to improve conditions for teaching and learning. The consultant, content, and presentation strategies are identical, but the faculty in one school embraces the concept and works to implement it while the teachers in the other respond with total indifference. These different reactions can only be attributed to the context or culture of the schools themselves. In the right school context, even flawed staff development activities (such as the much-maligned single-session workshop) can stimulate the reflection, collaboration, and experimentation that result in improvements. Conversely, in the wrong school context, even well-conceived and well-delivered activities are likely to be ineffective. While schools should certainly pay attention to the ideas that are presented to staff and the strategies used to help teachers master those ideas, schools should focus primarily on creating a context or culture that is conducive to professional growth and development. As Senge advises:

> *Learning is always an on-the-job phenomenon. Learning always occurs in the context of where you are taking action. So we need to find ways to get teachers working together; we need to create an environment where they can continually reflect on what they are doing and learn more and more what it takes to work as team.* (O'Neil, 1995, p. 20)

The context of staff development fosters individual and organizational renewal. When it is done well, staff development fosters individual and organizational renewal. In fact, Robert Waterman's (1987) description of the characteristics of a renewing organization also describes a school that uses staff development to seek and find better ways of fulfilling its vision. These characteristics include:

- *Informed optimism.* Staff development has an impact when educators believe in their ability to improve conditions for teaching and learning. If they lack this sense of self-efficacy, they are not likely to exert the necessary effort to master new skills or contribute to school improvement efforts.

- *Direction and empowerment.* Effective staff development empowers individual schools to create their own improvement initiatives, but those initiatives are directed by the insistence that the school plan must enhance its ability to function as a professional learning community.

- *Friendly facts.* Effective staff development programs are driven by data, by facts. Schools assess their initiatives at a number of different levels and seek to generate comparisons, rankings, measurements—anything that provides context and moves decision making beyond the realm of mere opinion.

- *A different mirror.* Effective staff development programs welcome different perspectives. Schools view the solicitation of the opinions of parents, students, and staff as an opportunity for growth. Furthermore, they are open, curious, and inquisitive and look beyond the school to external sources for new ideas.

- *Teamwork and trust.* Collaboration and teamwork are fundamental to good staff development practice. Effective models help break down the isolation and we/they barriers that are so destructive to growth.

- *Stability in motion.* At the same time that staff development encourages constant growth, it also reinforces a commitment to mission, vision, and values that remain constant. Furthermore, effective staff development does not look for the quick fix or the latest bandwagon. It fosters the pursuit of long-term training that results in individual mastery and organizational advancement.

- *Attitudes and attention.* Ineffective programs hope to improve performance through motivational speakers and exhortation. Programs have an impact when school leaders pay attention to the content, process, and context of staff development.

- *Causes and commitment.* The best staff development enables participants to see the relationship between the programs and practices that they are asked to pursue and the commitments they have made to improving their schools. The link between the specific program and the achievement of vision and goals is explicit.

Summary

High-quality staff development plays an integral part in the creation and operation of a professional learning community. The National Staff Development Council, United States Department of Education, and the National Foundation for the Improvement of Education have identified standards for quality staff development. The conclusions of these agencies offer a very consistent message regarding effective professional development and can be used by schools to audit their own practices.

The purpose of staff development is to help personnel become more individually and collectively effective in helping all students achieve the intended results of their education. Therefore, attention to developing the collective ability of the faculty to solve problems and achieve goals should be assigned a higher priority than independent individual growth.

The content of effective staff development programs should:

- Be based on research.
- Focus on both generic and discipline-specific teaching skills.
- Expand the repertoire of teachers to meet the needs of students who learn in diverse ways.

The process of effective staff development should:

- Attend to the tenets of good teaching.
- Provide the ongoing coaching that is critical to the mastery of new skills.
- Result in reflection and dialogue on the part of participants.
- Be sustained over a considerable period of time.

- Be evaluated at several different levels, including evidence of improved student performance.

The context of effective staff development should:

- Be focused on individual schools and have strong support from the central office.

- Be so deeply embedded in daily work that it is difficult to determine where the work ends and the staff development begins.

- Foster renewal.

Chapter 13

Passion and Persistence

At the heart of sustained morale and motivation lie
two ingredients that appear somewhat contradictory:
on the one hand, positive attitudes toward the future
and toward what one can accomplish through one's
own intentional acts, and on the other hand, recog-
nition that life is not easy and that nothing is ever
finally safe.

—John Gardner (1986, p. 10)

When presented with a challenge as complex as transforming schools into professional learning communities, most of us look for ways of reducing that challenge into more manageable steps. Because we need help in understanding the complexity of the problem, we seek linear, sequential procedures or checklists we can use to indicate progress. We gravitate toward the four building blocks of the learning community, the five criteria for evaluating a vision statement, the six characteristics of good teachers, the ten strategies for principals who function as leaders of a professional learning community, and so on. This tendency to seek sequential steps or checklists can help to sharpen our focus on what must be done. However, it is important to recognize the inherent dangers in this effort to simplify a complex task. Creating a professional learning community is a passionate, nonlinear, and persistent endeavor.

A Passionate Endeavor

When the challenge of creating a professional learning community is reduced to a recipe or formula, it is easy to overlook the fact that this task is a passionate endeavor. A school does not become a learning community simply by advancing through the steps on a checklist, but rather by tapping into the wellsprings of emotions that lie within the professionals of that school. The professional learning community makes a conscious effort to bring those emotions to the surface and to express explicitly what often is left unsaid. As John Gardner (1988) writes:

> One of the deepest truths about the cry of the human heart is that it is so often muted, so often a cry that is never uttered. To be sure there are needs and feelings that we express quite openly; lying deeper are emotions we share only with loved ones, and deeper still the things we tell no one. . . . It is strange that members of a species renowned for communicative gifts should leave unexpressed some of their deepest yearnings. (p. 6)

What are some of the needs and yearnings that the professional learning community seeks to address? There is a basic human desire to succeed in one's work, but the steady pronouncements of the failure of public education have dampened that desire within many educators. Furthermore, a lack of clear goals and agreed-upon indicators of achievement make it difficult for many schools to rebut their alleged "failure." The professional learning community calls for the clarity of purpose, the monitoring of results, and the celebration of progress that can restore the sense of achievement that people must feel in order to sustain their motivation.

There is also a basic human desire to belong, to feel a part of a collective endeavor. Schools have often failed to generate this sense of belonging because teachers have worked in isolation. The professional learning community tries to break down the walls of isolation and to foster collaborative relationships. Systems are put in place and relationships are encouraged that provide each staff member with someone to turn to for solace, help, and suggestions in meeting his or her challenges.

Above all else, there is a basic human desire to live a life of meaning, to serve a higher purpose, to make a difference in this world. It has been argued that this search for meaning, for significance, is the primary force in human life (Frankl, 1959). The desire to make a difference in the lives of their students is the single most powerful factor that attracts people to the teaching profession. But their belief in their ability to make a difference is often shaken when they encounter students who respond with indifference, confront external factors over which they seem to have little control, begin to question the relevance of the curriculum they are asked to teach, and work in a system that seems indifferent to them as individuals.

The professional learning community sets out to restore that belief by creating a community of caring and mutual concern. These schools focus not only on the content of the curriculum but also on the quality of connections between educators and students and among the educators themselves. It is only when students feel a connection with their teachers—when students believe that they are recognized, respected, and valued—that teachers are in a position to make a difference in students' lives. Furthermore, when educators connect with one another, they can accomplish far more collectively than they could ever hope to accomplish individually.

There are those who regard an appeal to the emotions as an inappropriate strategy for organizations—too "touchy-feely" for the serious business of school reform. These people are likely to call for systems, procedures, and benchmarks to be the cornerstones of reform. Indeed, these elements are essential to school improvement initiatives. But calls for more effective systems or for achieving higher test scores will not evoke passion, and school improvement must be a passionate undertaking if it is to be sustained. Educators hunger for evidence that they are successful in their work, that they are part of a significant collective endeavor, and that their efforts are making a difference in the lives of their students. When schools overlook the importance of appealing to these basic human needs to achieve, to belong, and to feel significant, they will be unable to generate the passion that is needed to forge a professional learning community.

A Nonlinear Endeavor

Step-by-step procedures and checklists can offer the illusion that creating a professional learning community is a linear task, but substantive change is never that simple. It is typically messy and redundant, requiring constant reexamination of conclusions and decisions. The exact meanings of specific provisions of the vision and values statements are likely to be debated periodically. Teachers immersed in developing assessment strategies, for example, may feel the need to reconsider course objectives they had adopted just a few months earlier. In the middle of the change initiative, there will be those who will suddenly question the need for change.

The process of creating a professional learning community is inherently dynamic and inefficient, and those who think that they can reduce it to a recipe for success are bound to be frustrated. The following description of life in general applies to the creation of a learning community as well:

Life is not neat, parsimonious, logical, nor elegant. Life
seeks order in a disorderly way. Life uses processes we
find hard to tolerate and difficult to believe in—mess
upon mess until something workable emerges. . . . It
takes a lot of repeated mess to get it right. (Wheatley
& Kellner-Rogers, 1996, p. 17)

Members of a professional learning community must be
prepared to slosh around together in the mess, to endure temporary discomfort, to accept uncertainty, to celebrate their
discoveries, and to move quickly beyond their mistakes. They
must recognize that even with the most careful planning, mis-
understandings will occur occasionally, uncertainty will prevail,
people will resort to old habits, and things will go wrong. At
those moments, they must give one another the benefit of the
doubt, maintain a sense of humor, and, above all, demonstrate
what Patrick Dolan (1994) refers to as "grace":

What we need, very often, more than anything else,
is a "grace" with one another. This grace comes from
understanding how difficult this business is, and from
making the very best assumptions about people and
their desire to change, understanding the reality of
past experience and the culture so often in place. It
is hard to make these changes, and we will never get
it right at the very beginning. . . . It is the giving of
grace to one another that very often allows us to move
through the early sticking moments and gather enough
momentum . . . [to] stay the course. (pp. 166–167)

A Persistent Endeavor

Weary school principals are likely to regard a call to create a learning community as simply another task to complete.
"Create a vision statement, develop value statements? Sure, send
me the forms," they often respond. Checklists can reinforce this

faulty perception. Principals can follow the steps of the checklist, file the appropriate documents with the central office—and then return to business as usual. Then, when improvements do not occur, they declare the learning community initiative is just another failed reform.

Once again, it is important to understand that a learning community is not created by completing a series of tasks but rather by beginning a process of perpetual renewal. This process calls on each member of the faculty to regard the continual search for better ways of fulfilling the school's mission and responding to change as integral parts of their daily responsibilities. It presents a constant challenge that will never be completely met.

Because of the factory model that has dominated the thinking of the twentieth century, there is a tendency to think of improvement in terms of production—develop a design, reduce the process into sequential steps, and proceed from step to step until the finished product has been created. The challenge of creating a professional learning community demands a new way of thinking about improvement because it does not accept the premise of a finished product. Toynbee's (1958) description of civilization provides a more appropriate metaphor: "It is a movement . . . and not a condition, a journey and not a destination, a voyage and not a harbor." And still another useful image can be drawn from the metaphor of farming:

> *The processes involved in school improvement are analogous to farming. We must plant the seeds of school improvement, cultivate, nurture, and care for them. We must practice patience and celebrate the unfolding of each blossom. We must believe the quality of the lives of our families, friends, and neighbors depends on the success of each harvest—because it*

does! We must realize one profitable crop will not be grounds for retirement. We must continually plan, monitor, and model the best behaviors and practices known. This will only happen if the process is cyclical, if it becomes internalized, if it is how we do business every day. (DuFour, Eaker, & Ranells, 1992, p. 11)

Thus, the creation of a professional learning community cannot be reduced to a "to do" list. It demands persistence! When Bennis and Nanus (1985) asked 90 successful leaders in a wide variety of endeavors about the personal qualities that had contributed to their success, the respondents did not focus on charisma or brilliance but on a willingness to accept challenges, commitment, constancy, and persistence. Each of the leaders had experienced setbacks and disappointments, but none ever used the term "failure" to describe attempts gone awry. They considered "mistakes" or "glitches" as situations they could learn from and thus improve the likelihood of success in their subsequent efforts. Educators must demonstrate this same persistence in their efforts to create professional learning communities. Those who believe they can "get it right" the first time are either naive or arrogant. It is not a project to be completed: it is a life's work.

A Final Critical Question

With the constant attacks and increasing demands on public education, it is understandable that some educators have succumbed to resignation and despair. When confronted with so much to do and so many obstacles to overcome, it is easy to lose heart and choose to do nothing. Almost every faculty includes members who have surrendered to cynicism and fatalism, but cynics and fatalists are generally incapable of creating a better future. If schools are to improve, they need educators who believe in the possibility of a better future—and in themselves.

The link between success and self-efficacy—the belief that one has mastery over one's life and can meet challenges as they come up—has been well established (Gardner, 1988; Goleman, 1995; Sternberg, 1996). Thus, perhaps the most critical question educators must confront as they consider an initiative to create a professional learning community is this one: Do we believe in our collective capacity to create a better future for our school?

While energized individuals can serve as catalysts for such a transformation, they cannot sustain it through the long haul. And while it is not imperative that every staff member become an ardent advocate for the change, it is imperative that the school develop a critical mass of personnel that accepts both the desirability and feasibility of transforming the school. The process will succeed only if educators can create a community of colleagues that supports and nourishes them through the inevitable difficulties. Each individual in the school must take a hard look at the person in the mirror and ask if that person believes in his or her ability to help create a professional learning community despite all the obstacles.

Self-efficacy is not the equivalent of an unrealistically rosy view of the future. Optimism must be tempered by tough-minded recognition of the difficulties that lie ahead. If creating a professional learning community is analogous to a "voyage," educators must prepare themselves to be buffeted by occasional ill winds along the way.

While some schools are content to lie at anchor and accept things as they are, and other schools simply drift from fad to fad, the members of a professional learning community will stay the course. They will recognize that they must overcome their history and respond to future problems that they could not possibly anticipate. Yet, they will set forth because, like

Oliver Wendell Holmes, they will have concluded that "what lies behind us and what lies ahead of us are insignificant compared to what lies within us." We wish them Godspeed.

Appendix A

Sample Vision Statements

This appendix provides two examples of vision statements developed by different schools: Adlai Stevenson High School in Lincolnshire, Illinois, and the Tintic School District in Eureka, Utah. As you consider these vision statements, remember that the product, the statement itself, is not nearly as important as the process. Those who use one of these statements in order to accelerate their school improvement initiative will have missed the major point. If a vision statement is adopted, but not developed, by a school's staff, its words will probably mean little or nothing at all to the staff. It is only when the teachers and constituents who develop the statement find meaning and ownership in its words that a vision statement will have an impact. This impact lies not in the eloquence of its statement, but in the meaning and direction it gives to the people in the school who developed it.

Stevenson High School Vision Statement

Community Relations

An Exemplary School

If Stevenson High School is to be an exemplary school, it must have a clear sense of the goals that it is trying to accomplish, the characteristics of the school it seeks to become, and the contributions that the various stakeholders in the school must make in order to transform ideals into reality. The following vision statement is intended to provide the standards that Stevenson High School should strive to achieve and maintain.

I. Curriculum

An exemplary school provides students with a common core curriculum complemented with a variety of elective courses and co-curricular activities. This balanced program stimulates intellectual curiosity, requires students to demonstrate that they have learned how to learn, and enables them to become productive and effective citizens. The school articulates the outcomes it seeks for all of its students and monitors each student's attainment of those outcomes through a variety of indicators. In such a school, the curriculum:

A. Addresses mastery of academic content that integrates acquisition of essential life skills.

B. Enables students to broaden their perspective in order to understand and appreciate diverse cultures within the school as well as cultures and conditions beyond those of their local community.

C. Stimulates active engagement on the part of students.

D. Recognizes and provides for individual differences and interests.

E. Integrates technology as a means to achieve specific curricular outcomes.

F. Reflects the District's support of innovation and commitment to continuous improvement.

II. Attention to Individual Students

Regardless of its size, an exemplary school recognizes the importance of each individual student. Those within the school make a concerted effort to communicate and demonstrate their concern for each student. As a result, each student feels that he or she is valued as a member of the school community. In an exemplary school:

A. Attention is paid to facilitating each student's transition to and through high school.

B. Each student is provided the information, assistance, and support that enables him or her to develop appropriate educational and career goals.

C. The behavior, academic progress, and emotional well-being of each student are continually monitored, and appropriate services are initiated as needed.

III. Personnel

An exemplary school operates on the premise that a school can only be as good as the personnel that it employs. Therefore, the Board and Administration are committed to recruiting and retaining individuals with exceptional expertise in their respective fields. In such a school:

A. All staff demonstrate their support of and commitment to the school's vision and values.

B. All staff have high expectations for student success and work individually and collaboratively to create conditions that promote student success.

C. All staff model the importance of lifelong learning through their commitment to ongoing professional development.

D. The Board of Education and Administration are proactive in promoting and protecting the District's vision and values.

IV. Students

In the final analysis, the effectiveness of any school is assessed on the basis of the conduct, character, and achievement of its students. In an exemplary school, students:

A. Accept responsibility for their learning, decisions, and actions.

B. Develop the skills to become more self-directed learners as they make the transition from freshman through senior year.

C. Become actively engaged in and give their best effort to academic and co-curricular pursuits.

D. Contribute to school and community service.

E. Conduct themselves in a way that contributes to a safe and orderly atmosphere and ensures the rights of others.

F. Are considerate of others—teachers, staff, fellow students, visitors, etc.

V. Climate

An exemplary school provides a warm, inviting climate that enables students to enjoy their high school experience and results in a shared sense of pride in the school. In such a school:

A. There is a commitment to provide an emotionally and physically safe, supportive environment.

B. There is an ongoing effort to providing a school that is free of alcohol, other drugs, and violence.

C. There are opportunities for high levels of participation in the curricular and co-curricular programs.

D. All individuals are treated with respect and consideration.

E. Relationships are characterized by caring and cooperation.

F. There is recognition and celebration of individual effort and achievement.

G. There is open communication between students, staff, administrators, and the Board of Education.

H. Well-maintained physical facilities meet the needs of students and the community and reflect pride in the school.

VI. Community Partnerships

An exemplary school recognizes the importance of establishing effective partnerships with the larger community—parents, residents, businesses, government agencies, and other educational systems. It strives to develop the community's allegiance to and ownership in the school. In such a school:

A. The community demonstrates its support for the vision and values of the school.

B. The community provides the resources that enable the school to offer exemplary academic and co-curricular programs and holds the school accountable for long-range financial planning to safeguard the community's investment in education.

C. The community participates in the life of the school by attending programs, volunteering service, and assisting in the processes that have been designed to enhance the various aspects of the school.

D. The community calls upon the school to establish effective two-way communication that both provides information and seeks feedback.

E. The community has ready access to the school's resources and facilities.

F. Parents play an active role in the education of their children, monitor their children's academic performance, and work with teachers to emphasize the importance of education.

G. Partnerships are established with business that reinforce the relevance of the academic and co-curricular programs and provide a direct link between the school and the workplace.

H. The school establishes effective linkages with sender districts and institutions of higher education.

Tintic School District Vision Statement

If the children of this community are to reap the benefits of an exemplary education, Tintic School District must have a clear sense of the goals it is trying to accomplish, the characteristics of the schools it seeks to provide, and the contributions that the various stakeholders in the District must make in order to transform these ideals into reality. The following vision statement is intended to provide the standards that Tintic should strive to achieve and maintain. These standards should serve as both the blueprint for our improvement efforts and the benchmarks by which we will evaluate our progress.

I. Leadership

Exemplary school districts require effective leaders—leaders who are able to build a *shared* vision that serves as a bridge between the district's present and the future that it desires. In such a district, the leaders:

A. Promote and protect the district's vision on a daily basis.

B. Establish priorities and focus that provide a sense of direction for the district.

C. Are committed to continuous improvement and providing the ongoing professional development essential to an improving school.

D. Facilitate teacher participation in the decision-making process.

E. Facilitate positive relationships between community members, parents, staff, students, and faculty.

F. Pursue the district's vision with persistence, tenacity, and courageous patience.

II. Staff

An exemplary school district operates on the premise that a school can only be as good as the personnel that it employs. Therefore, it is committed to recruiting and retaining outstanding educators who can advance the district's vision. In such a district, all staff members:

A. Are guided by shared goals and a sense of common purpose.

B. Have high expectations for student achievement and accept responsibility for helping students meet those expectations.

C. Collaborate with one another on a regular basis on curriculum, instruction, individual students, and school improvement initiatives.

D. Model the importance of lifelong learning by their commitment to their personal professional growth.

III. Curriculum and Instruction

An exemplary school district provides a diverse and balanced curriculum. This curriculum includes a core that specifies the knowledge and skills that all students are to attain. The district designs its curriculum and instruction to enable all students to acquire these outcomes through their student educational plan. In such a school district:

A. Curriculum and instruction are guided by specific, clearly stated, challenging goals for each grade level and course.

B. The scope (depth and breadth) and sequence (order or flow) of the curriculum are aligned from grade to grade and subject to subject so that teachers understand the relationship of their teaching assignment to the rest of the curriculum.

C. The academic progress of each student is closely monitored, and support is provided for those who require additional assistance.

D. Instructional strategies recognize individual learning styles, result in students who are actively engaged for the full class period, and promote independent learning.

E. Systematic processes of analysis, goal setting, and implementation are in place to demonstrate the district's commitment to continuous improvement.

IV. School Climate

An exemplary school district ensures that all of its schools provide an orderly yet inviting climate that is conducive to learning and protects instructional time. In the schools of such a district:

A. Relationships are based upon mutual respect and consideration.

B. There is a commitment to providing an emotionally and physically safe, supportive environment.

C. School rules are based upon a few fundamental principles that provide clear guidelines for student behavior.

D. The entire staff helps students understand the importance of the school rules by consistently enforcing those rules

E. There is a conscious effort to recognize and celebrate the efforts and achievements of students and staff.

V. Community Support

An exemplary school district has created an effective partnership with its community. The district is committed to addressing the needs of the community and establishes effective two-way communication to keep residents informed of district policies and initiatives. The community provides the district with the support that is essential to an improving district. In such a district:

A. The community has helped to develop and has endorsed the district's vision of the schools it strives to provide.

B. The community provides the resources—personnel, facilities, materials, equipment, and time—that enable the school district to offer exemplary programs.

C. The community has ready access to the school's resources and facilities.

D. Parents play an active role in the education of their children, monitor their children's academic performance, work with teachers to emphasize the importance of education, and model a commitment to lifelong learning.

VI. Students

In the final analysis, the effectiveness of a school district is determined on the basis of the conduct, character, and achievement of its students. In an exemplary school district, students:

A. Accept responsibility for their learning, decisions, and actions.

B. Set challenging goals and give their best effort to achieve them.

C. Believe in themselves and take pride in their achievements.

D. Demonstrate a desire to learn.

E. Become actively involved in school activities.

F. Conduct themselves in a way that contributes to a safe, orderly, positive school atmosphere and ensures the rights of others.

G. Form partnerships with their teachers in working to realize their full potential.

Appendix B

Curriculum Standards, Models, and Concepts

This appendix provides examples of useful sources for curriculum development. It is not intended to offer either a comprehensive listing of all useful resources or even a thorough analysis of those that are included. It is impossible to survey all of the curricular ideas and models available in today's educational arena. Providing materials such as these can be a valuable resource for teachers as they collaborate on curricular issues. Schools should be organized so that teachers do not have to tackle these issues in isolation. Both the structure and culture of schools should encourage teachers to collaborate with one another to find the right mix of curricular ideas for their students and their schools. This collaboration fosters the ownership and shared responsibility that make curriculum development a powerful force for school improvement.

Academic Content Standards

The academic content standards movement calls for a clearer identification of what students should know and be able to do and is critical of the fact that what students are taught in a specific subject or at a specific grade level varies greatly among schools and even among classrooms within a school. With its emphasis on specific knowledge and skills and explicit levels of performance, an examination of standards is an excellent place for a faculty to begin its study of "best thinking" about the curriculum in a learning community.

Content Knowledge: A Compendium of Standards and Benchmarks for K–12 Education (1996) and *Designing Standards Based Districts, Schools, and Classrooms* (1997) by John Kendall and Robert Marzano are two excellent resources for a study of content standards. These complementary works synthesize the curriculum recommendations of the major professional organizations for each content area. Kendall and Marzano (1997) also articulate standards in thinking and reasoning that should cut across all disciplines. These standards stipulate that students should be able to:

1. Understand and apply basic principles of presenting an argument.

2. Understand and apply basic principles of logic and reasoning.

3. Effectively use mental processes that are based on identifying similarities and dissimilarities (compares, contrasts, classifies).

4. Understand and apply basic principles of hypothesis testing and scientific inquiry.

5. Apply basic trouble-shooting and problem-solving techniques.

6. Apply decision-making techniques. (p. 38)

Kendall and Marzano also synthesize a variety of reports to identify standards for the knowledge and skills that are considered important for the workplace. These "workplace basics" include:

Working with Others

1. Contributes to the overall effort of a group.

2. Uses conflict resolution techniques.

3. Works well with diverse individuals and in diverse situations.

4. Displays effective interpersonal skills.

5. Demonstrates leadership ability.

Self-Regulation

1. Sets and manages goals.

2. Performs self-appraisal.

3. Considers risks.

4. Demonstrates perseverance.

5. Maintains a healthy self-concept.

6. Restrains impulsivity. (p. 41)

Another useful source for a faculty interested in best thinking in different disciplines is the second edition of *Content of the Curriculum,* edited by Allan Glatthorn (1995). This book offers the conclusions of experts in each discipline who were asked to address the following questions:

- What standards for and goals of the curriculum are recommended?

- To what extent do curriculum developments in cognitive psychology, technology, and assessment influence the content of the curriculum?

- What structure for the curriculum is recommended? What strand should be used in planning, how should the curriculum differ from level to level, and how much integration is recommended?

- What current issues divide the experts in the field and cause controversy among the public?

- What major research and evaluation studies have been carried out with respect to curriculum models?

- What major resources are available to curriculum planners?

Glatthorn concludes the book by offering practical guidelines for curriculum development.

Authentic Achievement

In *Authentic Achievement: Restructuring Schools for Intellectual Quality* (1996), Newmann and others offer standards for what they refer to as "authentic achievement and pedagogy." Newmann contends that authentic academic achievement for students is characterized by construction of knowledge, disciplined inquiry, and the value of achievement beyond school (pp. 23–24). He also specifies standards for assessment, instruction, and student performance that result in authentic student achievement. These standards include:

Standards for Authentic Pedagogy: Assessment Tasks

Construction of Knowledge

Standard 1: Organization of information. The task asks students to organize, synthesize, interpret, explain, or evaluate complex information in addressing a concept, problem, or issue.

Standard 2: Consideration of alternatives. The task asks students to consider alternative solutions, strategies, perspectives, or points of view in addressing a concept, problem, or issue.

Disciplinary Inquiry

Standard 3: Disciplinary content. The task asks students to show understanding and/or to use ideas, theories, or perspectives considered central to an academic or professional discipline.

Standard 4: Disciplinary process. The task asks students to use methods of inquiry, research, or communication characteristic of an academic or professional discipline.

Standard 5: Elaborated written communication. The task asks students to elaborate on their understanding, explanations, or conclusions through extended writing.

Value beyond School

Standard 6: Connection to the world beyond the classroom. The task asks students to address a concept, problem, or issue that is similar to one that they have encountered or are likely to encounter in life beyond the classroom.

Standard 7: Audience beyond the school. The task asks students to communicate their knowledge, present a product or performance, or take some action for an audience beyond the teacher, classroom, and school building. (p. 29)

Standards for Authentic Pedagogy: Instruction

Construction of Knowledge

Standard 1: Higher-order thinking. Instruction involves students in manipulating information and ideas by synthesizing, generalizing, explaining, hypothesizing, or arriving at conclusions that produce new meaning and understandings for them.

Disciplinary Inquiry

Standard 2: Deep knowledge. Instruction addresses central ideas of a topic or discipline with enough thoroughness to explore connections and relationships and to produce relatively complex understandings.

Standard 3: Substantive conversation. Students engage in extended conversational exchanges with the teacher or their peers about subject matter in a way that builds an improved and shared understanding of ideas or topics.

Value beyond School

Standard 4: Connections to the world beyond the classroom. Students make connections between substantive knowledge and either public problems or personal experiences. (p. 33)

Standards for Authentic Student Performance

Construction of Knowledge

Standard 1: Analysis.

> Mathematics: Student performance demonstrates thinking with mathematical content by organizing, synthesizing, interpreting, hypothesizing, describing patterns, making models or simulations, constructing mathematical arguments, or inventing procedures.

> Social studies: Student performance demonstrates higher-order thinking with social studies content by organizing, synthesizing, interpreting, evaluating, and hypothesizing to produce comparisons, contrasts, arguments, application of information to new contexts, and consideration of different ideas or points of view.

Disciplinary Inquiry

Standard 2: Disciplinary concepts.

Mathematics: Student performance demonstrates an understanding of important mathematical ideas that goes beyond application of algorithms by elaborating on definitions, making connections to other mathematical concepts, or making connections to other disciplines.

Social studies: Student performance demonstrates an understanding of ideas, concepts, theories, and principles from social disciplines and civic life by using them to interpret and explain specific, concrete information or events.

Standard 3: Elaborated written communication.

Mathematics: Student performance demonstrates a concise, logical, and well-articulated explanation or argument that justifies mathematical work.

Social studies: Student performance demonstrates an elaborated account that is clean and coherent and provides richness in details, qualifications, and argument. The standard could be met by elaborated consideration of alternative points of view. (p. 37)

Smart Schools

The concept of the "smart school" developed by David Perkins (1992) provides an excellent framework for thinking about the curriculum. According to Perkins' model, smart schools are:

Informed: Administrators, teachers, and indeed students in the smart school know a lot about human thinking and learning and how it works best. And they know a lot about school structure and collaboration and how that works best.

Energetic: The smart school requires spirit as much as information. In the smart school, measures are taken to cultivate positive energy in the structure of the school, the style of administration, and the treatment of teachers and students.

Thoughtful: Smart schools are thoughtful places in the double sense of caring and mindful. First of all, people are sensitive to one another's needs and treat each other thoughtfully. Second, both the teaching/learning process and school decision-making processes are thinking centered . . . putting thinking at the center of all that is crucial. (p. 3)

Perkins argues that the general goal of education is generative knowledge—"knowledge that serves people well in later academic and non-academic pursuits, knowledge that empowers the next generation to build even further" (p. 5). Generative knowledge requires teaching not only for retention, but also for understanding and application, or what Perkins calls "active use." The curriculum design that is best suited to this purpose is based on the premise that "learning is a consequence of thinking" (p. 8). Thus, a curriculum should be designed to generate "thoughtful learning" by creating experiences in which students think about and with what they are learning. This can best be accomplished through a "metacurriculum" that is infused in traditional subject matter and emphasizes:

Levels of understanding—paying attention not just to facts, but also to the problem-solving, epistemic (that is, justification and explanation), and inquiry levels of understanding.

Languages of thinking—using (1) a thinking vocabulary with terms such as hypothesis, evidence, belief; (2) strategies for decision making and problem solving; and (3) ways of thinking on paper, such as concept mapping, to foster more thoughtful classrooms.

Intellectual passions—fostering such dispositions as intellectual curiosity, willingness to seek and evaluate the reasoning of others, and reflection on one's own thinking process.

Integrative mental models—attempting to tie a subject matter or large parts of it together into a more coherent and meaningful whole and to identify interrelationships among subject matters.

Learning to learn—building students' capacity to conduct themselves more effectively as learners.

Teaching for transfer—teaching so that students apply what they learn in a particular subject in other subject areas as well as outside of school.

Perkins contends that determining what we try to teach is the most critical choice in curriculum development and argues that the metacurriculum of the smart school will require the elimination of some traditional content. Teaching for better understanding is more than just a matter of superior methods, he argues: "It requires teaching something more or something else, choosing differently what we try to teach. To teach for better understanding, we should teach different stuff" (p. 75).

The Coalition of Essential Schools

In 1984 the Coalition of Essential Schools was organized by Ted Sizer and his colleagues at Brown University in response to five years of research on high schools. Although the coalition does not offer a detailed curricular model, it does offer a set of guiding principles for its members:

1. The school should focus on helping adolescents learn to use their minds well. Schools should not attempt to be "comprehensive" if such a claim is made at the expense of the school's central intellectual purpose.

2. The school's goal should be simple: each student should master a number of essential skills and be competent in certain areas of knowledge. Although these skills and areas will, to varying degrees, reflect the traditional academic disciplines, the program's design should be shaped by the intellectual and imaginative powers and competencies that students need, rather than by conventional "subjects." The aphorism "less is more" should dominate: curricular decisions are to be directed toward the students' attempt to gain mastery rather than by the teachers' effort to cover content.

3. The school's goal should apply to all students, but the means to this goal will vary as these students themselves vary. School practices should be tailor-made to meet the needs of every group of adolescents.

4. Teaching and learning should be personalized to the maximum extent feasible. No teacher should have direct responsibility for more than 80 students: decisions about the course of study, the use of students' and teachers' time, and the choice of teaching materials and specific pedagogies must be placed in the hands of the principal and staff.

5. The governing metaphor of the school should be student as worker, rather than the more familiar metaphor of teacher as deliverer of instructional services. Accordingly, a prominent pedagogy will be coaching, to provoke students to learn how to learn and thus to teach themselves.

6. Students embarking on secondary school studies are those who show competence in language and elementary mathematics. Students of traditional high school age who do not yet have appropriate levels of competence to start secondary school studies will be provided with intensive remedial work so that they can quickly meet those standards. The diploma should be awarded on a successful final demonstration of mastery at graduation—an Exhibition. This Exhibition by the student of his or her grasp of the central skills and knowledge of the school's program may be jointly administered by the faculty and higher authorities. Because the diploma is awarded when earned, the school's program proceeds with no strict age grading and with no system of credits earned by time spent in class. The emphasis is on the students' demonstration that they can do important things.

7. The tone of the school should explicitly and self-consciously stress the values of unanxious expectation ("I won't threaten you, but I expect much of you"), of trust (unless it is abused), and of decency (the values of fairness, generosity, and tolerance). Incentives appropriate to the school's students and teachers should be emphasized, and parents should be treated as essential collaborators.

8. The principal and teachers should perceive of themselves first as generalists (teachers and scholars in general education) and next as specialists (experts in a particular discipline). Staff should expect multiple obligations (teacher-counselor-manager) and a sense of commitment to the entire school.

9. Administrative and budget targets should include substantial time for collective planning by teachers, competitive salaries for staff, and an ultimate per-pupil cost

not more than 10 percent higher than that at traditional schools. Administrative plans may have to show the phased reduction or elimination of some services now provided for students in many traditional comprehensive secondary schools. (Sizer, 1992, pp. 207–209)

The principles of focused intellectual purpose, limited goals, "less is more," mastery rather than coverage, demonstrated proficiencies, teacher as coach, and student as worker are important concepts that can and should contribute to a faculty's discussion of curriculum.

Accelerated Schools

The accelerated schools' model developed by Henry Levin of Stanford University was launched in 1986 as a comprehensive approach to school change specifically designed to improve schooling for children in at-risk situations. It has grown from a pilot project of two schools in the San Francisco area to almost 1,000 schools in 40 states. Instead of placing children in remedial classes, these schools accelerate student learning by providing all students with challenging activities that traditionally have been reserved only for students identified as gifted and talented.

Accelerated schools adhere to three principles:

Unity of purpose: All members of the school community— staff, parents, students, district office, and local community representatives—develop and work toward a shared vision of what they want the school to be and common goals that benefit all students.

Empowerment coupled with responsibility: Every member of the school community is empowered to share in decision making, in the responsibility for implementing decisions, and in being held accountable for the outcomes of a decision.

Building on strengths: Accelerated schools recognize and utilize the knowledge, talents, and resources of every member of the school community.

The model uses a systematic process designed to promote collaboration and informed decision making. After developing a shared vision for the school, accelerated schools identify discrepancies between that vision and the current conditions in the school, identify priority challenge areas, use an inquiry process to find and implement solutions, and then assess results.

At the center of the accelerated schools movement is the concept of the powerful learning triangle which challenges schools to consider what material will be taught, how it will be taught, and the context in which content will be taught. Curriculum and instruction are designed to result in powerful learning experiences which are:

1. Authentic: Activities and content that are relevant to students' lives.

2. Interactive: Enabling students to learn by exploration.

3. Learner centered: Focused around the needs of students rather than the needs of teachers or textbooks.

4. Inclusive: Incorporating all learning styles, language needs, cultural backgrounds, ethnicities and genders of the students.

5. Continuous: Building on prior knowledge and lessons, and leaving avenues open for further learning and exploration. (Levin, 1996)

These five core components of powerful learning are useful constructs as teachers work together to develop curriculum.

The Basic School

In 1995 the Carnegie Foundation for the Advancement of Teaching published *The Basic School: A Community for Learners* by Ernest Boyer. Boyer envisioned a restructuring of public education into three blocks. The Basic School would serve students in the early years of education and would focus on language and general education. The Common School would span the middle years and would be devoted to a core of general knowledge. The Transition School would represent the last two or three years of formal education and would provide students with beginning apprenticeships and preparation for collegiate study. In *The Basic School: A Community of Learners,* Boyer describes a concept of elementary schools organized around four priorities:

1. **The school as community.** The Basic School has a clear and vital mission, and those within the school work as a community to fulfill that mission. Each classroom represents a community where students and teachers come together to promote learning. Teachers serve as mentors to their students and have time and resources to engage in ongoing professional renewal. Parents are also viewed as members of the learning community and play a vital role within it.

2. **A curriculum with coherence.** Literacy is the first and most essential goal of the Basic School. Students also study fields of knowledge that are organized thematically within a framework called the Core Commonalities. Academic standards are established in literacy and the Core Commonalities, and benchmarks are developed to monitor student achievement.

3. **A climate for learning.** Class sizes are kept small, the teaching schedule is flexible, and student groupings are varied. Rich resources are available to stimulate learning.

4. **A commitment to character.** The Basic School addresses the ethical and moral dimensions of a child's life through attention to seven core virtues.

The Basic School presents a blueprint and overarching framework for the reform of elementary schools while encouraging individual schools to develop their own distinctive programs. It warrants serious consideration from those who seek to improve their elementary schools.

Dimensions of Learning

In the early 1990s, Robert Marzano and his colleagues began publishing a series of books and articles on the "dimensions of learning," which they described as an instructional framework based on the best of what research and theory say about learning (1992). This framework rests on the premise that there are five types, or dimensions, of thinking that are essential to successful learning:

1. Positive attitudes and perceptions about learning.

2. Acquiring and integrating knowledge.

3. Extending and refining knowledge.

4. Using knowledge meaningfully.

5. Productive habits of mind.

These dimensions of learning have significant implications for curriculum development.

Northwest Regional Educational Laboratory

A review of the studies of effective schooling practices presents consistent findings regarding the importance of a well-planned curriculum that is monitored regularly. A synthesis of this research, compiled by the Northwest Regional Educational Laboratory follows:

1. **The curriculum is based on clear goals and objectives.**

   • Learning goals and objectives are clearly defined and displayed; teachers actively use curriculum resources in the building for instructional planning.

   • Clear relationships between learning goals, instructional activities, and student assessments are established and written down.

   • Collaborative curriculum planning and decision making are typical. Special attention is focused on building good continuity across grade levels and courses; teachers know where they fit in the curriculum.

   • Staff, students, and community members know the scope of the curriculum and priorities within it.

   • Periodic curriculum alignment and review efforts are conducted to ensure congruence with school and district goals.

2. **Students are grouped to promote effective instruction.**

   • In required subjects and courses, students are placed in heterogeneous groups; tracks are avoided; underplacement is avoided.

   • Instructional aids and classroom grouping techniques are used to help keep the adult/student ratio low, especially during instruction aimed at priority objectives.

3. **School time is used for learning.**

   • School events are scheduled to avoid disruption of learning time.

   • Everyone understands time-use priorities; school communications highlight the need for time for learning; procedures are developed to maximize learning time.

- Time-use allocations are established among subjects taught; time-use guidelines are followed by staff.

- The school calendar is organized to provide maximum learning time. Prior to adoption, new instructional programs or school procedures are evaluated according to their potential impact on learning time.

- During the school day, unassigned time and time spent on non-instructional activities are minimal; the school day, classes, and other activities start and end on time.

- Student pull-outs from regular classes are minimal, either for academic or non-academic purposes. The amount of pull-out activity is monitored, and corrective action is taken as necessary to keep things in balance.

- Extra learning time is provided for students who want or need it; students can get extra help outside of regular school hours.

4. **Teachers and administrators continually strive to improve instructional effectiveness.**

    - Throughout the school, there is an ongoing concern for improving instructional effectiveness. No one is complacent about student achievement; there is an expectation that educational programs will be changed so that they work better.

    - School improvements are directed toward clearly defined student achievement goals and/or social behavior problems; strong agreement is developed within the school concerning the purpose of im-provement efforts.

    - Priority goals for improvement are set that give focus to planning and implementation. Goals that specify desired changes in achievement or social behavior are known and supported in the school community.

- The full staff is involved in planning for implementation; specific recommendations and guidelines provide the detail needed for good implementation; plans fit the local school context and conditions.

- Implementation is checked carefully and frequently; progress is noted and publicized; activities are modified as necessary to make things work better. Everyone works together to help the improvement effort succeed; staff members discuss implementation and share ideas and approaches.

- Resources are set aside to support improvement activities.

- School improvement efforts are periodically reviewed; progress is noted, and the improvement focus is renewed or redirected; success and new goals are reported. (Northwest Regional Educational Laboratory, 1990a, pp. 15–16)

Bibliography

Adelman, N., & Panton Walking Eagle, K. (1997). Teachers, time, and school reform. In A. Hargreaves (Ed.), *Rethinking educational change with heart and mind* (pp. 92–110). Alexandria, VA: Association of Supervision and Curriculum Development.

Alsalam, N., & Ogle, L. (Eds.). (1990). *The condition of education*. National Center for Educational Statistics. Washington, DC: U.S. Government Printing Office.

Bardwick, J. (1996). Peacetime management and wartime leadership. In F. Hesselbein, M. Goldsmith, & R. Beckhard (Eds.), *The leader of the future* (pp. 131–140). San Francisco: Jossey-Bass.

Barth, R. (1990). *Improving schools from within: Teachers, parents, and principals can make the difference*. San Francisco: Jossey-Bass.

Barth, R. (1991). Restructuring schools: Some questions for teachers and principals. *Phi Delta Kappan, 73*(2), 123–128.

Bell, T. (1984). *The nation responds: Recent efforts to improve education*. Washington, DC: United States Department of Education.

Bellon, J., Bellon, E., & Blank, M. (1992). *Teaching from a research knowledge base: A development and renewal process*. New York: Macmillan.

Bennis, W. (1997). 21st century leadership: Do you have what it takes? *Beyond Computing, 6*(4), 39–43.

Bennis, W., & Nanus, B. (1985). *Leaders: The strategies for taking charge.* New York: Harper and Row.

Bennis, W., & Townsend, P. (1995). *Reinventing leadership.* New York: William Morrow and Company.

Berliner, D. (1984). The glass half full: A review of research in teaching. In P. Hosford (Ed.), *Using what we know about teaching* (pp. 51–77). Alexandria, VA: Association for Supervision and Curriculum Development.

Berliner, D., & Biddle, B. (1995). *The manufactured crisis: Myths, fraud, and the attack on America's public schools.* Reading, MA: Addison-Wesley.

Bestor, A. (1953). *Educational wastelands.* Urbana, IL: University of Illinois Press.

Blankstein, A. M. (1992). Lessons from enlightened corporations. *Educational Leadership 49*(6), 71–75.

Bolman, L., & Deal, T. (1994). *Becoming a teacher leader.* Thousand Oaks, CA: Corwin Press.

Bolman, L., & Deal, T. (1995). *Leading with soul: An uncommon journey of spirit.* San Francisco: Jossey-Bass.

Boyer, E. (1995). *The basic school: A community for learning.* Princeton, NJ: The Carnegie Foundation for the Advancement of Teaching.

Bracey, G. (1997). *Setting the record straight: Responses to misconceptions about public education in the United States.* Alexandria, VA: Association for Supervision and Curriculum Development.

Burns, J. (1978). *Leadership.* New York: Harper and Row.

Carnegie Foundation Forum on Education and the Economy. (1986). *A nation prepared: Teachers for the 21st century.* Washington, DC: Carnegie Foundation.

Cawelti, G. (Ed.). (1995). *Handbook of research on improving student achievement.* Arlington, VA: Educational Research Service.

Champy, J. (1995). *Reengineering management.* New York: Harper Collins.

Center on Families, Communities, Schools and Children's Learning. (1994). *Research and Development Report.* Baltimore, MD: Johns Hopkins University.

Committee for Economic Development. (1994). *Putting learning first: Governing and managing the schools for high achievement.* New York: Committee for Economic Development.

Consortium on Productivity in the Schools. (1995). *Using what we know to get the schools we need.* New York: Teachers College Press.

Covey, S. (1989). *The seven habits of highly effective people: Restoring the character ethic.* New York: Franklin Press.

Covey, S. (1996). Three roles of the leader in the new paradigm. In F. Hesselbein, M. Goldsmith, & R. Beckhard (Eds.), *The leader of the future* (pp. 149–160). San Francisco: Jossey-Bass.

Cubberly, E. (1934). *Public education in the United States.* Boston: Houghton Mifflin.

Darling-Hammond, L. (1995). Policy for restructuring. In A. Lieberman (Ed.), *The Work of Restructuring Schools* (pp. 157–176). New York: Teachers College Press.

Darling-Hammond, L. (1996). What matters most: A competent teacher for every child. *Phi Delta Kappan, 78*(3), 193–200.

Darling-Hammond, L. (1997). *The right to learn.* San Francisco: Jossey-Bass.

Deal, T., & Kennedy, A. (1982). *Corporate cultures: The rites and rituals of corporate life.* Reading, MA: Addison-Wesley.

Deal, T., & Peterson, K. (1990). *The principal's role in shaping school culture.* Washington, DC: United States Department of Education.

Dillon-Peterson, B. (1986). Trusting teachers to know what is good for them. In K. Zumwalt (Ed.), *Improving teachers* (pp. 24–36). Alexandria, VA: Association for Supervision and Curriculum Development.

Dilworth, R. (1995). The DNA of the learning organization. In C. Sarita & J. Renesch (Eds.), *Learning organizations: Developing cultures for tomorrow's workplace* (pp. 243–254). Portland, OR: Productivity Press.

Donahoe, T. (1993). Finding the way: Structure, time, and culture in school improvement. *Phi Delta Kappan, 75*(4), 298–305.

Dolan, W. P. (1994). *Restructuring our schools: A primer on systemic change.* Kansas City, MO: Systems and Organization.

Doyle, W. (1992). Curriculum and pedagogy. In P. Jackson (Ed.), *Handbook of research in curriculum* (pp. 486–516). New York: Macmillan.

Drucker, P. (1992). *Managing for the future: The 1990s and beyond.* New York: Truman Talley Books.

Drucker, P. (1996). Not enough generals were killed. In F. Hesselbein, M. Goldsmith, & R. Beckhard (Eds.), *The leader of the future* (pp. xi–xv). San Francisco: Jossey-Bass.

DuFour, R. (1991). *The principal as staff developer.* Bloomington, IN: Solution Tree (formerly National Educational Service).

DuFour, R. (1995). Restructuring is not enough. *Educational Leadership, 52*(7), 33–36.

DuFour, R. (1997a). Make the words of mission statements come to life. *Journal of Staff Development, 18*(3), 54–55.

DuFour, R. (1997b). Moving toward the school as a learning community. *Journal of Staff Development, 18*(1), 52–53.

DuFour, R. (1997c). Seeing with new eyes. *Journal of Staff Development, 18*(4), 38–39.

DuFour, R., & Eaker, R. (1992). *Creating the new American school: A principal's guide to school improvement.* Bloomington, IN: Solution Tree (formerly National Educational Service).

DuFour, R., Eaker, R., & Ranells, M. (1992). School improvement and the art of visioning. *Tennessee Educational Leadership, XXIV*(1), 6–12.

Dukewits, P., & Gowin, L. (1996). Creating successful collaborative teams. *Journal of Staff Development, 17*(4), 12–16.

Eaker, R., & Awalt, K. (1997). Quality indicators reflect effective school improvement planning. *Tennessee Educational Leadership, XXIV*(1), 7–10.

Eaker, R., & Huffman, J. (1980). Helping teachers use research findings: The consumer-validation process, Occasional Paper No. 44. East Lansing, MI: Institute for Research on Teaching, Michigan State University.

Eastwood, K., & Louis, K. (1992). Restructuring that lasts: Managing the performance dip. *Journal of School Leadership, 2*(2), 213–224.

Educational Research Service. (1983). *Effective schools: A summary of research.* Arlington, VA.

Elam, S., Cramer, J., & Brodinsky, B. (1986). *Staff development: Problems and solutions.* Arlington, VA: American Association of School Administrators Press.

Elam, S., Rose, L., & Gallup, A. (1997). The 29th annual Phi Delta Kappa/Gallup poll of the public's attitudes toward the public schools. *Phi Delta Kappan, 79*(1), 41–56.

Elmore, R. (1996). In Miller, E., Idealists and cynics: The micropolitics of systemic school reform. *Harvard Education Letter, 12*(4), 1.

Enz, C. (1986). *Power and shared values in the corporate culture.* Ann Arbor, MI: University of Michigan Press.

Farkas, S., & Johnson, J. (1996). *Given the circumstances: Teachers talk about education today.* New York: Public Agenda.

Fielding, G., & Schalock, H. (1985). *Promoting the professional development of teachers and administrators.* Eugene, OR: Center for Educational Policy and Management.

Finn, C. (1991). *We must take charge: Our schools and our future.* New York: Free Press.

Fiske, E. (1992). *Smart schools, smart kids: Why do some schools work?* New York: Simon and Schuster.

Frankl, V. (1959). *Man's search for meaning.* New York: Pocket Books.

Fullan, M. (1991). *The new meaning of educational change.* New York: Teachers College Press.

Fullan, M. (1993). *Change forces: Probing the depths of educational reform.* London: Falmer Press.

Fullan, M. (1995). Leadership for change. In K. Leithwood (Ed.), *International handbook of educational leadership and administration.* Dordrecht, Netherlands: Kluwer Academic Publishers.

Fullan, M. (1997a). Broadening the concept of teacher leadership. In S. Caldwell (Ed.), *Professional development in learning-centered schools* (pp. 34–48). Oxford, OH: National Staff Development Council.

Fullan, M. (1997b). Emotion and hope: Constructive concepts for complex times. In A. Hargreaves (Ed.), *Rethinking educational change with heart and mind.* Alexandria, VA: Association for Supervision and Curriculum Development.

Fullan, M., & Hargreaves, A. (1991). *What's worth fighting for in your school?* Toronto: Ontario Public School Teachers' Federation.

Gardner, J. (1986). *The tasks of leadership.* Washington, DC: Independent Sector.

Gardner, J. (1988). *Leadership: An overview*. Washington, DC: Independent Sector.

Gardner, J. (1990). *On leadership*. New York: Free Press.

Georgiades, W., Fuentes, E., & Snyder, K. (1983). *A meta-analysis of productive school cultures*. Houston: University of Texas.

Gerstner, L., Semerad, R., Doyle, D. P., & Johnston, W. (1994). *Reinventing education: Entrepreneurship in America's public schools*. New York: Plume/Penguin.

Glasser, W. (1992). *The quality school: Managing students without coercion* (2nd ed.). New York: Harper Collins.

Glatthorn, A. (1994). *Developing a quality curriculum*. Alexandria, VA: Association for Supervision and Curriculum Development.

Glatthorn, A. (1995). *Content of the curriculum* (2nd ed.). Alexandria, VA: Association for Supervision and Curriculum Development.

Glickman, C. (1986). Developing teacher thought. *Journal of Staff Development, 7*(1), 6–21.

Goleman, D. (1995). *Emotional intelligence: Why it can matter more than IQ*. New York: Bantam Books.

Goodlad, J. (1984). *A place called school: Prospects for the future*. New York: McGraw-Hill.

Gutman, M. (1995). Beyond the bake sale. *America's Agenda, 5*(1), 21–25.

Handy, C. (1995). Managing the dream. In C. Sarita & J. Renesch (Eds.), *Learning organizations: Developing cultures for tomorrow's workplace* (pp. 45–55). Portland, OR: Productivity Press.

Hargreaves, A. (Ed.). (1997). *Rethinking educational change with heart and mind.* Alexandria, VA: Association of Supervision and Curriculum Development.

Henderson, A. (1987). *The evidence continues to grow.* Columbia, MD: National Committee for Citizens in Education.

Henderson, A., & Berla, N. (1995). *A new generation of evidence: The family is critical to student achievement.* Washington, DC: Center for Law and Education.

Hendricks, G., & Ludeman, K. (1996). *The corporate mystic.* New York: Bantam Books.

Heskett, J., & Schlessinger, L. (1996). Leaders who shape and keep performance-oriented cultures. In F. Hesselbein, M. Goldsmith, & R. Beckhard (Eds.), *The leader of the future* (pp. 111–120). San Francisco: Jossey-Bass.

Hodgkinson, H. (1996). *Bringing tomorrow into focus: Demographic insights into the future.* Washington, DC: Institute for Educational Leadership.

Hoffer, E. (1972). *Reflections on the human condition.* New York: Harper-Collins.

Interstate New Teacher Assessment and Support Consortium. (1991). *Model standards for beginning teacher licensure and development: A resource for state dialogue.* Washington, DC: Council of Chief State School Officers.

Interstate School Leaders Licensure Consortium. (1996). *Standards for school leaders.* Washington, DC: Council of Chief State School Officers.

Jacobs, H. (1997). *Mapping the big picture: Integrating curriculum and assessment K–12.* Alexandria, VA: Association for Supervision and Curriculum Development.

James, J. (1996, December). Thinking in the future tense. Keynote address presented at the annual conference of the National Staff Development Council, Vancouver, BC.

Joyce, B., & Showers, B. (1995). Learning experiences in staff development. *The Developer.* May, p. 3.

Kanter, R. M. (1982). The middle manager as innovator. *Harvard Business Review, 60*(4), 95–105.

Kanter, R. M. (1983). *The change masters: Innovation and entrepreneurship in the American corporation.* New York: Simon and Schuster.

Kanter, R. M. (1995). Mastering change. In C. Sarita & J. Renesch (Eds.), *Learning organizations: Developing cultures for tomorrow's workplace* (pp. 71–83). Portland, OR: Productivity Press.

Kanter, R. M. (1996). World-class leaders: The power of partnering. In F. Hesselbein, M. Goldsmith, & R. Beckhard (Eds.), *The leader of the future* (pp. 89–98). San Francisco: Jossey-Bass.

Kanter, R. M. (1997, October). Leading the change-adept organization with concepts, competence, and connections. Keynote address presented at the Lessons in Leadership Conference, Boston.

Kendall, J., & Marzano, R. (1996). *Content knowledge: A compendium of standards and benchmarks for K–12 education.* Aurora, CO: Mid-Continent Regional Educational Laboratory.

Kendall, J., & Marzano, R. (1997). *Designing standards-based districts, schools, and classrooms.* Aurora, CO: Mid-Continent Regional Educational Laboratory.

Kidder, T. (1989). *Among schoolchildren.* Boston: Houghton Mifflin.

Klein, S., Medrich, E., Perez-Ferreiro, V., & MPR Associates. (1996). *Fitting the pieces: Education reform that works.* Washington, DC: U.S. Government Printing Office.

Kofman, F., & Senge, P. (1995). Communities of commitment: The heart of learning organizations. In C. Sarita & J. Renesch (Eds.), *Learning organizations: Developing cultures for tomorrow's workplace* (pp. 15–43). Portland, OR: Productivity Press.

Kotter, J. (1996). *Leading change.* Boston: Harvard Business School Press.

Kouzes, J., & Posner, B. (1987). *The leadership challenge: How to get extraordinary things done in organizations.* San Francisco: Jossey-Bass.

Kouzes, J., & Posner, B. (1996). Seven lessons for leading the voyage to the future. In F. Hesselbein, M. Goldsmith, & R. Beckhard (Eds.), *The leader of the future* (pp. 99–110). San Francisco: Jossey-Bass.

Levin, B. (1994). Improving educational productivity: Putting kids at the center. *Phi Delta Kappan, 75*(10), 758–760.

Levin, H. (1996). What are accelerated schools? *Accelerated Schools Newsletter, 6*(1), 6.

Lezotte, L. (1997). *Learning for all.* Okemos, MI: Effective School Products.

Lieberman, A. (1990). Navigating the four C's: Building a bridge over troubled waters. *Phi Delta Kappan, 71*(7), 531–533.

Lieberman, A. (Ed.). (1995). *The work of restructuring schools.* New York: Teachers College Press.

Lipham, J. (1981). *Effective principal, effective school.* Reston, VA: National Association of Secondary School Principals.

Little, J. (1990). The persistence of privacy: Autonomy and initiative in teachers professional relations. *Teachers College Record, 91*(4), 509–536.

Louis, K. S., Kruse, S., & Marks, H. (1996). Schoolwide professional community. In Fred Newmann and Associates (Ed.), *Authentic achievement: Restructuring schools for intellectual quality* (pp. 179–203). San Francisco: Jossey-Bass.

Louis. K. S., Kruse, S., & Raywid, M. A. (1996). Putting teachers at the center of reform. *NASSP Bulletin, 80*(580), 9–21.

Marks, H., Doanne, K., & Secada, W. (1996). Support for student achievement. In Fred Newmann and Associates (Ed.), *Authentic achievement: Restructuring schools for intellectual quality* (pp. 209–227). San Francisco: Jossey-Bass.

Marzano, R. (1992). *A different kind of classroom: Teaching with dimensions of learning.* Alexandria, VA: Association for Supervision and Curriculum Development.

Marzano, R., Pickering, D., & McTighe, J. (1993). *Assessing student outcomes.* Alexandria, VA: Association for Supervision and Curriculum Development.

Matthews, D. (1997). The lack of a public for schools. *Phi Delta Kappan, 78*(10), 740–743.

Maxwell, J. (1995). *Developing the leaders around you: How to help others reach their full potential.* Nashville, TN: Thomas Nelson, Inc.

McLaughlin, C., & Davidson, G. (1994). *Spiritual politics: Changing the world from the inside out.* New York: Ballantine Books.

McLaughlin, M. (1995, December). Creating professional learning communities. Keynote address presented at the annual conference of the National Staff Development Council, Chicago.

Mehlinger, H. (1995). *School reform in the information age.* Bloomington, IN: Center for Excellence in Education.

Murphy, J., Evertson, C., & Radnofsky, M. (1991). Restructuring schools: Fourteen elementary and secondary teachers' perspectives on reform. *The Elementary School Journal, 92*(2), 135–148.

Nanus, B. (1992). *Visionary leadership.* San Francisco: Jossey-Bass.

National Association of Secondary School Principals. (1996). *Breaking ranks: Changing an American institution.* Reston, VA.

National Board for Professional Teaching Standards. (1994). *What teachers should know and be able to do.* Detroit, MI.

National Commission on Excellence in Education. (1983). *A nation at risk.* Washington, DC: U.S. Government Printing Office.

National Commission on Teaching and America's Future. (1996). *What matters most: Teaching for America's future.* New York.

National Foundation for the Improvement of Education. (1996). *Teachers take charge of their learning.* West Haven, CT.

National PTA. (1997). *National standards for parent/family involvement programs.* Chicago.

National Staff Development Council. (1995). *Standards for staff development: Middle level edition.* Oxford, OH.

Newmann, F., and Associates (1996). *Authentic achievement: Restructuring schools for intellectual quality.* San Francisco: Jossey-Bass.

Newmann, F., & Wehlage, G. (1995). *Successful school restructuring: A report to the public and educators by the Center for Restructuring Schools.* Madison, WI: University of Wisconsin.

Northwest Regional Educational Laboratory. (1990a). *Effective schooling practices.* Portland, OR.

Northwest Regional Educational Laboratory. (1990b). *Onward to excellence: Making schools more effective.* Portland, OR.

O'Neil, J. (1995). On schools as learning organizations: A conversation with Peter Senge. *Educational Leadership, 52*(7), 20–23.

Perkins, D. (1992). *Smart schools: From training memories to educating minds.* New York: Free Press.

Peters, T., & Austin, N. (1985). *A passion for excellence: The leadership difference.* New York: Random House.

Peters, T., & Waterman, R. (1982). *In search of excellence: Lessons from America's best-run companies.* New York: Harper and Row.

Peterson, K. (1988). Mechanisms of culture building and principal's work. *Education and Urban Society, 20*(3), 250–261.

Pinchot, G., & Pinchot, E. (1993). *The end of bureaucracy and the rise of the intelligent organization.* San Francisco: Berrett-Koehler.

Poplin, M., & Weeres, J. (1992). *Voices from inside: A report on schooling from inside classrooms.* Claremont, CA: Institute for Education in Transformation.

Purkey, S., & Smith, M. (1983). Effective schools: A review. *Elementary School Journal, 83*(4), 427–452.

Rolls, J. (1995). The transformational leader: The wellspring of the learning organization. In C. Sarita & J. Renesch (Eds.), *Learning organizations: Developing cultures for tomorrow's workplace* (pp. 101–110). Portland, OR: Productivity Press.

Ross, R., Smith, B., & Roberts, C. (1994). The team learning wheel. In P. Senge, et al., *The fifth discipline fieldbook: Strategies and tools for building a learning organization* (pp. 59–64). New York: Doubleday.

Sagor, R. (1997). Collaborative action research for educational change. In A. Hargreaves (Ed.), *Rethinking educational change with heart and mind*. Alexandria, VA: Association for Supervision and Curriculum Development.

Salisbury, D., & Conner, D. (1994). How to succeed as manager of an educational change project. *Educational Technology, 34*(6), 12–19.

Sarason, S. (1995). Foreword. In A. Lieberman (Ed.), *The work of restructuring schools*. New York: Teachers College Press.

Sarason, S. (1996). *Revisiting the culture of the school and the problem of change*. New York: Teachers College Press.

Schein, E. (1992). *Organizational culture and leadership*. San Francisco: Jossey-Bass.

Schein, E. (1996). Leadership and organizational culture. In F. Hesselbein, M. Goldsmith, & R. Beckhard (Eds.), *The leader of the future* (pp. 59–69). San Francisco: Jossey-Bass.

Schlechty, P. (1990). *Schools for the 21st century: Leadership imperatives for educational reform*. San Francisco: Jossey-Bass.

Schlechty, P. (1993). On the frontiers of school reform with trailblazers, pioneers, and settlers. *Journal of Staff Development, 14*(4), 46–51.

Schlechty, P. (1997). *Inventing better schools: An action plan for education reform*. San Francisco: Jossey-Bass.

Schmoker, M. (1996). *Results: The key to continuous school improvement*. Alexandria, VA: Association for Supervision and Curriculum Development.

Schneider, J., & Houston, P. (1993). *Exploding the myths: Another round in the education debates.* Arlington, VA: American Association of School Administrators.

Senge, P. (1990). *The fifth discipline: The art and practice of the learning organization.* New York: Doubleday Currency.

Senge, P. (1996). Leading learning organizations. In F. Hesselbein, M. Goldsmith, & R. Beckhard (Eds.), *The leader of the future* (pp. 41–58). San Francisco: Jossey-Bass.

Senge, P., Ross, R., Smith, B., Roberts, C., & Kleiner, A. (1994). *The fifth discipline fieldbook: Strategies and tools for building a learning organization.* New York: Doubleday.

Sergiovanni, T. (1984). Leadership and excellence in schooling. *Educational Leadership, 41*(5), 4, 6–13.

Sergiovanni, T. (1994). *Building community in schools.* San Francisco: Jossey-Bass.

Showers, B., Joyce, B., & Bennett, B. (1987). Synthesis of research on staff development: A framework for future study and a state-of-the-art analysis. *Educational Leadership, 45*(3), 77–87.

Shulman, L. (1996). Quoted in National Commission on Teaching and America's Future, *What matters most: Teaching for America's future.* New York: National Commission on Teaching and America's Future.

Sizer, T. (1991). No pain, no gain. *Educational Leadership, 48*(8), 32–34.

Sizer, T. (1992). *Horace's school: Redesigning the American high school.* Boston: Houghton Mifflin.

Sizer, T. (1996). Hard-won lessons from the school reform battle: A conversation with Ted Sizer. *Harvard Education Newsletter, XII*(4), 3.

Smith, W., & Andrews, R. (1989). *Instructional leadership: How principals make a difference.* Alexandria, VA: Association for Supervision and Curriculum Development.

Sparks, D. (1995). A paradigm shift in staff development. *Journal of Staff Development, 15*(4), 2–4.

Sparks, D., & Hirsh, S. (1997). *A new vision for staff development.* Oxford, OH: National Staff Development Council and Alexandria, VA: Association for Supervision and Curriculum Development.

Sternberg, R. (1996). *Successful intelligence: How practical and creative intelligence determine success in life.* New York: Simon and Schuster.

Stiggins, R., Webb, L. D., Lange, J., McGregor, S., & Cotton, S. (1997). *Multiple assessment of student progress.* Reston, VA: National Association of Secondary School Principals.

Taylor, F. W. (1911). *Principles of scientific management.* New York: Harper and Brothers.

Thompson, J. (1995). The renaissance of learning in business. In C. Sarita & J. Renesch (Eds.), *Learning organizations: Developing cultures for tomorrow's workplace* (pp. 85–99). Portland, OR: Productivity Press.

Toynbee, A. (1958). *Civilization on trial.* New York: Meridian Books.

Ulrich, D. (1996). Credibility x capability. In F. Hesselbein, M. Goldsmith, & R. Beckhard (Eds.), *The leader of the future* (pp. 209–219). San Francisco: Jossey-Bass.

United States Department of Education. (1984). *The nation responds: Recent efforts to improve education.* Washington, DC.

United States Department of Education. (1994). *GOALS 2000.* Washington, DC.

United States Department of Education. (1995a). *An invitation to your community: Building community partnerships for learning.* Washington, DC.

United States Department of Education. (1995b). *Building bridges: The mission and principles of professional development.* Washington, DC.

Urbanski, A. (1997, March). Keynote address presented at the Symposium on World Class Educators for the 21st Century, Chicago.

Wasley, P., Hampel, R., & Clark, R. (1995). When school change influences student achievement. Unpublished manuscript cited in S. Sarason, *Revisiting the culture of the school and the problem of change.* New York: Teachers College Press.

Waterman, R. (1987). *The renewal factor.* New York: Bantam Books.

Wehlage, G., Newmann, F., & Secada, W. (1996). Standards for authentic achievement and pedagogy. In Fred Newmann and Associates (Ed.), *Authentic achievement: Restructuring schools for intellectual quality* (pp. 21–48). San Francisco: Jossey-Bass.

Wehlage, G., Osthoff, G., & Porter, A. (1996). Support from external agencies. In Fred Newmann and Associates (Ed.), *Authentic achievement: Restructuring schools for intellectual quality* (pp. 264–285). San Francisco: Jossey-Bass.

Wheatley, M., & Kellner-Rogers, M. (1996). *A simpler way.* San Francisco: Berrett-Koehler.

Wheelis, A. (1973). *How people change.* New York: Harper Torchbooks.

Wildman, T., & Niles, J. (1987). Essentials of professional growth. *Educational Leadership, 44*(5), 4–10.

Revisiting Professional Learning Communities at Work™: New Insights for Improving Schools
Richard DuFour, Rebecca DuFour, and Robert Eaker
This 10th anniversary sequel to *Professional Learning Communities at Work™* offers advanced insights on deep implementation, the commitment/consensus issue, and the human side of PLC. **BKF2524**

Getting Started
Robert Eaker, Richard DuFour, and Rebecca DuFour
Act on your PLC plans using the clear starting point and conceptual framework offered in this essential PLC resource. **BKF120**

Learning by Doing
Richard DuFour, Rebecca DuFour, Robert Eaker, and Thomas Many
Perplexing problems become workable solutions as collaborative teams take action to close the knowing-doing gap and transform their schools into PLCs. **BKF214**

Whatever It Takes
Richard DuFour, Rebecca DuFour, Robert Eaker, and Gayle Karhanek
Elementary, middle, and high school case studies illustrate how professional learning communities respond to students who aren't learning despite their teachers' best efforts. **BKF174**

Solution Tree | Press

a division of
Solution Tree

Visit solution-tree.com or call 800.733.6786 to order.